W...
Organizational
Psychology

Psychologists have been fascinated by the world of work, and the changing relationship between people, technology and the workplace, since the onset of the industrial revolution. And in providing a complete and contemporary overview of this evolving and fascinating field, the new edition of *Work and Organizational Psychology* is the perfect textbook, outlining not only the key theoretical ideas, but also how they relate to the role of psychologists advising today's organizations.

The only textbook to integrate the fields of HRM and organizational behaviour, this new edition is thoroughly revised to cover new technological advances such as virtual workplaces and virtual employees. In an era of rapid socio-economic change, there is also expanded coverage of the role of workplace diversity, employee commitment and globalization, as well as updated chapters on key concepts such as motivation, leadership, group behaviour and well-being at work.

Also including a chapter on career development, the book is supported by a range of pedagogical features, spotlighting issues of theoretical, ethical or contemporary interest, whilst also enabling students to engage in active learning. Lucid and comprehensive, the second edition of *Work and Organizational Psychology* will be the cornerstone for any student of this dynamic field.

Ian Rothmann is Professor of Industrial Psychology and Director of the Optentia Research Focus Area at the North-West University, Potchefstroom, South Africa. Ian's research interest is the assessment and development of human potential and flourishing in institutions. He is author/co-author of 165 peer-reviewed journal articles and chapters in handbooks.

Cary L. Cooper is Distinguished Professor of Organizational Psychology and Health at Lancaster University Management School, UK. He is the author and editor of more than 125 books and is one of Britain's most quoted business experts. He was awarded the CBE by the Queen in 2001 for his contributions to organizational health and safety; and in 2014 he was awarded a Knighthood for his contribution to the social sciences.

Topics in Applied Psychology

Series Editor: Graham Davey, Professor of Psychology at the University of Sussex, UK, and nt of the British Psychological Society.

Topics in Applied Psychology is a series of accessible, integrated textbooks ideal for courses in applied psychology. Written by leading figures in their field, the books provide a comprehensive academic and professional overview of the subject area, bringing the topics to life through a range of features, including personal stories, case studies, ethical debates and learner activities. Each book addresses a broad range of cutting-edge topics, providing students with both theoretical foundations and real-life applications.

Clinical Psychology
Second Edition
Graham Davey

Educational Psychology
Second Edition
Tony Cline, Anthea Gulliford and Susan Birch

Work and Organizational Psychology
Second Edition
Ian Rothmann and Cary Cooper

Sport and Exercise Psychology
Second Edition
Andy Lane

Health Psychology
Second Edition
Charles Abraham

Criminal Psychology
Second Edition
David Canter

Work and Organizational Psychology

Second edition

**Ian Rothmann
and Cary L. Cooper**

Routledge
Taylor & Francis Group

LONDON AND NEW YORK

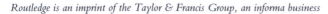

Second edition published 2015
by Routledge
27 Church Road, Hove, East Sussex BN3 2FA

and by Routledge
711 Third Avenue, New York, NY 10017

Routledge is an imprint of the Taylor & Francis Group, an informa business

First edition published by Hodder Education 2008

British Library Cataloguing in Publication Data
A catalogue record for this book is available from the British Library

Library of Congress Cataloging in Publication Data
Rothmann, S. (Sebastiaan), 1959–
Work and organizational psychology / Cary Cooper, Ian Rothmann. –
2 Edition.
pages cm. – (Topics in applied psychology)
Includes bibliographical references and index.
1. Psychology, Industrial. 2. Organizational behavior. I. Cooper, Cary
L. II. Rothmann, S. (Sebastiaan), 1959– Organizational and work
psychology. III. Title.
HF5548.8.R67 2015
1 58.7 – dc23
2014038390

ISBN: 978-1-84872-219-4 (hbk)
ISBN: 978-1-84872-220-0 (pbk)
ISBN: 978-1-315-71747-0 (ebk)

Typeset in Bembo and Univers
by Florence Production Ltd, Stoodleigh, Devon, UK

Printed and bound by CPI Group (UK) Ltd, Croydon, CR0 4YY

Contents

Series preface

Psychology is still one of the most popular subjects for study at undergraduate degree level. As well as providing the student with a range of academic and applied skills that are valued by a broad range of employers, a psychology degree also serves as the basis for subsequent training and a career in professional psychology. A substantial proportion of students entering a degree programme in Psychology do so with a subsequent career in applied psychology firmly in mind, and as a result the number of applied psychology courses available at undergraduate level has significantly increased over recent years. In some cases these courses supplement core academic areas and in others they provide the student with a flavour of what they might experience as a professional psychologist.

The original series of *Texts in Applied Psychology* consisted of six textbooks designed to provide a comprehensive academic and professional insight into specific areas of professional psychology. The texts covered the areas of *Clinical Psychology, Criminal and Investigative Psychology, Educational Psychology, Health Psychology, Sports and Exercise Psychology*, and *Work and Organizational Psychology*, and each text was written and edited by the foremost professional and academic figures in each of these areas.

These texts were so successful that we are now able to provide you with a second edition of this series. All texts have been updated with details of recent professional developments as well as relevant research, and we have responded to the requests of teachers and reviewers to include new material, and new approaches to this material. Perhaps most significantly, all texts in the series will now have back-up web resources.

Just as in the first series, each textbook is based on a similar academic formula that combines a comprehensive review of cutting-edge research and professional knowledge with accessible teaching and learning features. The books are also structured so they can be used as an integrated teaching support for a one-term or one-semester course in each of their relevant area of applied psychology. Given the increasing importance of applying psychological knowledge across a growing range of areas of practice, we feel this series is timely and comprehensive. We hope you find each book in the series readable, enlightening, accessible and instructive.

Graham Davey
University of Sussex, Brighton, UK
August 2014

Preface

Work and organizational psychology is an academic subject and a profession which focuses on human behaviour related to organizations, work and productivity. It applies psychological principles to the workplace. The purpose of this book is to introduce the undergraduate psychology student to both academic and professional aspects of work and organizational psychology.

The book begins with a chapter to give the reader an insight into the domain of work and organizational psychology, the development of the field of work and organizational psychology, tasks and competencies of organizational and work psychologists, and careers in work and organizational psychology. The rest of the book is divided into thirteen chapters which address the fields of work and organizational psychology. Organizational psychology includes individual differences and diversity (Chapter 2), motivation (Chapter 3), group behaviour (Chapter 4), communication (Chapter 5), leadership (Chapter 6), well-being and dysfunctional behaviour at work (Chapter 13), and organizational design, development and culture (Chapter 14). Work psychology includes human resource planning and job analysis (Chapter 7), recruitment and selection (Chapter 8), induction, training and development (Chapter 9), compensation management (Chapter 10), performance appraisal (Chapter 11) and career development (Chapter 12).

As with all the books in the Topics in Applied Psychology series, this text is written as a support for a one-term or one-semester course in work and organizational psychology, and contains all the teaching and learning features appropriate to the series, including focus boxes on research methods in work and organizational psychology and issues of theoretical, ethical or contemporary interest, and activity boxes that provide the student with the opportunity to engage in active learning. Each chapter also ends with extensive support for further reading, including relevant journal articles, books, websites and videos. This should enable the interested student to engage with a topic in some depth.

Ian Rothmann
Cary Cooper
June 2014

1 Introduction to work and organizational psychology

This first chapter introduces the reader to the field and history of *work and organizational psychology*, and the tasks and competencies of work and organizational psychologists. The first section describes the field of work and organizational psychology in terms of its two major subfields, namely *work psychology* (often referred to as 'human resource management') and organizational psychology (often referred to as 'organizational behaviour'). We then look at how the various schools of thought about human behaviour in work and organizational context developed since the early 1900s, including *scientific management*, *classical organizational theory*, the Hawthorne studies, the human relations approach, the *socio-technical systems approach*, contingency theories, theories about *organizational transformation*, *organizational culture*, the learning organization, teamwork, *total quality management* and *positive psychology*. The chapter then proceeds to the tasks of work and organizational psychologists. Finally, we look at the challenges for and competencies of work and organizational psychologists.

LEARNING OUTCOMES

When you have completed this chapter you should be able to:

1 Define work and organizational psychology.
2 Describe the tasks of a work and organizational psychologist.
3 Review the development of the field of work and organizational psychology.
4 Summarize the activities of a work and organizational psychologist.
5 Explain the challenges for work and organizational psychologists.
6 Discuss the competencies of a work and organizational psychologist.
7 Identify the attractions and drawbacks of careers in work and organizational psychologists.

DEFINITION OF WORK AND ORGANIZATIONAL PSYCHOLOGY

Work and organizational psychology is defined as an applied division of psychology concerned with the study of human behaviour related to work, organizations and productivity (Cascio, 2001). Work and organizational psychologists are involved in research on employees and the application of psychological principles of that research to the workplace to help to optimize an organization's success (Schultz and Schultz, 2014).

Work and organizational psychologists help individuals and organizations to fulfil their potential and to produce outputs efficiently and at a high level of quality in the following ways:

- Develop, validate and apply methods to recruit and select *individuals* who will match their jobs; orientate, train and develop them and equip them with the knowledge, skills and attitudes required by jobs; monitor and evaluate their performance; motivate, lead and reward them; maintain and promote their health, safety and well-being; and assist them with their career development.
- Apply work and organizational psychology knowledge to benefit organizations by promoting efficiency, improving morale and increasing organizational profits. For example, work and organizational psychologists save costs for organizations by reducing absenteeism, voluntary turnover, work slowdowns, faulty products, poor service and accidents.

Work and organizational psychology comprises two branches, namely *work psychology* (also referred to as 'human resource management') and *organizational psychology* (also referred to as 'organizational behaviour'. Human resource management is a philosophy about how people should be managed. It is a strategic, integrated and coherent approach to the employment, development and well-being of people working in organizations (Armstrong and Taylor, 2014). Organizational behaviour is defined as the study of what people do in organizations and how their behaviours affect organizations' functioning and performance (Robbins and Judge, 2013).

Organizational psychology is directed at the behaviour of individuals, groups and organizations in the work situation. It focuses on the following topics (see Figure 1.1 for the chapters in which these subfields are discussed):

- *Individual differences and diversity management.* Individual differences refer to differences between people regarding any characteristic, such as a personality trait, through which an individual could be distinguished from others. Diversity includes the mixture of many dimensions which makes people unique and different from each other.
- *Motivation.* The term motivation refers to the factors which determine or regulate behaviour.
- *Communication.* Communication is defined as the process by which a person, group or organization transmits information to another person.
- *Leadership.* Leadership is the process whereby one individual influences other group members towards the attainment of defined group or organizational goals.

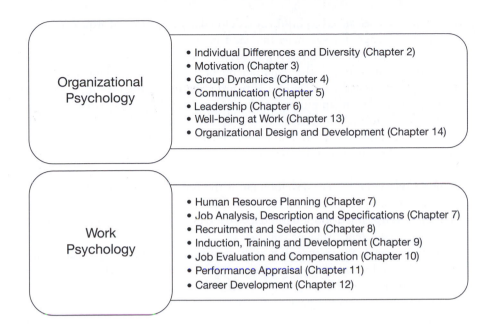

FIGURE 1.1 Fields of work and organizational psychology

- *Group dynamics.* Group dynamics refers to the dynamics of interaction in social groups.
- *Health and well-being.* A healthy work environment is one in which no diseases occur. Well-being is a state in which individuals feel and function well in different life domains.
- *Organizational design, development and culture.* Organizational design is defined as the formal system of communication, authority and responsibility adopted by an organization which constitutes its internal structure. Organizational development is defined as a long-range effort to improve an organization's ability to cope with change and its problem solving and renewal processes through effective management of the organizational culture.

Figure 1.1 shows that work psychology focuses on topics which are typically covered in textbooks on human resource management, including:

1 *Human resource planning.* Human resource planning is a planned analysis of the present and future human resource needs of an organization and the implementation of action plans in order to ensure the adequate supply of human resources.
2 *Job analysis, description and job specifications.* Job analysis is defined as the process of gathering job information by breaking the job down into its components. A job description is a written summary of the key performance areas of a specific job. A job specification is a written explanation of the minimum requirements needed for effective performance on a given job.

3   *Recruitment and selection.* Recruitment is defined as the process of attracting suitable candidates to apply for vacancies that exist in an organization. Selection involves the sorting out of applicants for a vacant job and the elimination of those applicants who do not fit the requirements of the job and/or the organization.

4   *Induction, training and development.* Induction is defined as the introduction of new employees to the organization, work unit and job. Training is the systematic application of formal processes to help people to acquire and develop knowledge, skills, behaviours and attitudes. Development is defined as the growth of a person's ability and potential through the provision of learning and educational experiences.

5   *Career development.* Career development is the process of guiding the placement, movement and the growth of employees through assessment, planned training activities and planned job assignments. It includes personal career planning and organizational career management.

6   *Job evaluation and compensation.* Job evaluation involves rating of jobs through the use of a job evaluation plan and conversion of relative job values to a definite wage rate. The total remuneration employees receive from work is called compensation. Compensation means the provision of a suitable return for services.

7   *Performance appraisal.* Performance appraisal is the process by which the organization determines how effectively the employee is performing the job.

THE DEVELOPMENT OF THE FIELD OF WORK AND ORGANIZATIONAL PSYCHOLOGY

Various approaches and theories contributed to the field of work and organizational psychology and also to its identity. Early contributions (including the scientific management approach) stressed efficient performance according to economic principles. *Classical organization theory* was concerned with the effective organization of people. The Hawthorne studies, in turn, stressed the social nature of human beings. This was followed by the *human relations movement*, which paid attention to aspects such as human needs, attitudes, motives and relationships. In contrast to an emphasis primarily on structure or the human side of organizations, organizational thought in the past few decades has emphasized the integration of these two perspectives. More recent development in the field of organization development (including the *systems approach* and *contingency theory*) also contributed to the field of work and organizational psychology. Lastly, the developments in *positive psychology* and *positive organizational scholarship* also impacted on the field of work and organizational psychology. Next, these developments will be reviewed in more detail.

Early contributions

Since the Industrial Revolution of the nineteenth century, relatively large numbers of people started working together voluntarily in manager–subordinate relationships. The Industrial Revolution brought much technological change to the workplace. During this era, the emphasis was on the job being performed, not on the person performing the job. Engineers focused on the development of efficient machines. They argued that if the machines which were used for the production of goods could be improved, greater efficiency would follow. Efficiency problems led engineers to start considering the people who were operating the machines. This in turn led to the implementation of time and motion studies. Through these studies attempts were made to design jobs so that they could be performed in the most efficient manner (Schultz and Schultz, 2014).

Scientific management

Scientific management is the name of the approach to work and organizational psychology initiated by Frederick Winslow Taylor. Scientific management was concerned with maximizing efficiency and getting the highest possible production out of employees (Armstrong and Taylor, 2014). As an industrial engineer, Taylor was concerned with inefficiencies in manual labour jobs and believed that by scientifically studying the specific motions that made up the total job, a more rational, objective and effective method of performing the job could be determined. This approach emphasized the design of jobs to ensure that work tasks were planned in a systematic manner. Employees were carefully selected and trained for their jobs. Taylor also realized that motivation in work settings was very important. During this period, managers saw their job as increasing efficiency and were less interested in the well-being of workers (Schultz and Schultz, 2014).

Taylor's ideas had a profound influence on the management practices and business thinking of his time, because they facilitated job specialization and mass production. However, labour unions opposed his ideas, because the goal of scientific management was to get more output from employees. Some government members thought that the implementation of his ideas would lead to the dehumanization of the workplace and to workers becoming robots.

Classical organization theory

Classical organization theory was concerned with the question as to how large numbers of workers and managers could be effectively organized into an overall organizational structure. Max Weber was one of the most prominent contributors to the thinking concerning classical organization theory. He was of the opinion that a bureaucratic form of organization structure would work for all types of organizations (Armstrong and Taylor, 2014).

Early in the 1900s, Hugo Munsterberg, a German psychologist who subsequently emigrated to the USA and who is regarded by some as one of the 'founding fathers' of work and organizational psychology, argued that the field of psychology could provide important insights into areas such as the selection and motivation of employees. At the same time a vocational guidance expert by the name of Mary Parker Follett argued that organizations should strive harder to meet their employees' needs and that management should become more democratic in its dealings with employees (Schultz and Schultz, 2014).

The Hawthorne studies

The Hawthorne studies were carried out between 1924 and 1932 at Western Electric's Hawthorne plant in Chicago, USA. Two staff members of Harvard University, namely Elton Mayo and Fritz Roethlisberger, were, from 1927, involved in the Hawthorne studies. The Hawthorne studies took work and organizational psychology beyond selection and placement to complex problems of motivation, interpersonal relations and organizational dynamics (Hsueh, 2002). The findings of the study surprised the researchers: social and psychological factors were potentially of greater importance in the work environment than lighting, temperature and/or humidity. The Hawthorne studies opened up new research areas to explore, such as motivation and leadership. Although these studies have been criticized for a lack of scientific rigour, there is no denying that they had a major impact on the field of work and organizational psychology.

The human relations movement

The human relations movement paid attention to aspects such as human needs, attitudes, motives and relationships. According to this approach, people respond primarily to their social environment, motivation depends more on social needs than on economic needs, and satisfied employees work harder than dissatisfied workers (Schultz and Schultz, 2014). The values of the human relations movement are, to a certain extent, best mirrored by Theory Y of Douglas McGregor (1960) which he set out in his book *The Human Side of Enterprise*. In this book he identified two opposing perspectives which he believed typified managerial views of employees. Theory Y represents an optimistic and a positive view of human nature. McGregor also refers to Theory X, which represents a much more negative and pessimistic view of human nature.

The human relations movement has also been criticized. For instance, a happy (satisfied) worker is not necessarily a productive worker. In some instances it might turn out that because a worker is able to be productive, he or she might be satisfied. The human relations movement in some instances led managers to believe that workers wanted them to act as mothers/fathers. This practice is known as *paternalism*. Workers often resent a paternalistic manager. Many of the assumptions of the human relations movement were also rather simplistic and situation specific.

Integrative perspectives

In contrast to an emphasis primarily on structure or the human side of organizations, organizational thought in the past few decades has emphasized the integration of these two perspectives.

The socio-technical systems approach

Trist and Bamforth (1951) described a change in technology in a British coal mine. In the mine, workers were used to working independently in small, self-contained units in which they organized the work themselves. However, the technology for mining coal improved in a way that required management to increase job specialization and

RESEARCH METHODS 1.1

The Hawthorne studies

The first of the Hawthorne studies was designed by industrial engineers who wanted to study the effects of different levels of lighting, temperature and humidity on productivity. For example, in the lighting experiment they used an experimental group and a control group of women workers. The control group worked in a control room in which the lighting was kept constant. The experimental group worked in a test room in which the lighting level was systematically manipulated. At first, the lighting in the test room was systematically increased. As has been expected, the productivity in the test room increased. However, the unexpected happened in the sense that the productivity in the control room also increased. What was surprising was the fact that when the lighting in the test room was subsequently decreased, the productivity in both rooms continued to increase. It was obvious that something else beside the lighting levels (e.g. the human factor) was playing a role.

Elton Mayo started a series of studies which received the name the Relay Room studies. The subjects in these experiments were again female employees who worked in a special test room. In these studies, the impact of thirteen different factors on productivity was examined. These factors included the length of rest pauses, length of the work-day, length of the work-week, method of payment, place of work and a free mid-morning lunch. The results showed that the productivity of the group increased with almost every change in work conditions. Even when the initial standard conditions were again instituted, productivity continued to increase.

Question: What is meant by the Hawthorne effect in research? Read the following article before you respond:

Wickström G. and Bendix, T. (2000) 'The "Hawthorne effect" – what did the original Hawthorne studies actually show?' *Scandinavian Journal of Work, Environment and Health*, 26(4), 363–367.

decrease the workers' participation in job assignments. The coal miners hated the specialization, because they preferred working closely with each other and performing a variety of tasks. The researchers compared the performance of work groups, the jobs of which had become specialized by the new technology, with work groups which had kept their former social structure. They found that absenteeism in the specialized group was several times greater and productivity much lower than in the groups that had maintained their group organization. The socio-technical systems researchers concluded that neither technology, nor human relations, could be excluded when trying to understand a work system (Armstrong and Taylor, 2014).

Systems theory

Systems theory offers an integrated and comprehensive view of organizational functioning. The general systems model (Katz and Kahn, 1978) represents an organization as an open system, one that interacts with environmental forces and factors (Armstrong and Taylor, 2014). A system has four characteristics, namely (Clegg *et al.*, 2005):

1   It comprises a number of interdependent and interrelated subsystems (e.g. individual employees, work teams, departments).
2   It is open and dynamic. The organization continually receives new energy in the form of new resources (people, materials and money) or information (concerning strategy, environment and history) from the environment. These inputs are then transformed into outputs. The transformation of inputs creates changes in individual, group and organization behaviour and attitudes (e.g. performance, morale, satisfaction, turnover and absenteeism).
3   It strives for equilibrium. When organizations become unbalanced or experience disequilibrium, such as when changes in the environment make current staffing inadequate, organizations attempt to return to a steady state, which may differ from the original state of equilibrium.
4   It has multiple purposes, objectives and functions, some of which are in conflict. Organizations which survive adapt to a particular situation. They respond to changes in the environment with appropriate changes in the system.

Contingency theory

In organizations, contingency theory emphasizes the fit between organizational processes and the characteristics of the situation. Therefore there is *no best way* to manage people or situations. The best way to manage people or situations depends on the situation in which the organization finds itself (Armstrong and Taylor, 2014). Early contingency research looked at the fit between an organization's structure and its environment. Burns and Stalker (1961) described two different types of management systems: mechanistic and organic. Mechanistic systems have characteristics such as those described in the scientific and classical management traditions. Organic systems are much more flexible and loosely structured, and allow more employee influence over decisions than do mechanistic systems. Mechanistic systems are appropriate to stable environmental conditions, while organic systems are appropriate to changing organizations. Mintzberg (1983) emphasized the importance of fitting organization structure to various contingencies. Thus contingency theory has also extended to leadership, group dynamics, power relations and work design. Fiedler (1967) developed a contingency theory of leadership, which states that leadership effectiveness depends on the situation in which the leader finds himself or herself (including the characteristics of followers).

Developments in the field of organizational development

Various developments in the field of organizational development contributed to the field of work and organizational psychology. These developments include an interest in organizational transformation, organizational culture, the earning organization, teams and total quality management (Anderson, 2012).

The organization development literature distinguishes between first-order and second-order change. First-order change refers to incremental modifications within an established framework or operating method (e.g. implementing a computer system that automates existing work processes). Second-order change concerns transformational changes that modify established frameworks or operating methods (Anderson, 2012). Organizational transformation entails second-order change and is multi-dimensional, multilevel, discontinuous and radical organization change. For example, rethinking how the organization uses a computer system, including redefining roles, processes, objectives and values would be considered second-order change.

Efforts to define, measure and change organizational culture have become more sophisticated. Schein (1985) has done much work on organizational culture, and has devised interventions to help leaders and employees identify those cultural conventions and assumptions which will assist the organization in attaining its goals. An organization's strategy and culture should be in alignment for the organization to succeed (Anderson, 2012).

Stimulated by the works of Argyris et al. (1985), Argyris and Schön (1978) and Senge (1990), there has been considerable interest in the conditions under which individuals, teams and organizations learn. It is clear that some organizations learn better than others (Anderson, 2012). A learning organization is an organization which has developed the continuous capacity to adapt and change. Argyris (1990) has focused on the defensive routes of organization members. Senge (1990) writes about the learning disabilities which plague organizations. One learning disability is exclusively focusing on one's own job with little sense of responsibility for the collective product. Another is to do a lot of blaming of 'the enemy out there' for things which are wrong.

Although the study of teams was always important in work and organizational psychology, there is currently a deepened interest in self-managed or self-directed teams. This interest was caused by the pressure on organizations to improve quality, to become more flexible, to reduce layers of management and to enhance employee morale (Anderson, 2012). Laboratory training methods have been found to be useful in training team members in effective membership and leadership behaviour, and in training supervisors and managers in delegation and empowerment.

Total quality management is a company-wide effort seeking to install and make permanent a climate where employees continuously improve their ability to provide products and services, which customers will find of value, on demand. Total quality management programmes involve personal and organizational culture change and work and organizational psychologists help to facilitate this change.

Positive psychology

At the beginning of the twenty-first century, the prevailing values perspective in work and organizational psychology, emphasizing a utilitarian, cost-benefit approach, has strongly influenced research and practice (Wright and Wright, 2002). A consequence of the utilitarian perspective has been that applied research tends to focus unduly on the identification of financial costs to the organization of distressed, dissatisfied and unhappy employees. The cause of this employee dissatisfaction and unhappiness was typically seen as being deeply imbedded in the emotional maladjustment of the employee, as opposed to aspects of the job itself (Wright, 2003). As a result, the cure for this maladjustment usually involves some type of prevention-based employee therapy (Wright and Cropanzano, 2000). The movement towards positive psychology has resulted in a bigger awareness of happiness of people in work and organizational contexts (Linley *et al.*, 2011; Rothmann, 2013; Swart and Rothmann, 2012).

Positive psychology is defined as the scientific study of what enables individuals and institutions to flourish by focusing on the optimal expression of potential through positive well-being, positive traits and positive institutions (Seligman and Csikszentmihalyi, 2000). It is a movement in psychology which emphasizes what is right with people rather than what is wrong with them (Nelson and Cooper, 2007). At the subjective level, positive psychology is about valued subjective experiences: well-being, contentment and satisfaction, hope and optimism, and flow and happiness (Seligman and Csikszentmihalyi, 2000).

In line with the development of positive psychology, various disciplines have developed which take a proactive approach to work and organizational psychology research. These disciplines include positive organizational scholarship (POS; Cameron and Spreitzer, 2012), positive organizational behaviour (POB; Luthans, 2002a) and positive organizational psychology (Donaldson and Ko, 2010). Luthans (2002b: 59) defines POB as 'the study and application of positively oriented human resource strengths and psychological capacities that can be measured, developed and effectively managed for performance improvement'. POS emphasizes the positive characteristics

FIGURE 1.2 Positive psychology studies the factors that contribute to human flourishing

Source: © bilderpool/Shutterstock.com

FOCUS 1.1

Some findings from positive work and organizational psychology studies

- Authentic leadership has a positive effect on psychological capital (i.e. employees' levels of self-efficacy, resilience, hope and optimism). Psychological capital contributes to job satisfaction, talent retention and job performance (Luthans, 2012).
- The availability of job resources (e.g. good supervisor relations, role clarity and challenging tasks) and personal resources (e.g. dispositional optimism) lead to employee engagement (Barkhuizen *et al.*, 2014).
- Flourishing employees (compared with employees who are not flourishing) are more satisfied with their jobs, have a lower intention to leave, show more organizational citizenship behaviour, show less counterproductive behaviour, are more committed to their organizations, and are more productive at work (Boehm and Lyubomirsky, 2008; Diedericks and Rothmann, 2014; Swart and Rothmann, 2012).
- Manager support and trust affect employees' psychological need satisfaction and intentions to leave their organizations (Rothmann *et al.*, 2013).

of the organization that facilitates its ability to function. Positive organizational psychology (POP) is defined as 'the scientific study of positive subjective experiences and traits in the workplace and positive organizations, and its application to improve the effectiveness and quality of life in organizations' (Donaldson and Ko, 2010: 278).

A review of the POS literature points to a focus on six areas in research, namely:

1 Relations among individual behaviours and features of employees and their engagement in their work and organizations.
2 Positive behaviours of leaders, e.g. positive emotions and building positive visions and the effects thereof on flourishing of employees.
3 The relation between organizational virtuousness and organizational performance.
4 Interpersonal relationships in relation to organizational performance.
5 Psychological capital.
6 Relations between positive and negative phenomena in organizations.

(Glińska–Neves and Stankiewicz, 2013)

THE TASKS OF WORK AND ORGANIZATIONAL PSYCHOLOGISTS

The primary task of work and organizational psychologists is to apply psychological principles and research to workplace phenomena by using a scientific approach. Science is defined by its methods and procedures, not by its subject matter (Schultz and Schultz, 2014). When work and organizational psychologists deal with the

Tasks of a work and organizational psychologist

Four broad tasks of the work and organizational psychologists are distinguished, namely:

1 Explaining individual, group and organizational behaviour.
2 Measuring behaviour and predicting potential.
3 Contributing to individual, group and organization development.
4 Translating research findings and empowering potential users thereof.

behaviour of people at work, they do so objectively and systematically. They use qualitative observation as well as quantitative measurement and statistics to conduct research and intervene in the workplace (Brewerton and Millward, 2004). Furthermore, they are concerned about the effectiveness of the organization and the well-being of individuals. Lastly, work and organizational psychologists operate with an implicit multilevel model, i.e. they recognize that in addition to individual influences on individual behaviour and attitudes, higher order units such as teams and the organizational context have influence (Ryan, 2003). The tasks of work and organizational psychologists are shown in Focus 1.2.

Explaining individual, group and organizational behaviour

The first task of a work and organizational psychologist is to explain individual, group and organizational functioning based on theories and models. For example, the work and organizational psychologist can meet with clients or managers to discuss the nature of a problem (e.g. the turnover rate among employees is too high), conduct interviews or send out questionnaires to employees to determine the nature of their job tasks, conduct a study to determine what training is needed, survey employees to determine how they feel about their jobs and identify solutions to an organization's problem (e.g. too much employee absence).

Measuring behaviour and predicting potential

Work and organizational psychologists observe and record the behaviour of employees under well-controlled and systematic conditions. Over the years psychological measures have become essential tools for implementing change. The term 'test' refers to group and individually administered standardized measures of aptitudes, achievement, intelligence, personality, social, language, perception and motor skills (Oakland, 2004). Strong evidence exists to support the merit of tests for providing policy-makers with information for decision-making, aiding psychologists in the individual screening and diagnostic process, credentialing and licensing candidates in professions and specialties, and providing organizations with data for employee selection, promotion and evaluation of training (Hambleton and Oakland, 2004). Work and organizational psychologists should ensure that assessment materials and measures are reliable, valid, equivalent and unbiased (Smith *et al.*, 2001). Assessment materials and measures could be inequivalent or biased as a function of culture and other differences (Bryson and Hosken, 2005).

Contributing to individual, group and organizational development

Work and organizational psychologists must deal with worker resistance to new ideas and support employees and their supervisors or managers (Schultz and Schultz, 2014). They have to plan and implement interventions that will contribute to individual, group and organization development. To contribute to organizational development, work and organizational psychologists need to conceptualize organizational effectiveness and develop measures thereof. Characteristics of effective organizations include profitability, return on investment, market share, growth, adaptability and innovation, and perhaps the ultimate objective: survival. An organization is effective when it offers its consumers the services and products desired with reasonable conditions of price, quality and delivery date.

From a POS perspective, work and organizational psychologists should contribute to building and maintaining positive institutions. According to Cameron and Spreitzer (2012), positive organizations have a purpose and a shared vision (of the moral goal of the organization), provide safety (protection against threat, danger and exploitation), and ensure fairness (equitable rules governing reward and punishment), humanity (care and concern) and dignity (treatment of all as individuals regardless of their position).

Translating research findings and empowering potential users thereof

Although a large body of research findings exists, potential users often do not act on them. This might be attributed to a lack of knowledge and understanding of research findings, a lack of implementation skills, a lack of motivation and/or limitations created by the prevailing organizational culture. Many industrial leaders uphold dysfunctional paradigms which may profoundly diminish the effectiveness of work and organizational psychology teaching, practice and research (Watkins, 2001). Reacting to the opinions of industrial leaders, without at least considering work and organizational success factors to support their reasoning, may potentially be devastating to the subject. Work and organizational psychologists must present their contributions in a way that can be understood by users of their services (Schultz and Schultz, 2014).

CHALLENGES FOR WORK AND ORGANIZATIONAL PSYCHOLOGISTS

The environment in which individuals and organizations find themselves is rapidly changing. Technological advances, more diverse populations, changing business and economic conditions, and the changing nature of work lead to more and different demands and responsibilities for work and organizational psychologists (Robbins and Judge, 2013; Schultz and Schultz, 2014).

Virtual workplaces

Due to technological developments, large numbers of employees work offsite. Mobile phones and computers can be used to telecommute from home offices, and employees can communicate by phone, and send text messages and emails from cars, hotel rooms, even when they are on vacation. Many jobs can be performed within electronic reach of the office. Online material be downloaded and printed, databases can be accessed, and employees and their work assignments can be tracked at any time. The downside of these technological developments is that employers often expect employees to be available beyond working hours. Therefore employees might find it difficult to escape from job demands.

Virtual employees

Employees are less likely to have full-time contracts and life-long job security is no longer guaranteed by organizations. More employees are likely to be contingent workers, freelancers, independent contractors or part-time seasonal labourers. Many workers prefer contingent work because it provides independence, challenges and opportunities to acquire new knowledge and skills.

Employee commitment

Today's employees want empowerment, involvement and participation. Employees are expected to master the tasks of a specific job, but they also need personal and interpersonal competence which they can transfer from one job to another. They have to constantly upgrade their skills and participate in multidisciplinary teams. These changes have implications for the ways in which supervisors and managers perform their roles. Supervisors and managers often depend on the power of instruction to influence their people. Research showed that supervisors and managers spend almost 85 per cent of their time telling people what to do (Daniels, 2000). Telling people what to do is not sufficient: support and trust demand other behaviours from supervisors and managers. When employees participate in making decisions and experience satisfaction, their autonomy needs are more engaged in their work and they are less inclined to quit (Rothmann *et al.*, 2013). An important challenge for work and organizational psychologists is to prepare and support supervisors and managers to empower and involve employees.

New skills

Computers, faxes, mobile phones, electronic notebooks, emails and the Internet have changed the nature and functions of many jobs and resulted in new types of jobs. Modern jobs require computer literacy and well-educated employees. However, many individuals in industrialized and developing countries are functionally illiterate, and lack basic skills in reading, writing and mathematics. The shortage of individuals who have acquired basic skills presents an important challenge for work and organizational psychologists who have to ensure that employees have the required knowledge and skills to perform high-tech jobs.

Globalization

Globalization is defined as the process of increasing the connectivity and interdependence of the world's markets and businesses (Berry *et al.*, 2002). Because of globalization, businesses that had previously only sold goods domestically can start selling products and/or services to other countries. Globalization results in shifting jobs to places with lower labour costs and competition, an international pool of immigrant workers employed by multinational organizations, and an increase in cross–cultural contacts (Mathews, 2012). Work and organizational psychologists are challenged by the need for the retraining of employees who will lose their jobs because of globalization, as well as preparing employees to manage international assignments.

Workplace diversity

Globalization and developments in information technology, mass media and transport have led to more exposure from people in one culture to the way of life of people in other cultures. Research by Gallup has shown that approximately 700 million adults would want to migrate to another country in the world permanently if they were afforded the opportunity (www.gallup.com/poll/124048/700-Million-Worldwide-Desire-Migrate-Permanently.aspx). More than 150 million adults worldwide reported that they would like the United States as their desired future residence, while 7 per cent of respondents chose the United Kingdom. Other desired destination countries included Canada, France, Saudi Arabia, Australia, Germany and Spain. Furthermore, major shifts in the composition of workforces in terms of gender and ethnicity in organizations are taking place. As a consequence, organizations have to become more sensitive to differences in cultures, languages, backgrounds and expectations. The challenges for work and organizational psychologists are to select and train employees, to redesign jobs, to optimize management practices and to deal with morale.

Another aspect of diversity concerns the value of employees. Three generations with different values, namely Baby Boomers, Generation X and Generation Y are distinguished (Schultz and Schultz, 2014). Baby Boomers were born between 1946 and 1964. Because they had to be very competitive to find jobs and promotions, many became workaholics. They work long hours and often compromise family commitments. Individuals classified as Generation X were born between 1965 and 1979 and chose not to follow their parents' commitment to work. They are sophisticated computer users, value autonomy and independence, and tend to question authority. Individuals in Generation Y were born after 1980 and are typified as self–centred, and they require constant feedback and recognition. They are entrepreneurial and want to do meaningful work. Work and organizational psychologists should understand the expectations of employees of different generations.

THE COMPETENCY PROFILE OF WORK AND ORGANIZATIONAL PSYCHOLOGISTS

The competency profile of work and organizational psychologists is addressed on the websites of various psychological associations, including the American Psychological

Association (www.apa.org) and the Canadian Society for Industrial and Organizational Psychology (http://psychology.uwo.ca/csiop). A competency profile can be defined as a list of competencies required in a specific job or profession. Competencies are the work-related knowledge, skills, attitudes and behaviour needed to effectively perform in a role. Knowledge is the awareness and understanding of facts, truths or information gained through learning, experience and/or introspection. A skill is the ability to perform a work-related activity which contributes to the effective work performance. An attitude involves beliefs, feelings, values and dispositions to act in certain ways. Behaviour is the manner of acting or controlling yourself.

The education and training of work and organizational psychologists are rooted in the various foundations, namely: a) psychological science (including biological bases of behaviour, cognitive-affective bases of behaviour, social bases of behaviour and individual differences); b) research methods; c) theory and methods of psychological and behavioural measurement; and d) advanced statistical theory. Based on these foundations, the competency areas of work and organizational psychologists are reported in Focus 1.3.

FOCUS 1.3

Competencies of work and organizational psychologists

- *Knowledge of work and organizational psychology theory and research.* The work and organizational psychologist should understand psychological theory and research, and demonstrate the ability to assimilate new psychological knowledge as well as knowledge of ethical considerations. This competency includes the following aspects: individual differences; work motivation; attitude theory measurement and change; human resource planning, recruitment, selection and placement; career development; job analysis, description and evaluation; health, safety and well-being in organizations; human factors and performance in work; individual, group and organizational assessment methods; decision theory; training and development; performance management; group and team behaviour; leadership; compensation and benefits; organizational theory; organizational development; ethical, legal and professional contexts.
- *Research and statistical skills.* The work and organizational psychologist should demonstrate the ability to use research methods and statistics, understand published research and show the ability to think critically. This competency includes research methodology and statistical analysis.
- *Professional skills.* The work and organizational psychologist should demonstrate the ability to apply knowledge to real-life situations, demonstrate effective oral and written communication skills, and show an awareness of career options. This competency includes consulting and business skills, knowledge of careers, and oral and written communication skills.

In Figure 1.3, the competencies of work and organizational psychologists are classified based on three areas, namely, knowledge of work and organizational psychology theory, research and statistical skills, and professional skills.

Knowledge of work and organizational psychology includes an understanding of theory and research (as described in Focus 1.3), the ability to assimilate new psychological knowledge, and knowledge of ethical considerations. Research and statistical skills include the ability to use research methods and statistics, an understanding of published research and critical thinking. Professional skills include effective oral and written communication skills, an awareness of career options and the ability to apply knowledge to real–life situations.

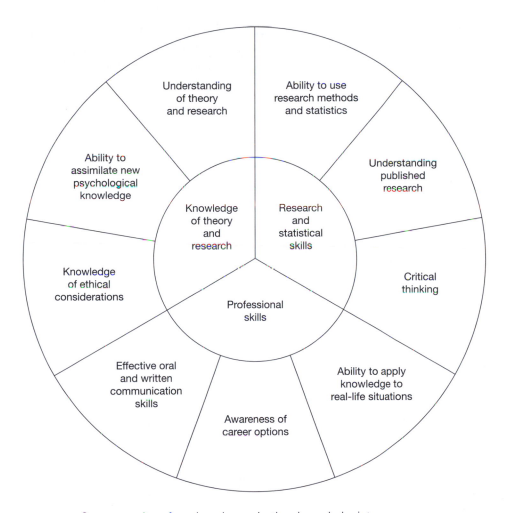

FIGURE 1.3 Competencies of work and organizational psychologists

CAREERS IN WORK AND ORGANIZATIONAL PSYCHOLOGY

Careers in work and organizational psychology are characterized by both rewarding and frustrating aspects (www.wcupa.edu): The attractions of careers in work and organizational psychology include the following:

- There are many career opportunities in work and organizational psychology. One can work in a human resource department in various types of private and public organizations, work in management, or work for consulting companies.
- Careers in work and organizational psychology are challenging because it is a new field and because the field presents opportunities for learning, variety and autonomy.
- Work and organizational psychologists are in demand because organizations realize that human potential management is the key to business success.
- Work and organizational psychologists could work for organizations or they may become entrepreneurs and initiate their own businesses.

The drawbacks of careers in work and organizational psychology include the following:

- Many jobs in work and organizational psychology require a master's degree or a doctorate in work and organizational psychology.
- Work and organizational psychologists are at risk for developing burnout because of the nature of people work they do.
- Work and organizational psychologists often become intensely involved with people and those who do not like dealing with people might find the careers in the field frustrating.
- Organizations and employees often depend on work and organizational psychologists to help them, and they might experience intense frustration if people do not want to change.

ACTIVITY 1.1

Challenges for and competencies of work and organizational psychologists

Identify the major challenges for work and organizational psychologists in the next ten years. List the competencies needed by work and organizational psychologists. Compare your competencies with those required of work and organizational psychologists and identify the most important gaps between your competency profile and the profile as specified.

ETHICS 1.1

Ethical conduct

Ethics are the basic rules or first principles that have been proposed to ensure a 'good' society, i.e. one in which people are willing to co-operate for the benefit of all. Ethical behaviour conforms to accepted standards of conduct. Ethical reasoning involves the sorting out of principles that help determine what is right in the face of a human dilemma. An ethical dilemma is a situation or problem facing an individual where complex and often conflicting principles of behaviour are in play.

Minimum ethical guidelines for work and organizational psychologists

A professional must always:

- Support, promote and apply the principles of human rights, equity, dignity and respect in the workplace, i.e. must respect people as individuals and inherently of equal worth regardless of race, origin, gender, sexual orientation or any of the grounds enunciated under the relevant human rights code.
- Hold in strict confidence all confidential information acquired in the course of the performance of their duties and not divulge confidential information unless required by law and/or where serious harm is imminent.
- Strive to balance organizational and employee needs and interests in the practice of their profession, i.e. a professional must support and represent the best interests of their employer or client (employee), and acknowledge and respect their fiduciary duty in this relationship with the highest standards of honesty and integrity.
- Question pending individual, group and organizational actions when necessary to ensure that decisions are ethical and are implemented in an ethical manner.
- Either avoid or disclose a potential conflict of interest that might influence or might be perceived to influence personal actions or judgements. A professional is in a conflict of interest situation when he or she tends to favour, for reasons that are extraneous to the interests of the organization, a client (employee) whom he or she is currently representing, or a course of action not in the best interests of the organization or the client.

SUMMARY

- Work and organizational psychology is defined as an applied division of psychology concerned with the study of human behaviour related to work, organizations and productivity.
- Work and organizational psychology comprises two branches, namely organizational psychology and work psychology. Organizational psychology focuses on individual differences and diversity management, motivation, communication, leadership, group behaviour, health and well-being, organizational design and organization development. Work psychology focuses on human resource management, including human resource planning, job analysis, description and job specifications, recruitment and selection, induction and training, career development, job evaluation and compensation, and performance appraisal.
- Various approaches and theories contributed to the field of work and organizational psychology. Early contributions stressed efficient performance according to economic principles. Classical organization theory was concerned with the effective organization of people. The Hawthorne studies, in turn, stressed the social nature of human beings. This was followed by the human relations movement, which paid attention to aspects such as human needs, attitudes, motives and relationships. In contrast to an emphasis primarily on structure or the human side of organizations, organizational thought in the past few decades has emphasized the integration of these two perspectives. More recent developments in the field of organization development and the positive psychology movement also contributed to the field of work and organizational psychology.
- Four tasks of the work and organizational psychologists are distinguished, namely explaining individual, group and organizational behaviour, measuring behaviour and predicting potential, contributing to organization development, and translating research findings and empowering potential users thereof.
- The competencies of work and organizational psychologists are classified based on three areas, namely knowledge of work and organizational psychology theory, research and statistical skills, and professional skills.
- Careers in work and organizational psychology are characterized by both rewarding and frustrating aspects.

KEY CONCEPTS AND TERMS

- Attitude
- Bias
- Behaviour
- Classical organization theory
- Competency
- Contingency theory
- Culture
- Diversity
- Effectiveness
- Efficiency
- Equity
- Human relations movement
- Human resource management
- Knowledge
- Learning organization
- Organizational behaviour
- Organizational culture
- Organizational psychology
- Organizational transformation
- Positive organizational behaviour
- Positive psychology
- Scientific management
- Skill
- Socio-technical systems approach
- System
- Total quality management
- Work psychology

SAMPLE ESSAY TITLES

- What is the relevance of positive psychology for work and organizational psychologists?
- What are the main tasks and competencies of work and organizational psychologists?

FURTHER READING

Books

Arnold, J., Silvester, J., Patterson, F., Robertson, I., Cooper C.L. and Burnes, B. (2005). *Work Psychology: Understanding Human Behavior in the Workplace* (4th edn). Harlow, Essex: Pearson Education.

Grenville-Cleave, B. (2012). *Positive Psychology: A Practical Guide*. Toronto, Ontario: Icon Books.

Steger, M.F. and Dik, B.J. (2010). 'Work as meaning'. In: Linley, P.A., Harrington, S. and Page, N. (eds) *Oxford Handbook of Positive Psychology and Work*. Oxford: Oxford University Press, 131–142.

Journal articles

Luthans, F. (2012). 'Psychological capital: Implications for HRD, retrospective analysis, and future directions'. *Human Resource Development Quarterly*, 23(1), 1–8.

1 | Organizational psychology

2 Individual differences and diversity management

This chapter focuses on individual-level variables that may affect individuals, groups and organizations. The first section describes personality, taking into account a cross-cultural perspective. More specifically, the five-factor or 'Big Five' personality model (which distinguishes between five personality dimensions, namely extroversion, emotional stability, conscientiousness, agreeableness and openness to experience) is introduced. We then look at values and the implications thereof for organizations. The chapter then proceeds to attitudes and how they can be measured and managed in organizations. This is followed by a discussion of mental abilities. Finally, we focus on diversity in the workplace.

LEARNING OUTCOMES

When you have completed this chapter you should be able to:

1 Explain what is meant by 'personality' and evaluate the elements of the most commonly accepted model of personality – the five-factor model.
2 Describe how personality affects job performance and other work-related outcomes.
3 Understand the relationship between attitudes and behaviour, especially regarding performance on the job.
4 Understand how work and organizational psychologists are helping companies to assess and manage job attitudes and their impact on organizational performance.
5 Explain what job attitudes are and be familiar with the assumptions that underlie them.
6 Motivate why diversity in the workplace matters, know the different types of diversity, and identify how work and organizational psychologists could help organizations to manage diversity.

PERSONALITY

Definition of personality

The word 'personality' is derived from the word *persona*, which has Greek and Latin roots and refers to the theatrical masks worn by Greek actors (Pervin and John, 2001). In the broadest sense, the term 'personality' refers to the enduring, inner characteristics of individuals who organize their behaviour (Derlega *et al.*, 2005). Most uses of the term can be summarized in terms of two major themes:

1   The first meaning of the term originates from the perspective of an observer and involves an individual's public presence and social reputation.
2   The second meaning refers to the inner self or being of an individual: one's private, vital and essential nature. With time, personality in this sense has come to mean the deep and enduring structures of an individual that form the central core of the self (Derlega *et al.*, 2005).

The measurement of personality becomes complicated by the fact that these two perspectives are not easily integrated and require quite different measurement strategies, since one emphasizes the outer visible aspects, while the other focuses on the inner dynamic whole for the outer perspective on personality.

HISTORY OF PERSONALITY THEORY AND RESEARCH

Trait theorists are concerned with the measurement of psychological characteristics (Arnold *et al.*, 1995) and this approach forms the basis of the psychometric approach to personality analysis, as portrayed by the use of factor analysis, where the factors are conceptualized as measurements of traits.

Within the framework of the trait theories, human behaviour is characterized by consistent patterns of behaviour known as traits, factors, dimensions or types. The trait approach can be divided into two paradigms, namely ideographic and nomothetic. Ideographic theorists (e.g. Allport, 1961) believe that every human being has their own unique set of traits that are fundamental to their personality. Nomothetic theorists (e.g. Cattell, 1965), on the other hand, believe that the exact same set of traits exists within each individual, but they differ from each other in the way and intensity to which each trait is manifested.

Cattell (1965) considered language a valuable tool to gather information regarding personality. He used a lexical approach to generate an original list of trait names. By means of factor analysis he identified sixteen core personality traits and developed the well-known personality assessment questionnaire, the Sixteen Personality Questionnaire (16PF). The development of the 16PF has played an important role in the development of the Big Five factor model.

An etic, emic or combined etic–emic approach to the conceptualization of personality may be employed (Cheung *et al.*, 2011). The *etic* approach emphasizes 'universals' or 'core similarities' in all human beings. The *emic* approach, on the other hand, supposes a culture-specific orientation (Berry, 1989). Unique cultural behaviour can be detected when an emic approach is used.

The cross-cultural generalizability of personality characteristics has most often been investigated by means of an imposed etic approach, which implies that assessment instruments developed in Western countries were adopted in other cultural contexts, assuming that the underlying theories and constructs are universal.

According to Church and Lonner (1998: 36), an etic strategy may increase the chances of finding cross-cultural comparability and exclude culture-specific dimensions. However, an imposed etic strategy may be biased towards the discovery of universals and may miss personality dimensions that are specific to particular cultures. Moreover, the specific values and tendencies of the Western culture may unknowingly lead to the de-emphasis or omission of some universal constructs. The emic approach seeks to identify an optimal way of structuring personality variables reflecting the indigenous patterns of each culture (Saucier, 2003).

Cheung *et al.* (2011) suggest that a combined etic and emic approach be used, which combines methodological rigor and cultural sensitivity. Such an approach is helpful in delineating the universal and culture-specific aspects of constructs.

CONCEPTUALIZATION OF PERSONALITY

The Big Five personality model

Since the mid-1980s research has focused on the use of the five-factor model (FFM) to classify personality (Barrick *et al.*, 2001). The FFM of personality represents a structure of traits, developed and elaborated over the last five decades (McCrae and Costa, 1995). Researchers agree that most personality measures could be categorized according to the FFM of personality (referred to as the 'Big Five' personality dimensions) (Goldberg, 1990). Research showed that the five personality factors have a genetic basis (Digman, 1989) and that they are probably inherited (Jang *et al.*, 1996).

According to the FFM, five basic personality dimensions underlie all others (see Focus 2.1).

Theory and research show that Big Five factors impact on motivation, which in turn affects performance. Personality is something that is expressed in attitudes and behaviours. A conscientious person does not perform highly because of the property of conscientiousness. Usually it is assumed that personality is a *distal* predictor of performance, operating through the more *proximal* processes of motivation. Self-efficacy (Bandura, 1977) and goals (Locke and Latham, 2002) are important motivational constructs in work and organizational psychology. Self-efficacy impacts both on goals and performance. Research shows the effects of both conscientiousness and emotional stability on self-efficacy and goals (Judge and Ilies, 2002).

It is necessary to acknowledge that the FFM is not unanimously accepted. According to Block (1995), factor analysis (which is a statistical technique used to uncover relationships among personality descriptive terms) is not an appropriate and adequate base to decide the theoretical constructs of personality. Other researchers have criticized the model on the basis of the number of factors (Eysenck, 1992; Tellegen and Waller, 1995). Are there three, five, sixteen or more factors? However, Costa and

The Big Five personality dimensions

- *Extroversion*: a personality dimension describing someone who is sociable, talkative and assertive.
- *Agreeableness*: a personality dimension describing someone who is good-natured, co-operative and trusting.
- *Conscientiousness*: a personality dimension describing someone who is responsible, dependable, persistent and achievement oriented.
- *Emotional stability*: a personality dimension which characterizes someone who is calm, enthusiastic, secure (positive) to tense, nervous, depressed and insecure (negative).
- *Openness to experience*: a personality characteristic which characterizes someone who is imaginative, sensitive and intellectual.

McCrae (1995) and Barrick *et al.* (2001) state that the Big Five has been reproduced a great number of times, through different factor analysis methods, by different researchers, with different instruments and in different languages.

A fundamental question for work and organizational psychologists interested in the measurement of personality and culture is whether personality traits are universal or *culture-specific*. The results from several studies indicated that the Big Five structure is less universal than supposed at the beginning of the 1990s (Digman, 1997; Goldberg, 1993). Some researchers found quite different personality structures in different cultures (Caprara *et al.*, 2001). In a large-scale South African study it was found that personality traits can be classified in terms of nine clusters, namely Conscientiousness, Emotional Stability, Extroversion, Facilitating, Integrity, Intellect, Openness, Relationship Harmony and Soft-Heartedness (Nel *et al.*, 2012).

Using a combined emic–etic approach, Valchev *et al.* (2013) investigated similarities and differences in the indigenous personality concepts of ethnocultural groups in South Africa. Nine personality clusters were found in all groups, yet the groups differed in their use of the model's components: Blacks referred more to social–relational descriptions, specific trait manifestations and social norms, whereas Whites referred more to personal-growth descriptions and abstract concepts, and Indians had an intermediate pattern. The results suggest that a broad spectrum of personality concepts should be included in the development of common personality models and measurement tools for diverse cultural groups.

Personality assessment as a tool in decision-making

Personality predicts aspects of job performance that may not be strongly related to knowledge, skills or abilities. Personality traits predict what a person will do, as opposed to what he or she can do. Borman and Motowidlo (1997) distinguish between two types of performance, namely task performance and contextual performance.

- *Task performance* refers to 'the effectiveness with which job incumbents perform activities that contribute to the organization's technical core' (Borman and Motowidlo, 1997: 100). For a salesperson, task performance will include components such as product knowledge, time management and task knowledge.
- *Contextual performance* includes 'volunteering to carry out task activities that are not formally part of the job and helping and co-operating with others in the organization to get tasks accomplished' (Borman and Motowidlo, 1997: 100). Contextual performance includes the following aspects: a) persisting with enthusiasm and extra effort as necessary to complete own task activities; b) volunteering to carry out activities that are not formally part of the job; c) helping and co-operating with others; d) following organizational rules and procedures, and e) endorsing, supporting and defending organizational objectives. Organizational citizenship behaviours, which indicate contextual performance, are defined as the willingness to 'go above and beyond' the call of duty. Unlike other selection tools, little or no evidence of adverse impact (different selection ratios between demographic groups) has been shown when personality traits are used to predict organizational citizenship behaviour.

There are various reasons why personality matters in the workplace (Barrick and Mount, 2005: 359):

- Managers care about personality; few managers will be willing to appoint a person who is anxious, unstable or irresponsible.
- Meta-analytic techniques assisted researchers to develop an understanding of the relationship between personality and performance.
- Personality contributes incremental validity in the prediction of job performance beyond that accounted for by other predictors.
- Meta-analytic derived estimates of the relation between a specific personality trait and performance is an underestimation.
- Small differences exist between racial and ethnic groups.
- Longitudinal data showed that personality traits predicted multiple facets of career success over a span of fifty years.
- Personality traits are significant predictors of organizational citizenship behaviour, turnover, absenteeism, safety and leadership effectiveness.

VALUES

Definition of values

Values are among the most stable and enduring characteristics of individuals. They are the basis on which attitudes and personal preferences are formed. An organization, too, has a value system, usually called its organizational culture.

Values are types of *beliefs*, centrally located within one's total belief system, about how one ought or ought not to behave, or about some end state of existence worth attaining (Rokeach, 1973). Values are general beliefs about desirable or undesirable ways of behaving and about desirable or undesirable goals or end states (Lonner and

ACTIVITY 2.1

Use of personality tests for personnel selection

Study the following article and answer the questions that follow:

> Meiring, D., Van de Vijver, F. J. R., Rothmann, S. and Barrick, M. (2005). Construct, item and method bias of cognitive and personality tests in South Africa. *South African Journal of Industrial Psychology*, 31(1), 1–8. (Article available online at http://sajip.co.za/index.php/sajip/article/view/182)

Questions:
What were the major findings of Meiring *et al.* (2005) regarding the use of personality tests imported from Europe for use in South Africa?

Do you think that the South African Police Service could use the personality test described in the study for selection purposes? Motivate your answer.

RESEARCH METHODS 2.1

Meta-analytical studies of the relationship between personality and work outcomes

Early researchers believed the personality–job performance relationship was weak. The reasons for this were that weak analytic techniques were employed, inappropriate measures of personality were used, no theoretical framework existed on which research findings could be based, and it was believed that behaviour is determined more by situations than by traits. Some people have argued that situations drive behaviour. However, psychologists would now agree that behaviour is best understood by taking into consideration both the person and the situation. It seems that personality has a much larger effect on performance than previously supposed.

The results of various studies showed that various Big Five personality dimensions are related to job performance. In the USA, Barrick and Mount (1991) found that Conscientiousness is a valid predictor across occupations and across criteria, and that the other personality factors only generalize their validity for some occupations and some criteria. Barrick and Mount found that Extroversion is a valid predictor for managers, Emotional Stability is a valid predictor for police, and Agreeableness is a valid predictor for police and managers. Openness to Experience did not show validity for any occupational group. Extroversion is a valid predictor of training proficiency, as are Emotional Stability, Agreeableness and Openness to Experience. The relative non-validity of Emotional Stability may have been due to a type of range restriction based on a 'selecting-out' process in the applicant pool, where the applicants low in Emotional Stability were already excluded from the applicant pool (Barrick and Mount, 1991).

Tett *et al.* (1991) found that all personality dimensions are valid predictors of job performance. However, Extroversion and Conscientiousness have lower validity coefficients, whereas Neuroticism, Openness to Experience and Agreeableness have higher validities. Salgado (1997) conducted a *meta-analysis* of the Big Five dimensions in relation to performance for three criteria (i.e. supervisory ratings, training ratings and personnel data) and for five occupational groups using thirty-six validity studies conducted in Europe. Results indicated that Conscientiousness and Emotional Stability were valid predictors for all performance criteria and for most occupational groups. Openness to Experience and Agreeableness showed validity for training criterion. Extroversion showed generalized validity for managers and police, although the validity for managers was very low.

Barrick *et al.* (2001) summarized the results of fifteen meta-analytic studies. They found that the validity of Conscientiousness in predicting job performance was the highest (of the personality traits studied) and that it generalized across all criterion types and all occupations studied. The validity of Emotional Stability was distinguishable from zero, but its overall relationship with performance was smaller than the effect for Conscientiousness. Barrick *et al.* suggested that a reason for the relatively low validity of Emotional Stability is that it might be a considerably broader construct than previously considered, and that it should include aspects such as self-esteem, self-efficacy and locus of control. Extroversion, Agreeableness and Openness to Experience predicted some aspects of performance in some occupations.

Malpass, 1994). Schwartz (1994) defines values as constructs that determine what people will strive for in their lives and what they are prepared to sacrifice. Values are trans–situational criteria or goals ordered by importance as guiding principles in life.

Values and culture

Values can be seen as culturally bound. This becomes clear when one looks at the different values and attitudes of different culture groups. According to Smith and Bond (1993), individuals who find themselves in a specific culture are also bound in a specific social environment. This social environment is home to their own unique norms, language, systems and values. This results in members of similar culture groups sharing many cultural and social values. Individual values and value priorities are, however, also formed by the individual's unique personal experience (Schwartz, 1999). This may result in individuals within a certain culture group having different and unique values and value priorities.

Recent studies have shown that values and value priorities are not displayed only by people, but that nations, countries and other social categories also display distinct value profiles or patterns (Roe and Ester, 1999). According to research, cultural dimensions of values reflect the basic issues or problems that societies must face in order to regulate human activities (Hofstede, 2001; Schwartz, 1999). Values are the foundation of cultural norms and set the standard for appropriate behaviour in specific situations (Schwartz, 1999).

Cultural values manifest in two main areas, namely collectivism and individualism. Traditional Western thinking tends to rate success and achievement very highly and is a good example of typical individualism (Duckitt and Foster, 1991). The opposite can be found in an African thinking pattern, where the emphasis falls on traditions and conformity. Collectivism is therefore more important. In these societies the needs of the group are more important than those of the individual (Smith and Bond, 1993).

Models of values

Different value models have been developed by various researchers and all these models are evidence that values are part of culture. Kluckhohn and Strodtbeck (1961) were the first to develop a model on values. According to their model, there are different value systems within different culture groups. They identified five main problems that can be found across all cultural groups, namely:

- What is the essence of being human?
- What is the relationship between humans, nature and the supernatural?
- What should the time focus of humans be?
- What is acceptable for human activity?
- What is the essence of human interpersonal relations?

According to Kluckhohn and Strodtbeck (1961), these five problems are present within all cultures. Priorities may, however, vary within different groups.

Rokeach (1973) placed values in hierarchical order within every individual. He distinguished between two main sets of values, namely terminal values and instrumental values. Terminal values are values that people find important in order to live a meaningful life. In order to achieve one's terminal values, instrumental values must

ACTIVITY 2.2

A theory of cultural values

Access the following link and study the information that is to be found therein – http://usdkexpats.org/theory/schwartzs-culture-model. Then answer the questions that follow:

Questions:
1 Which cultural values are distinguished by Schwartz?
2 What are the implications of these values for work contexts?

be applied. Instrumental values are the values individuals use to achieve the end state of their objectives. In all culture groups a total of thirty-six terminal and instrumental values are present, but the hierarchal order may vary (Hoag and Cooper, 2006).

Outcomes of values in organizations

Employees who hold values which are congruent with their organization's values are more productive and satisfied. Holding values which are inconsistent with company values is a major source of conflict, frustration and non-productivity. People sometimes lose touch with their own values, behaving in ways which are inconsistent with those values. Not being aware of one's own value priorities can lead to misdirected decisions and frustration in the long term. Because values are seldom challenged, people forget value priorities and behave in ways that do not fit the values. Until people encounter a threat to their values, they seldom seek to clarify them. Becoming mature in value development requires that individuals develop a set of internalized principles by which they can govern their behaviour. The development of those principles is enhanced and value maturity is increased as value-based issues are confronted, discussed and thought about.

ATTITUDES

Definition of attitudes

An attitude represents a predisposition to respond in a favourable or unfavourable way to persons or objects in one's environment (Fishbein and Ajzen, 1975). When we say we 'like' something or 'dislike' something, we are in effect expressing an attitude towards the person or object. Fishbein (1967) defines an attitude as a learned implicit response that varies in intensity and tends to guide (mediate) an individual's overt responses to an object. In Fishbein's conceptualization, attitude refers only to the evaluation of a concept and there is a mediating evaluative response to every stimulus. Consequently, people have attitudes towards all objects which may be positive, negative or neutral.

Research has shown that job attitudes of employees were very stable over a five-year period (Staw and Ross, 1985). Employees with negative job attitudes tended to remain negative, even those who changed jobs or occupations. In contrast, employees with positive job attitudes remained positive after five years.

Attitudes should not be confused with values. Values represent global beliefs that influence behaviour across situations, while attitudes relate only to behaviour directed towards specific objects, persons or situations. Values and attitudes are generally, but not always in harmony. Three important assumptions underlie the concept of attitudes, namely:

1   An attitude is a hypothetical construct. We cannot actually see attitudes, although we can often see their consequences. Therefore, the existence of attitudes must be inferred from people's statements and behaviours.

2   An attitude is a unidimensional construct. It can be measured along a continuum which ranges from very positive to very negative.

3   Attitudes are believed to be somewhat related to subsequent behaviour.

Attitudes and behavioural intentions

An attitude is defined as an evaluation of a psychological object (Ajzen, 2001). The work of Ajzen and Fishbein (1977, 1980) is frequently cited as a theoretical framework concerned with attitude formation, behavioural intentions and the prediction of overt behaviours. According to this work, beliefs about aspects of a job (e.g. 'I do not have sufficient advancement opportunities in my job') lead to an attitude (e.g. 'I am dissatisfied with my job'), which in turn results in behavioural intentions (e.g. 'I'm intending to quit my job'). Behavioural intentions are then often translated into actual behaviour, such as leaving the organization, assuming that the person is able to carry out the intention. The model of behavioural intention is given in Figure 2.1.

Figure 2.1 shows that behavioural intentions are influenced by one's attitude towards the behaviour as well as the perceived norms about exhibiting the behaviour. Attitudes and subjective norms are influenced by personal beliefs.

- *Beliefs influence attitudes*. Beliefs are the result of direct observation and inferences from previous learned relationships. Attitudes are based on salient or important beliefs that may change as relevant information is received. Figure 2.1 shows that an individual will have positive attitudes towards performing a behaviour when he or she believes that the behaviour is associated with positive outcomes. If the employee believes that quitting a job will lead to positive outcomes (e.g. better advancement opportunities), he or she will be more likely to quit.

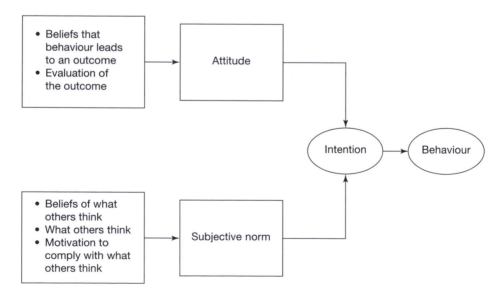

FIGURE 2.1 A model of behavioural intention

Source: Based on Ajzen and Fishbein, 1980

- *Beliefs influence subjective norms.* Subjective norms are an outcome of beliefs that specific individuals or groups think that the individual should (or should not) perform the behaviour. Subjective norms can exert a powerful influence on the behavioural intentions of individuals who are sensitive to the opinions of role models.

According to Breckler (1984), who presented an alternative model of attitudes, attitudes have three different components: affective, behavioural and cognitive. The affective component consists of the feelings that a particular topic arouses. The behavioural component consists of a tendency to act in a particular way with respect to a particular topic. The cognitive component consists of a set of beliefs about a topic – beliefs that can be expressed in words. The affective components of attitudes can be very strong and pervasive. Like other emotional reactions, these feelings can be strongly influenced by direct or vicarious classical conditioning. The affective component of attitudes tends to be rather resistant to change. The cognitive components of attitudes can be acquired quite directly by reading a fact or opinion, or reinforcement by other people. Behavioural components of attitudes are not as clear cut as once believed. People do not always behave as their expressed attitudes and beliefs would lead us to expect.

Attitude change

Although one can regard attitudes as causes of behaviour, behaviour may also affect attitudes. Festinger's (1957) theory of cognitive dissonance attempts to explain the impact of behaviour on attitude formation and change. According to Festinger, when an individual perceives a discrepancy between their attitudes and our behaviour, between behaviour and self-image, or between one attitude and another, an unpleasant state of dissonance results, a state that people are motivated to eliminate. A person can achieve dissonance reduction by: a) reducing the importance of one of the dissonant elements; b) adding consonant elements; or c) changing one of the dissonant elements. For example, an employee believes that they are a good performer, but receives poor performance ratings. Because the obvious prediction is that good performers get good ratings, the discrepancy causes the employee to experience dissonance. To reduce dissonance, the employee may decide that performance ratings are not important and that performance is not closely related to ratings. They are using strategy 1, reducing the importance of one of the dissonant elements. Or the employee may believe that their supervisor was unfair or that they had difficult circumstances at home which affected their performance. In this case, they are using strategy 2, reducing dissonance by adding consonant elements. Finally, the employee can use strategy 3 to change one of the dissonant elements (by performing better or by revising their opinion of their performance).

Assessing and managing attitudes

Work and organizational psychologists can assist managers to appreciate the dynamic relationships between beliefs, attitudes, subjective norms and behavioural intentions when attempting to foster productive behaviour (Conner and Clawson, 2004).

Although attitudes are often resistant to change, they might rest on incorrect beliefs, which could be indirectly influenced by education and training experiences. Subjective norms can also be redirected through clear and credible communication and role models.

Work and organizational psychologists can play the following roles in assessing and managing attitudes in organizations:

- *Attitude surveys.* The most obvious attitude-related activity of work and organizational psychologists is to develop, administer, analyse and report on the results of attitude surveys. Organizations use surveys to learn about employees' attitudes on employment issues such as compensation, quality of supervision, work/non-work balance. A weakness of attitude surveys is that management of organizations often fails to use the data and to implement recommended changes.
- *Job design.* Work and organizational psychologists assist organizations to design jobs in such a way that positive attitudes could be built.
- *Personnel selection.* Work and organizational psychologists are instrumental in developing reliable and valid prediction tools that incorporate attitudinal components.
- *Change management.* Work and organizational psychologists assist with change management in organizations by using attitude surveys to assess how employees view changes and their attitudes toward them.

ABILITIES

Definition of an ability

An ability is a broad and stable characteristic which is responsible for a person's maximum rather than typical performance on mental and physical tasks. An ability is the capacity to perform a physical or mental function.

Intelligence and cognitive abilities

Intelligence is regarded as a cognitive ability. Wechsler (1944) defined intelligence as 'the aggregate or global capacity of the individual to act purposefully, to think rationally and to deal effectively with his environment'. It is described as the general ability to perform cognitive tasks. Sternberg (1994) defined intelligence as the cognitive ability of an individual to learn from experience, to reason well, to remember important information and to cope with the demands of daily living. Intelligence is affected by the environment and more specifically schooling, socioeconomic status, healthy nutrition and the technologically complex society (Azar, 1996).

According to Sternberg (1994), intelligence comprises three interrelated abilities, namely analytical ability, creative ability and practical ability. The analytical ability solves familiar problems by using strategies that manipulate the elements of a problem or the relationship among the elements (e.g. comparing and analysing). The creative ability solves new kinds of problems that require thinking about the problem and its elements in a new way (e.g. inventing and designing). The practical ability solves problems that apply what individuals know to everyday contexts (e.g. applying and using).

Intelligence is considered as a set of skills which consists of behaviours that are modifiable. Three abilities are distinguished, namely a practical problem-solving ability, a verbal ability and social competence.

- *Practical problem-solving ability* includes behaviours such as good and logical reasoning, identifying connections among ideas, seeing all aspects of a problem, keeping an open mind and responding thoughtfully to others' ideas, and sizing up situations well.
- *Verbal ability* includes behaviours such as speaking clearly and articulating well, studying hard, reading widely with high comprehension, writing without difficulty, setting aside time for reading and displaying good vocabulary.
- *Social competence* includes behaviours such as accepting others for what they are, admitting mistakes, displaying interest in the world at large, being on time for appointments, thinking before speaking and doing, making fair judgements and assessing well the relevance of information to a problem at hand.

Dunette (1976) distinguished seven mental abilities that underlie performance of employees, namely verbal comprehension (i.e. the ability to understand the meaning of words and to comprehend verbal material), word fluency (i.e. the ability to produce specific words that fulfil certain requirements), numerical ability (i.e. the ability to make quick and accurate arithmetic computations), spatial ability (i.e. the ability to visualize how geometric shapes would look if transformed), memory (having a good memory for symbols and words), perceptual speed (i.e. the ability to perceive similarities and differences) and inductive reasoning (i.e. the ability to reason from specifics to general conclusions).

Abilities and performance

Ability tests are valid predictors of job performance and can be used for employee selection (Schmidt and Hunter, 1981). In a later study it was found that general mental ability is one of the best predictors of job performance (Schmidt and Hunter, 1998).

DIVERSITY

Diversity refers to the multitude of individual differences and similarities that exist among people. Diversity includes the mixture of many dimensions which make people unique and different from each other (Thomas, 1996).

Dimensions of diversity

Diversity has primary and secondary dimensions (Loden, 1996). These dimensions are described in Focus 2.2.

There is also a difference between valuing diversity and managing diversity. Valuing diversity refers to the awareness, recognition, understanding and appreciation of

FOCUS 2.2

Primary and secondary dimensions of diversity

Primary dimensions of diversity refer to human differences which affect the early socialization of individuals and have a powerful and sustained impact throughout their lives. Primary dimensions of diversity include gender, ethnicity, race, mental and physical abilities, sexual orientation and age.

Secondary dimensions of diversity refer to personal characteristics that include an element of personal choice. These dimensions are less visible to others, and their power to influence individuals' lives is less constant and more individualized. Secondary dimensions of diversity include education, language, religion, income, experience, geographic location, organizational role and communication style.

FIGURE 2.2 The workforce of organizations is increasingly becoming diverse

Source: © Konstantin Chagrin/Shutterstock.com

human differences (Thomas, 1996). It takes place through training and development of workers to improve interpersonal relationships among diverse groups (Nemetz and Christensen, 1996). In contrast, managing diversity entails enabling people to perform to their maximum potential by changing an organization's culture and infrastructure to allow people to be productive.

Managing diversity is different from affirmative action. Managing diversity focuses on maximizing the ability of all employees to contribute to organizational goals. Affirmative action focuses on specific groups because of historical discrimination, such as people of colour and women. Affirmative action is an artificial intervention which aims at giving organizations a chance to correct injustices, imbalances and mistakes of the past. Affirmative action emphasizes legal necessity and social responsibility; managing diversity emphasizes business necessity. While managing diversity is also concerned with under-representation of women and people of colour in the workforce, it is more inclusive and acknowledges that diversity must work for everyone.

Importance of diversity management

Diversity management is important because it enables organizations to grow and be sustainable in an increasingly competitive marketplace (Agars and Kotke, 2005). The most important reasons for the management of diversity at work include the following.

- *A diverse workforce*. More women are entering the workforce, people of colour represent a growing share of the workforce, there is a mismatch between the educational attainment and occupational requirements of occupations, the workforce is ageing, more people with disabilities are entering the labour market, and sexual orientation and political views can also create tensions in the workplace.
- *The service economy*. In the USA it is estimated that 75 per cent of employees work in the service industry (Janoski *et al.*, 2014). The interpersonal nature of service transactions makes similarities between employee and customer more important. As the population in general becomes more diverse, employees who can communicate most efficiently with those clients become a business advantage.
- *Globalization*. Globalization has increased the contact with clients and co-workers from other countries. An understanding of cultural differences can not only facilitate communication, but can also avoid potentially embarrassing or even insulting situations.
- *The changing labour market*. To deal with the changing labour market, employers are developing new recruiting strategies to target older employers, minorities and immigrants. They are developing more flexible benefits packages (more flexible hours, working from home, leaves of absence) to accommodate the new diversity they must manage.

In racial diverse settings a psychologically safe work environment where employees feel confident in expressing their true selves without fear of being judged as inferior or incompetent is important (Singh *et al.*, 2013). Psychological safety is a principal motivator of employee performance behaviours in a racially diverse work setting. Positive organizational contexts (such as diversity climate and psychological safety) hold a greater significance for minorities and are more effective in shaping their performance behaviours.

The role of work and organizational psychologists in managing diversity

The most common intervention used by work and organizational psychologists to help organizations manage diversity is *diversity training*. Training for managers will focus on how to recruit and hire a more diverse workforce. This training often entails raising awareness of new sources or outlets that allow employers to find a greater pool of applicants. Manager training will also focus on how to manage the diversity of the

---

ACTIVITY 2.3

Individual differences and diversity management

Individual differences will influence a person's experience of the workplace. For example, introverts and extroverts might experience workplace challenges very differently.

1 Identify a person who functions in a team in a medium to large organization and who is regarded as an introvert. Schedule an interview with the person. What you want to learn from this interview is how the individual experiences their work environment. Several issues to explore include:
   • How does the individual prefer to interact with others in the team?
   • How does the individual prefer others to interact with him or her?
   • Does he or she feel appreciated by others in the workplace? Elaborate.
   • What challenges does he or she experience in the workplace because of his or her introversion?
   • What strategies does he or she apply to overcome these challenges?

2 Identify a person who functions in a team in a medium to large organization and who is regarded as an extrovert. Schedule an interview with the person. What you want to learn from this interview is how the individual experiences their work environment. Several issues to explore include:
   • How does the individual prefer to interact with others in the team?
   • How does the individual prefer others to interact with him or her?
   • Does he or she feel appreciated by others in the workplace? Elaborate.
   • What challenges does he or she experience in the workplace because of his or her extroversion?
   • What strategies does he or she apply to overcome these challenges?

Present your findings to the class.

newly hired workers. Specifically, training will focus on how to integrate the new employees into the existing workforce and how to raise the awareness of the current employees as to the benefits of greater diversity. This often requires a shift in the style of management. The focus of management shifts from treating everyone equally to treating everyone equitably, given the differences that each employee brings to the job. Training for all employees goes through several steps. The first step entails raising awareness that differences do exist. The second step focuses on how these differences influence working together to get the job done. The third step focuses on how these differences can be used to enhance productivity without treating people unfairly.

SUMMARY

- Personality has been defined as the enduring, inner characteristics of individuals who organize their behaviour. An etic or emic approach to the conceptualization of personality may be employed. The five-factor model of personality represents a structure of traits, including extroversion, agreeableness, conscientiousness, emotional stability and openness to experience. Personality predicts aspects of job performance that may not be strongly related to knowledge, skills or abilities. There are various reasons why personality matters in the workplace. The results of several studies showed that various Big Five personality dimensions are related to job performance.
- Values are constructs that determine what people will strive for in their lives and what they are prepared to sacrifice. Values can be seen as culturally bound. Values and value priorities are not displayed only by people; nations, countries and other social categories also display distinct value profiles or patterns. Cultural values manifest in two main areas, namely collectivism and individualism. Different value models have been developed by various researchers and all these models are evidence that values are part of culture. Employees who hold values that are congruent with their organization's values are more productive and satisfied.
- An attitude represents a predisposition to respond in a favourable or unfavourable way to persons or objects in one's environment. Research has shown that job attitudes of employees were very stable over years. Beliefs about aspects of a job lead to an attitude, which in turn results in behavioural intentions. Behavioural intentions are often translated into actual behaviour. Although attitudes are often resistance to change, they might rest on incorrect beliefs, which could be indirectly influenced by education and training experiences.
- An ability is a broad and stable characteristic that is responsible for a person's maximum rather than typical performance on mental and physical tasks. Intelligence is regarded as a cognitive ability. Seven abilities underlie performance of employees, namely verbal comprehension, word fluency, numerical ability, spatial ability, memory, perceptual speed and inductive reasoning. Ability tests are valid predictors of job performance.
- Diversity refers to the multitude of individual differences and similarities that exist among people. Diversity has primary and secondary dimensions. Diversity

management is important because it enables organizations to grow and be sustainable in an increasingly competitive marketplace. The most common intervention used to help organizations manage diversity is diversity training.

KEY CONCEPTS AND TERMS

- Ability
- Agreeableness
- Attitude
- Attitude change
- Attitude survey
- Behavioural intention
- Beliefs
- 'Big Five' personality model
- Conscientiousness
- Contextual performance
- Emic approach
- Emotional stability
- Etic approach
- Extroversion
- Intelligence
- Meta-analysis
- Openness to experience
- Organizational citizenship behaviour
- Personality
- Task performance
- Value

SAMPLE ESSAY TITLES

- Is personality a predictor of work-related outcomes? Motivate your answer.
- What are the contents and methodology of a diversity training programme?

FURTHER READING

Books

Chamorro-Premuzic, T. (2007). *Personality and Individual Differences*. London: Blackwell.

Journal articles

Barrick, M.R., Mount, M.K. and Li, N. (2013). The theory of purposeful work behavior: The role of personality, higher-order goals, and job characteristics. *Academy of Management Review*, 38(1), 132–154.

Cheung, F.M., Van de Vijver, F.J.R. and Leong, F.T.L. (2011). Toward a new approach to the study of personality in culture. *American Psychologist*, 66(7), 593–603.

Pendry, L.F., Driscoll, D.M. and Field, S.C.T. (2007). Diversity training: Putting theory into practice. *Journal of Occupational and Organizational Psychology*, 80, 27–50.

Valchev, V.H., Van de Vijver, F.J.R., Nel, J. A, Rothmann, S. and Meiring, D. (2013). The use of traits and contextual information in free personality descriptions of ethno-cultural groups in South Africa. *Journal of Personality and Social Psychology*, 104(6), 1077–1091.

3 Motivation and satisfaction

This chapter focuses on motivation and job satisfaction. The first section describes motivation and theories thereof. Early theories of motivation are introduced, followed by contemporary theories. Early theories include Maslow's theory of needs hierarchy, Herzberg's two-factor theory, McGregor's Theory X and Theory Y, and McClelland's theory of needs. These theories tried to explain what motivates people. Contemporary theories include equity theory, expectancy theory, goal-setting theory, self-determination theory, engagement theory, self-efficacy theory and reinforcement theory. The chapter then proceeds to motivation principles and the application thereof in organizations. Finally, we focus on job satisfaction.

LEARNING OUTCOMES

When you have completed this chapter you should be able to:

1 Define motivation.
2 Compare and evaluate the different theories of motivation.
3 Explain how the different theories of motivation can be used to influence the behaviour of people in organizations.
4 Define job satisfaction and explain the factors which influence job satisfaction.
5 Give a description of the consequences of job satisfaction.
6 Explain the relationship between job satisfaction, motivation and performance.

DEFINITION OF MOTIVATION

Motivation is a set of energetic forces that originate both within and outside an individual to initiate work-related behaviour and to determine the direction, intensity and duration thereof (Latham and Pinder, 2005).

The definition of motivation has three key elements, namely intensity, direction and persistence (Robbins and Judge, 2013). Intensity describes how hard a person tries;

direction entails whether effort is channelled in areas that benefit the organization, while persistence refers to how long a person can maintain effort.

THEORIES OF MOTIVATION

One way in which to 'classify' work motivation theories is by distinguishing between early and contemporary theories (Robbins and Judge, 2013).

Early theories

The hierarchy of needs theory of Maslow

Maslow (1971) proposed that the needs of a person are arranged in a hierarchical order of importance. The most important needs appear at the bottom of the hierarchy. Once a given level of need is satisfied, it no longer serves to motivate. The following needs are distinguished (Greenberg, 2011):

1   *Physiological needs.* Physiological needs (e.g. hunger, thirst and sleep) are the most basic of all the needs.
2   *Safety/security needs.* Safety/security needs involve the protection from physical danger and economic instability. The appropriate encouragement in this field is stable working conditions, the prospect of increasing cost of living being covered by an increase in salary, that provision shall be made for illness, disability and old age by contributing towards medical, insurance and pension schemes.
3   *Social needs.* Social needs refer to the need to affiliate with other people. They refer to the need to have friends, to be loved by others and to be accepted by other people. The group of which the individual is a member plays a very important role in satisfying these needs.
4   *Esteem/ego needs.* These needs can be divided into two groups, namely self-esteem needs and needs concerning (receiving) esteem from others. The first group is concerned with needs which are related to a person's self-value and self-respect (e.g. achievement, independence and freedom). The second group is concerned with needs that are related to reputation or prestige that others ascribe to the person (e.g. status, recognition and respect).
5   *Self-actualization needs.* Self-actualization needs are found at the top of the hierarchy of needs. Self-actualization needs are associated with the desire to become all that one is capable of being.

Maslow's theory has not been subjected to much research. In cases where it has been researched in organizations, the data gathered do not seem to strongly support the theory. There seems to be an overlap between the different categories of needs. Some people are of the opinion that the physiological and the safety/security needs should be grouped together in one category, and that the higher order needs should be grouped together in another category. It is also possible that many of people's different needs may be partially satisfied and partially unsatisfied at the same time.

FIGURE 3.1 Money can be used to satisfy various needs

Source: © Edler von Rabenstein/Shutterstock.com

The two-factor theory of Herzberg

Frederick Herzberg proposed this theory, which is also known as the motivation–hygiene theory (Herzberg *et al.*, 1959). Herzberg wanted to know the answer to the following question: What do people want from their jobs? Herzberg and his colleagues interviewed about 200 engineers and accountants. The participants were asked to describe occasions when they had felt particularly good about their jobs and describe occasions when they had felt particularly bad about their jobs. Job factors which tended to be consistently related to job satisfaction were achievement, recognition, the work itself, responsibility, advancement and growth. Job factors that tended to be consistently related to job dissatisfaction were company policy and administration, supervision, interpersonal relations with supervisor, work conditions, salary, factors in personal life, status and job security.

Herzberg and his colleagues made a distinction between motivators and hygiene factors, because the factors which lead to satisfaction and thus to motivated behaviour (the motivators – if they are present) are distinct from those that lead to dissatisfaction (the hygiene factors – if they are absent). Also, based on the above findings, the researchers were led to believe that the opposite of satisfaction (when the motivators are present) is not dissatisfaction, but rather 'no satisfaction' (when the motivators are absent), and that the opposite of dissatisfaction (when the hygiene factors are absent) is not satisfaction, but rather 'no dissatisfaction' (when the hygiene factors are present). Once the hygiene factors are in order, they form a kind of a base or platform on which to build the motivators.

Although the motivators appear to be distinct from the hygiene factors (81 per cent of the factors which contributed to job satisfaction were motivators and 69 per cent of the factors which contributed to dissatisfaction were hygiene factors), hygiene factors sometimes lead to satisfaction (19 per cent of the factors which contributed to job satisfaction were hygiene factors) and motivators sometimes lead to dissatisfaction (31 per cent of the factors which contributed to dissatisfaction were motivators). Aspects such as a good remuneration, good supervision and a pleasant work environment are important factors to prevent employees from becoming dissatisfied. If employees become dissatisfied, they will tend to become demotivated. On the other hand, employee motivation is a result of factors such as the nature of the work they perform, the recognition they receive for tasks well done, the responsibility they carry, the opportunity they have to achieve and the promotion they receive. In practice, then, one should attend to both the motivators and the hygiene factors.

Herzberg placed a lot of emphasis on personal growth as a motivating factor. There are, however, limits to what can be achieved in organizations regarding making use of the motivators (e.g. changing the nature of employees' jobs). There might be employees who do not wish to have their jobs enriched or changed. Some employees do not have the skills needed to handle these enriched or changed jobs. Criticism directed at the theory is that the procedure which Herzberg used is limited by its methodology. When things are going well, people tend to take credit themselves. Contrarily, they blame failure on the external environment. Furthermore, the theory provides an explanation of job satisfaction rather than motivation (Robbins and Judge, 2013).

Theory X and Theory Y

Douglas McGregor (1960) proposed two distinct views of human beings, namely Theory X and Theory Y. Theory X represents a negative and pessimistic view of human nature, which in many ways is consistent with the assumptions of scientific management. Theory Y represents an optimistic and a positive view of human nature.

Under Theory X, managers assume that:

- people do not like work and try to avoid it;
- managers have to control, direct, coerce and threaten employees to get them to work towards organizational goals;
- people prefer to be directed, to avoid responsibility, to want security: they have little ambition.

Under Theory Y, managers assume that people:

- do not naturally dislike work: work is a natural part of their lives;
- are internally motivated to reach objectives to which they are committed;
- are committed to goals to the degree that they receive personal rewards when they reach their objectives;
- will both seek and accept responsibility under favourable conditions;
- have the capacity to be innovative in solving organizational problems;
- are bright, but under most organizational conditions their potentials are underutilized.

McGregor (1960) believed th[...]
X assumptions. He proposed prac[...]
relations and a challenging job which a[...]
no evidence exists for the validity of the[...]
that Theory Y will lead to higher work m[...]

McClelland's theory of needs

McClelland (1955, 1984, 1987) did extensive rese[...]
affiliation and achievement. Let us now take a closer [...]

- *The need for power.* This need for power is characteriz[...]
  impact, to be influential and to have control over one's en[...]
  high in the need for power enjoy being in charge, strive for in[...]
  prefer to be placed into competitive and status–oriented situatio[...]
  more concerned with prestige and gaining influence over oth[...]
  effective performance.
- *The need for affiliation.* The need for affiliation has to do with the desire[...]
  strong interpersonal ties and to get close (on a psychological basis) to other p[...]
  It thus is the need for human companionship, and to be liked and accepted[...]
  others. They strive for friendship, prefer co-operative situations rather than[...]
  competitive ones and desire relationships involving a high degree of mutual
  understanding.
- *The need for achievement.* The need for achievement has to do with the desire to
  reach goals or to accomplish tasks more effectively than in the past. A person with
  a high need for achievement sets him- or herself goals which are neither too easy
  (because then there is very little challenge involved) or too difficult (because then
  there is little chance that he or she will reach the goal). At the same time these
  goals should constitute a challenge to the person, so that he or she needs to make
  use of his or her abilities. Such a person also wants immediate and concrete
  feedback on his or her performance. A person with a high need for achievement
  tends to be preoccupied with his or her work, even when they are away from the
  work situation. The last principal characteristic of a person with a high need for
  achievement is the tendency for such a person to take personal responsibility for
  getting things done.

High achievers are strongly motivated when jobs have a high degree of personal
responsibility and feedback, and a moderate degree of risk. However, individuals with
a high achievement need do not necessarily make good managers, because they are

ACTIVITY 3.1

Usefulness

If we call the theories of Maslow, Herzberg and McClelland 'need' theories, what
are the similarities between these theories?

t Theory Y assumptions are more valid than Theory
ices such as participative decision-making, good
low employees to take responsibility. However,
assumptions of Theory X and Theory Y or
tivation (Robbins and Judge, 2013).

rch about the needs for power,
ook at each of these needs.

d by the desire to have
ironment. Individuals
fluence over others,
s, and tend to be
ers than with
to form
eople.
by

rthermore, high-
ss (Robbins and
best be assessed
might be difficult
used to measure

e theory is that
that they have
eliminate the
is based on the
e belief that a
f that a person
2012). When
es for pay and
e any inequity

whether they
e input(s) the
puts, and this
person sees as the ratio of
outcomes to inputs of the person/people/situation(s) they compare themselves with. The inputs are the characteristics the person brings with him or her to the job, for example race, sex, age, education or experience. It is important to note that these characteristics are subjectively perceived by the person. The outcomes are those things the individual receives from the job, such as pay/salary, promotions and fringe benefits (Robbins and Judge, 2013).

What is rather complicated about equity theory is the role of the specific person or situation which the individual chooses to compare him- or herself with (this person/situation is called the referent). It thus implies that the referent who or which is chosen plays an important role in equity theory. An equity comparison typically occurs whenever organizations allocate extrinsic rewards, especially monetary incentives or pay increases. Inequity is perceived whenever people feel the rewards received for their work are unfair given the rewards other persons are getting. The comparison others may be co-workers in the group, workers elsewhere in the organization, and even persons employed by other organizations. According to Adams (1963), these comparisons can result in any of three states (see Focus 3.1).

What happens when a person feels inequity? He or she is motivated to reduce this inequity (Armstrong and Taylor, 2014). On the other hand, if a person feels equity, he or she tends to try to maintain the current situation. The first two methods of reducing inequity are rather straightforward. A person may increase/decrease his or her effort, depending on the type of inequity that is felt. A person might try to alter the outcomes. This may take on a demand for a higher pay/salary, seeking other ways

States of inequity

- *Overpayment* inequity occurs when a perso[n]
  greater than the corresponding ratio of the ot[her]
  person compares him- or herself. According to [equity theory, such a]
  person will tend to feel guilty.
- *Underpayment* inequity occurs when a person's ou[tcome/input is]
  less than the corresponding ratio of the other person [with whom that]
  person compares him- or herself. According to equity t[heory, such a]
  person will tend to feel angry.
- *Equitable payment* occurs when a person's outcome/input [is equal to]
  the corresponding ratio of the other person with whom that [person]
  compares him- or herself. According to equity theory, such a p[erson will]
  tend to feel satisfied.

in which to develop and grow, or it might even go as far as stealing. In these ways a person alters his or her own ratio. A more complex situation arises wh[en a] person wants to alter the perceptions of self and of others. This means that a pers[on] has to change his or her original view of the ratio between his or her own outcome[s] and inputs, or change his or her original view of the ratio of the comparison–other regarding the comparison–other's outcomes and inputs. Another way of reducing inequity is to exchange the current comparison–other for another comparison–other, who would provide a more valid basis for comparison. Of course, a person might, as a last resort, simply decide to leave the situation by resigning or by asking for a transfer to another job or department (Moorhead and Griffin, 2012).

People who feel overpaid (positive inequity) have been found to increase the quantity or quality of their work. Those who feel underpaid (negative inequity) reduce their work efforts to compensate for the missing rewards, which means they are less motivated to work hard in the future. The way rewards are perceived by their recipients will largely determine how they affect satisfaction and performance. Because feelings of inequity are based on individual perceptions, it is not the reward's absolute value or what a manager thinks that counts. It is what the recipients think that determines motivational outcomes. Rewards perceived as equitable should have a positive result; those perceived as inequitable may create dissatisfaction and reduced performance.

From the above-mentioned methods of reducing inequity it is clear that some involve behavioural responses (like stealing), while others involve psychological responses (like thinking differently about the situation). As many people would feel uncomfortable with stealing from their organization, they might try to lessen the inequity by thinking differently about the situation. This implies some kind of psychological process of altering their perception.

Most of the research about the equity theory thus far has concentrated on pay/salary, equity/inequity. Strong support was found for equity theory. However, recent research

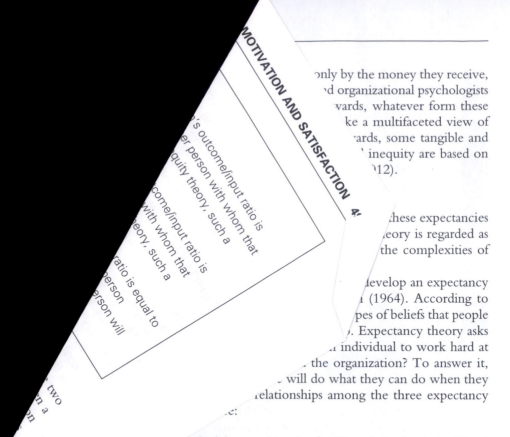

only by the money they receive,
organizational psychologists
vards, whatever form these
ke a multifaceted view of
ards, some tangible and
inequity are based on
12).

these expectancies
eory is regarded as
the complexities of

levelop an expectancy
(1964). According to
pes of beliefs that people
. Expectancy theory asks
individual to work hard at
the organization? To answer it,
will do what they can do when they
relationships among the three expectancy

s belief that working hard will result in the desired level
being achieved (effort–performance expectancy). If a person
harder he or she works, the more he or she will accomplish, then
y that such a person holds a high effort–performance expectancy. On
her hand, a person might be able and willing to work hard, but might not
ave the necessary skills or training, or has to work with faulty equipment. Such
a person is more likely to hold a very low effort–performance expectancy.

- *Instrumentality (I)*: A person's belief that successful performance will be followed by rewards and other potential outcomes (performance–outcome expectancy). Even if a person works hard and performs at a high level, his or her motivation is likely to decrease if that performance is not suitably rewarded by the organization. In this instance, the person is likely to hold a low belief that high performance is instrumental in bringing about rewards. A case in point is when a person has reached the top of his or her salary scale, and no further advancement opportunities exist for him or her.
- *Valence (V)*: The value a person assigns to the possible rewards and other work-related outcomes (rewards–personal goal relationship). Valence refers to the degree to which organizational rewards satisfy an individual's personal goals or needs and the attractiveness of those potential rewards for the individual. If a person would rather like to receive a promotion as a reward for his or her efforts, but knows that the reward will (only) be in the form of a bonus, such a person is likely to hold a low rewards–personal goal belief. Their motivation is likely to be low.

$$\text{Motivation} = E \times I \times V$$

Note that a zero at any location at the right side of the equation will result in zero motivation. The manager must give attention to each of the components of motivation. Consider the following ways (see Focus 3.2):

Applying expectancy theory

- *Maximize expectancy*: Make the person feel competent and capable of achieving the desired performance level. This can be done by selecting workers with ability, training workers to use their abilities, supporting work efforts and clarifying performance goals.
- *Maximize instrumentality*: Make the person confident in understanding which rewards and outcomes will follow performance accomplishments. Clarify psychological contracts, communicate performance outcome possibilities and explain that rewards are contingent on performance.
- *Maximize valence*: Make the person understand the value of various possible rewards and work outcomes. Identify individual needs and adjust rewards to match these needs.

According to expectancy theory, motivation is not equal to job performance. Motivation is only one of several factors which influence job performance. Skills and abilities, and role perceptions, also play an important role in job performance. In one of the examples we have already mentioned something about the role of skills and abilities. Role perceptions have to do with what people think is expected of them. If a person thinks that he or she is expected to carry out certain tasks, but his or her supervisor expects him or her to do other tasks, then such a person might be seen as not performing his or her work adequately (Greenberg, 2011).

Next, an 'extended' version of expectancy theory, namely that of Porter and Lawler (1968), will be discussed. Initially, an individual's effort to a great degree depends upon the attractiveness (valence) of the potential reward he or she can expect if he or she exerts him- or herself, and upon the perceived probability (expectancy) that the effort will lead to a certain reward. Together with the individual's abilities and traits, and role perceptions, effort leads to performance, which in turn leads to receiving of rewards. The individual then judges how equitable the rewards are. If the rewards are perceived as being equitable, the individual will feel satisfied. Next time around, the degree of satisfaction with the rewards (a bonus) influences the value that the individual attaches to the rewards. Also, the performance that followed from the effort influences the way in which the individual perceives the probability that a certain effort will lead to certain rewards.

According to the 'extended' expectancy theory, performance leads to rewards, and these in turn lead to satisfaction with the rewards. It is also clear that satisfaction indirectly influences (future) performance. Also, it is clear that this version of expectancy theory incorporates some of the notions of equity theory. Porter and Lawler

(1968) recommend that one should attempt to measure the values of possible rewards, the perceptions of effort–reward probabilities, and role perceptions. Organizations should also take a critical look at the way in which employees are rewarded. They also stress that one should look closely at the relationship between levels of satisfaction and levels of performance.

Regarding the relationship between motivation and performance, barriers to performance should be overcome by ensuring that: a) people possess the necessary abilities, skills and knowledge to do their jobs; b) it is physically and practically possible for people to carry out their jobs; c) the interdependence of jobs with other people or activities is taken into account; and d) ambiguity surrounding the job requirements is kept to a minimum. Regarding the relationship between performance and satisfaction, the following guidelines have been suggested: a) determine what rewards each employee values; b) define what the desired standard of performance is; c) make it possible for employees to attain the desired standard of performance; and d) link the valued rewards to the attained levels of performance.

Goal-setting theory

Task goals in clear and desirable performance targets form the basis of the goal-setting theory of Locke and Latham (1984). According to this theory, task goals can be highly motivating if they are specific and not too difficult. Goals affect performance through four mechanisms (Locke and Latham, 2002), namely:

- they direct attention and effort to goal-relevant activities and away from goal-irrelevant activities;
- they have an energizing function;
- they affect persistence; and
- they affect action indirectly by leading to arousal, discovery and/or use of task-relevant knowledge and strategies.

Moderators of the goal–performance relationship include the following (Locke and Latham, 2002):

- *Goal commitment.* The goal–performance relationship is the strongest when people are committed to goals. Workers tend to be committed to goals when they regard them as important and when their levels of self-efficacy are high.
- *Feedback.* For goals to be effective, people need summary feedback that reveals progress in relation to their goals.
- *Task complexity.* Goal effects are dependent upon the ability to discover appropriate task strategies.

The essential elements of goal-setting theory and high performance are illustrated in Figure 3.2.

A manager must work with subordinates to set the right goals in the right ways. The following guidelines can be used:

- *Set specific goals.* They lead to higher performance than more generally stated ones such as 'do your best'.

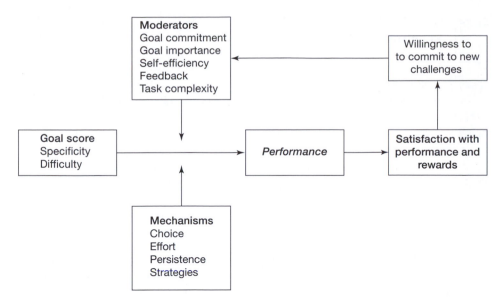

FIGURE 3.2 Elements of goal-setting theory and high performance

Source: Locke and Latham (2002). Copyright © American Psychological Association. Reproduced with permission.

- *Set challenging goals.* As long as they are viewed as realistic and attainable, more difficult goals lead to higher performance than easy goals.
- *Build goal acceptance and commitment.* People work harder towards goals that they accept and believe in; they tend to resist goals that seemed forced on them.
- *Clarify goal priorities.* Make sure that expectations are clear as to which goals should be accomplished first and why.
- *Reward goal accomplishment.* Do not let positive accomplishments pass unnoticed; reward people for doing what they set out to do.

Self-determination theory

According to self-determination theory (SDT), motivation ranges from autonomous and stemming from within the self (self-concordant), to controlled and stemming from outside pressure (Deci and Ryan, 2008b). Intrinsic motivation occurs when an activity is undertaken out of interest, enjoyment or inherent satisfaction, is divided into three parts, namely intrinsic motivation to know, intrinsic motivation towards accomplishment and intrinsic motivation to experience stimulation. The basic premise of SDT is that the satisfaction of the three psychological needs, namely autonomy, competence and relatedness (see Focus 3.3), is a prerequisite for intrinsic motivation (Deci and Ryan, 2008a, 2008b). Satisfying all three needs is important for optimal functioning and well-being.

Activities that are not intrinsically motivating require extrinsic motivation. Extrinsic motivation relates to activities undertaken for other reasons than interest in the activity, and can be classified as integration, identification, introjections and external regulation (Ryan and Deci, 2002). *Integrated regulation* occurs when an activity is

Psychological needs

* The need for *autonomy* refers to the desire to experience freedom and choice when carrying out an activity.
* The need for *competence* refers to individuals' inherent desire to feel effective in interacting with the environment.
* The need for *relatedness* refers to the innate need of individuals to feel connected to others, to love and care for others, and to be loved and cared for. This need is satisfied when individuals experience a sense of communion and develop close and intimate relationships with others.

recognized as worthwhile because it is seen as a means to an end. *Identification* occurs when individuals identify that an activity is worthwhile for a specific reason. *Introjected regulation* is governed by rewards and restrictions implemented by individuals themselves. *External regulation* is governed by rewards and restrictions implemented by others. The latter type of motivation is the lowest type of motivation on the self-determination continuum.

Psychological need satisfaction will enhance employees' intrinsic motivation and promote internalization of extrinsic motivation (Gagné and Deci, 2005). A work environment characterized by autonomy support will elicit overall need satisfaction (i.e. of all three needs) and result in greater work engagement and well-being. Employees who perceived their managers as being more autonomy supportive exhibited greater job satisfaction and better well-being (Rothmann *et al.*, 2013). Competence and relatedness are necessary for motivation, whether being autonomous or controlled motivation, and are implicit in autonomy support (Deci and Ryan, 2000). Focus 3.4 shows examples of behaviour of supervisors and managers that support psychological need satisfaction.

Employees' intrinsic motivation and internalization of extrinsic motivation contribute to two components of organizational commitment, namely identification with an organization and internalization of its values. Thus, psychological need satisfaction can be regarded as an important mediator between managerial autonomy support and turnover intention (Van den Broeck *et al.*, 2008).

Engagement theory

According to the personal engagement theory of Kahn (Kahn and Heaphy, 2014), individuals invest personal energies into role behaviours and express their selves (Kahn and Heaphy, 2014) physically, cognitively and emotionally during role performance. Engagement is characterized by three dimensions, namely a physical dimension (having a high energy level), an emotional dimension (being dedicated) and a cognitive dimension (getting absorbed in work).

According to the personal engagement theory of Kahn (1990), various factors might shape the engagement of employees through three psychological conditions, namely meaningfulness, safety and availability (Kahn and Heaphy, 2014). Focus 3.5 shows the definitions of the three psychological conditions.

FOCUS 3.4

Behaviour that supports psychological need satisfaction

Autonomy support
- Encourage employees to speak up when they disagree with a decision.
- Encourage employees to participate in important decisions.
- Provide direction when needed.
- Provide a meaningful rationale for doing a task.
- Emphasize choice rather than control.

Competence support
- Support employees' attempts to acquire additional training or education.
- Provide helpful feedback about employees' performance.
- Encourage employees to develop new skills and/or strengthen current skills.
- Praise good work and inspire employees.
- Make it clear what employees should be doing.

Relatedness support
- Treat people fairly and in a humane way.
- Protect employees' interests.
- Be accessible and trustworthy.
- Communicate in a way that employees understand.
- Listen carefully to different points of view before coming to conclusions.

FOCUS 3.5

Psychological conditions for personal engagement

- Psychological *meaningfulness* relates to the value that people attach to a work goal compared with their own personal goals.
- Psychological *safety* is defined as the experience of being able to act in a way that is natural, and to be able to use and employ all skills and knowledge in a role without having to fear ridicule or negative consequences.
- Psychological *availability* is the ability to engage as a result of having the cognitive, emotional and physical resources.

According to the model of Kahn (1990), person–environment fit, job enrichment and co-worker relations affect personal engagement via experiences of psychological meaningfulness. Supervisor and co-worker relations affect personal engagement via experiences of psychological safety. Personal resources and work/life interference affect personal engagement via experiences of psychological availability (May *et al.*, 2004; Rich *et al.*, 2010; Rothmann and Welsh, 2013).

Because organizations are defined by relationships among people who co-ordinate their activities in the service of tasks, goals and missions, relational contexts shape personal engagement in work roles (Kahn and Heaphy, 2014). Relationships shape meaningfulness by deepening individuals' experiences of the purposes of their work (in teams, in leader–follower situations and in relations with beneficiaries of your job) and by heightening their sense of belongingness (social identification) at work. Experienced safety is shaped through empathic acknowledgement and an enabling perspective. Relationships shape availability through energizing interactions and emotional relief (Kahn and Heaphy, 2014).

According to the Job Demands-Resources (JD-R) model (Demerouti *et al.*, 2001), every occupation has specific characteristics (job demands and job resources) associated with the well-being of people. Employee engagement results when job resources (e.g. supervisor and co-worker support) are available and when job resources are exceeding job demands (Schaufeli and Bakker, 2004). Personal resources (e.g. optimism) have also been studied in relations to models of employee engagement (Xanthopoulou *et al.*, 2009). For example, research has shown that employees who are optimistic were inclined to perceive that job resources are available, while pessimists were inclined to perceive a lack of job resources (Barkhuizen *et al.*, 2014).

Employee engagement is associated with various positive organizational outcomes, including higher customer loyalty, lower absenteeism, higher productivity and profitability, as well as lower rates of staff turnover (Harter *et al.*, 2002). Employee engagement predicts positive organizational outcomes, e.g. productivity, job satisfaction, motivation, commitment, low turnover intention, customer satisfaction, return on assets, profits and shareholder value (Rich *et al.*, 2010).

Self-efficacy theory

Self-efficacy refers to a belief in the probability that one can successfully execute some action or task to achieve some result. The construct self-efficacy is linked to social cognitive theory (Wood and Bandura, 1989). In difficult situations, people with low self-efficacy are likely to reduce their effort or to give up. In contrast, people with high self-efficacy will try harder to master a challenge.

Self-efficacy is a powerful motivator of behaviour because efficacy expectations at a given point in time determine the initial decision to perform a task, the effort expended and the level of persistence that emerges in the face of adversity. Self-efficacy can also be viewed as a general, stable cognition (trait) that individuals hold and carry with them, that reflects the expectation that they possess the ability to perform tasks successfully in a variety of achievement situations.

Efficacy beliefs may be enhanced by mastery experiences, vicarious experience, verbal persuasion and positive emotional states. Hence motivational programmes should include these elements, for instance, practical exercises to provide experiences of vocational success (mastery experiences), role models of good performance (vicarious experiences), coaching and encouragement (verbal persuasion) and reducing fear of rejection or failure (managing emotional states). Enactive mastery (i.e. getting experience with a task or job) is the most important source of increasing self-efficacy. Employees who have done a task successfully in the past will be more confident to perform it confidently in the future.

Reinforcement theory

Reinforcement theory entails a behaviouristic approach to motivation. Behaviourists believe that living systems function according to the principles of operant conditioning. In other words, behaviour is followed by a consequence and the nature of the consequence modifies the organism's tendency to repeat the behaviour. Skinner's classic laboratory studies showed that rats in a cage learn to acquire food by repetitively touching a mechanical device.

The implication of reinforcement theory for work and organizational psychologists is that behaviour might be reinforced by the consequences thereof. For example, pay can motivate people to show specific behaviours. However, the process is probably much more difficult than simply a stimulus and response. Reinforcement probably has an important influence on behaviour, but is not the only influence on behaviour.

IMPLICATIONS OF MOTIVATIONAL THEORIES

Next, some implications of motivational theories and research findings will be discussed, based on the theories as discussed in this chapter as well as recent reviews of the topic (Latham and Pinder, 2005).

Personal motives and values

A motivating environment can be created by ensuring that the motives and values of the worker match those of the organization and the job. This can be done by giving a realistic preview of the job or training the worker to accept these motives and values. Jobs might be simple, repetitive and require little brain power to do. If someone for this type of work is found, the candidate should be told exactly what the job entails and then a candidate who will be satisfied doing that kind of work should be selected.

Goal setting

Work and organizational psychologists can assess the motivational climate of their working environment by asking, 'Do workers understand and accept performance expectations?'. The foundation of an effective motivation programme is proper goal setting. Effective goal setting has three critical components: goal-setting process, goal characteristics and feedback.

- *Goal-setting process.* Goals must be understood and accepted if they are to be effective. Workers are more likely to accept goals if they feel they were part of the generation process. This is especially important if the work environment is unfavourable for goal accomplishment (for example, when the goal is inconsistent with accepted practice or when it requires new skills).
- *Goal characteristics.* Research has shown that goal characteristics significantly affect the likelihood that the goal will be accomplished. Effective goals are specific, consistent and appropriately challenging. Specific goals are measurable, unambiguous and behavioural.

- *Feedback.* Feedback provides opportunities for clarifying expectations, adjusting goal difficulty and gaining recognition. Therefore, it is important to provide benchmark opportunities for individuals to determine how they are doing. These progress reports are particularly critical when the time required to complete an assignment or reach a goal is very long.

Facilitating subordinates' performance

One key ingredient of an effective goal programme is a supportive work environment. After goals have been set, the work and organizational psychologist's focus should shift to helping accomplishment. Help may come in many forms, including making sure that the worker has the required abilities for the job, providing the necessary training, securing needed resources and encouraging co-operation and support from other work units. In other words, work and organizational psychologists should assist in making the paths leading towards the targeted goals easier for workers to travel.

Appropriate use of rewards and discipline

An important step in developing an effective motivational programme is to encourage goal accomplishment by linking performance to outcomes (rewards and discipline). Two principles are important, namely: a) rewards should be linked to performance, rather than seniority or membership; and b) discipline could be used to decrease counterproductive behaviour and rewards could be used to reinforce constructive behaviour.

If an organization is rewarding all people the same or on some basis other than performance, then high performers are likely to feel that they are receiving less than they deserve. The most important individuals in any organization are its high performers. Therefore, motivational schemes should be geared to keeping high performers satisfied. This principle raises a voice of caution regarding the practice of eliminating distinctions between workers. Although there are obvious motivational benefits to employees who feel they are receiving the same rewards despite seniority level or level of authority, this philosophy, when carried to an extreme, ends up demotivating high performers.

Managers and supervisors must recognize that their daily interactions with subordinates are important motivators (Clawson, 2006). The following types of responses to employee behaviour must be considered:

- *Extinction.* Extinction is behaviour followed by no response at all, but can be a difficult strategy to carry out. Often a non-response is interpreted as either a positive or negative response. If behaviour persists, it is reinforced. Thus, if an employee is chronically late or continually submits sloppy work, the manager must ask where the reinforcement for this behaviour is coming from.
- *Disciplining.* Discipline involves responding negatively to an employee's behaviour with the intention of discouraging future occurrences. Discipline should be used to extinguish unacceptable behaviour. However, once an individual's behaviour has reached an acceptable level, negative responses will not push the behaviour up to the exceptional level. Failure to reprimand and redirect inappropriate

behaviour may lead to undesirable outcomes. It poses a serious threat to the work unit's morale and it does not improve the poor performer's behaviour.

- *Rewarding*. The rewarding approach consists of linking desired behaviour with employee-valued outcomes. For example, when a worker completes a report in time, the manager praises their promptness. It is only through positive reinforcement that workers have control over achieving what they want.

Providing attractive rewards

It is a mistake to assume that all workers value the same outcomes. Workers could be allowed to select from a benefits menu. A flexible reward system helps managers not to project their own preferences on to subordinates.

External motivators are controlled by someone other than the worker. The manager or supervisor can show appreciation for a job well done, offer job security, show personal loyalty to workers and provide good working conditions. Although managers control the components of a job, they have no direct control over whether a specific worker finds a job interesting. The outcomes associated with an interesting job come from internal motivators – factors inherent in the job itself, not from any particular actions of the manager or supervisor.

No matter how many externally controlled rewards managers or supervisors use, if workers find their jobs to be uninteresting and unfulfilling, performance will suffer. Attention to internal motivators is particularly critical in situations where managers or supervisors have relatively little control over the organizational incentive system. Job design is the process of matching job characteristics and workers' skills and interests. According to the model of Hackman and Oldham (1976), internal satisfying tasks are high on skill variety, task identity, task significance, autonomy and feedback. These core job characteristics result in three critical psychological states, namely experienced meaningfulness, experienced responsibility and knowledge of results. These critical psychological states promote job satisfaction, internal work motivation and work performance. Autonomy and feedback have a greater impact on the motivational potential of a job compared with the other three characteristics.

The more variety in skills a person can use in doing the work, the more the person perceives the task as meaningful. The more an individual can do a complete job from beginning to end (task identity), and the work affects the work or lives of other people (task significance), the more the employee will view the job as meaningful. The more autonomy in the work (freedom to choose when and how to do the job), the more responsibility they feel for their successes and failures. Increased responsibility results in increased commitment to one's work. Autonomy can be increased by beginning flexible work schedules, decentralizing decision-making or removing selected formalized controls, such as the ringing of a bell to indicate the beginning and end of a workday. The more feedback individuals receive about how well their jobs are being done, the more knowledge of results they have. Knowledge of results may be enhanced by increasing employees' direct contact with clients or by giving them feedback on how their jobs fit in and contribute to the total operation of the organization.

Other models of job design are the job demands–control model (Karasek, 1979) and psychological empowerment theory. The job demands–control model proposes that job demands might be less harmful and demotivating when they are accompanied by high levels of control. Psychological empowerment theory (Spreitzer, 1995) distinguished empowerment practices (e.g. job enrichment) from psychological empowerment (the cognitive-motivational states that arise from these practices). Psychological empowerment theory proposes that competence or self-efficacy (meaning believing that goals to be accomplished are meaningful), choice (feeling a sense of self-determination and choice over tasks) and impact (believing that actions make a difference) mediate the link between objective work conditions and psychological outcomes. This model implies that the psychological states (rather than just the objective work conditions) can be measured and promoted.

Equitable distribution of rewards

Once the appropriate rewards have been determined for each worker, the work and organizational psychologist must assist managers and supervisors in considering how to distribute the rewards. Any positive benefits of attractive rewards will be cancelled if workers feel that they are not receiving their fair share. Equity refers to the workers' perceptions of the fairness of rewards. Evaluations of fairness are based on a social comparison process in which workers individually compare what they are getting out of the work relationship (outputs) with what they are putting into the work relationship (inputs).

If workers experience feelings of inequity, they will behaviourally or cognitively adjust their own, or fellow workers', inputs and/or outputs. This may lead to a decrease in motivation and performance. For example, if workers believe that they are underpaid, they may, as part of a cognitive strategy, rationalize that they are not really working as hard as they thought they were, thus reducing the perceived value of their own inputs. Or they may convince themselves that their co-workers are working harder than they thought they were. Behaviourally workers can request a pay raise, or they can decrease their inputs by leaving a few minutes early each day, decreasing their effort, deciding not to complete an optional training programme or finding excuses not to accept difficult tasks.

Subordinates' perceptions of equity should be monitored because they may uncover faulty comparison processes. For example, people may be using inappropriate comparisons (with more senior or better educated individuals), they may misunderstand the value placed on various inputs (e.g. experience versus expertise, quantity versus quality) or they may have unrealistic views of their own performance. The important thing to keep in mind about equity and fairness is that we are dealing with perceptions. Whether these perceptions are accurate or distorted, until proven otherwise they are accurate in the mind of the perceiver.

Providing timely awards and accurate feedback

It is the timing of the reinforcement that lets the worker know which behaviour is being encouraged. Giving a reward at the wrong time can increase undesirable behaviour. For example, giving a long-overdue, fully warranted rise to a worker during an interview in which he or she is complaining about the unfairness of the reward system may reinforce complaining rather than good work performance. Moreover, failure to give a reward when desired behaviour occurs will make it even more difficult to increase that behaviour in the future.

Formal administrative procedure in organizations often delays for months the feedback on the consequences of worker performance. This delay between performance and feedback decreases the effectiveness of rewards or discipline. Immediate and spontaneous rewards are important.

Social and group factors

The interpersonal and group process must support the worker's efforts to achieve objectives. The use of self-managed work groups and giving responsibility for a whole task can motivate workers. The motivational climate in the group can be improved by giving attention to the composition of the group. The homogeneous composition of groups, team building and the selection and development of leaders can affect motivation.

Role of supervisors and managers

The quality of supervision and management is an important component of creating a motivational environment. Most supervisors and managers have little understanding of their influence on work engagement, commitment and/or intentions to stay or leave. An important task of managers is to optimize the emotional climate in their teams and enhance employee engagement by showing the following behaviours:

- Acknowledge and reward good performance instead of only correcting substandard performance.
- Be fair towards employees because this will strengthen the psychological contract.
- Put problems on the agenda and discuss these in an open, constructive and problem-solving way, both in work meetings and in individual talks.
- Inform employees on a regular basis and as early and complete as possible in face-to-face meetings about important issues.
- Coach employees by helping them with setting goals, planning their work, pointing out pitfalls and giving advice as necessary.
- Interview employees on a regular basis about their personal functioning, professional development and career development.

JOB SATISFACTION

In this section we will look at job satisfaction in terms of its definition, contributing factors and consequences thereof.

Definition of job satisfaction

Job satisfaction is a pleasurable or positive emotional state resulting from the appraisal of one's job or job experience (Locke, 1976). This definition incorporates both cognitive ('an appraisal of one's job') and affective ('emotional state') elements (Weiss,

2002). Most studies on job satisfaction (and specifically the measurement thereof) have focused on the cognitive element. Weiss (2002: 6) defined job satisfaction as 'a positive (or negative) evaluative judgment one makes about one's job or job situation'.

Factors which influence job satisfaction

Job satisfaction depends on many work-related factors, including the nature of the work itself, pay, promotional opportunities, supervision, co-worker relations and job security (Schultz and Schultz, 2014). The nature of the work seems to be a major source of job satisfaction, especially characteristics such as feedback, and interesting and challenging work. Pay seems to be a major factor in job satisfaction, because the money a person receives not only gives him or her the opportunity to satisfy their basic needs, but also to satisfy higher level needs. Promotional opportunities seem to have a varying effect on job satisfaction. Supervision is a moderately important source of job satisfaction.

Relationships with co-workers are not essential to job satisfaction. However, if the work group is difficult to get along with, it will have a negative effect on job satisfaction. Working conditions seem to have a modest effect on job satisfaction. If working conditions are good, there will be no job satisfaction problems; if they are bad, there will be. It actually seems as if employees generally do not give much thought to working conditions, unless they are extremely bad.

A person's needs and aspirations can affect satisfaction. If an employee wants to be in a high-status position, gaining such a position will probably enhance his or her level of job satisfaction. The instrumental benefits of the job, or the extent to which it (the job) enables the employee to achieve other ends also play an important role in satisfaction (Moorhead and Griffin, 2012).

The consequences of job satisfaction and job dissatisfaction

Research showed a moderate inverse relationship between satisfaction and turnover. High job satisfaction does seem to help to keep turnover low, but will not, in and of itself, keep it low (Robbins and Judge, 2013). If, on the other hand, there is high job dissatisfaction, turnover is likely to be high. The reason for this moderate relationship between satisfaction and turnover is the fact that other factors (e.g. the state of the economy) play a role in an employee's decision to keep or quit his or her job.

There is an inverse relationship between satisfaction and absenteeism – that is, when employees are highly satisfied, they tend to be less absent from work; when they are highly dissatisfied, they tend to be more absent from work. Again, there are other factors which influence this relationship. One such factor might be the degree to which an employee feels that his or her work is important. If a person feels that his or her work is important, he or she will be less likely to be absent from work (Robbins and Judge, 2013).

There is a large-scale study (Faragher et al., 2005) which indicates a strong relationship between job satisfaction and employee health. Research showed positive relationships between job satisfaction and life satisfaction, happiness, positive affect and the absence of negative affect (Bowling et al., 2010). The causal relationship from subjective well–being to job satisfaction was stronger than the causal relationship from job satisfaction to subjective well–being.

A more 'problematic' relationship is that of satisfaction and performance. Research results showed that in some cases there is a negative relationship between satisfaction and performance, in some cases there is a positive relationship between satisfaction and performance, and in some cases there are very few signs of such a relationship. During the mid-1950s, Brayfield and Crockett (1955) found that the median correlation between satisfaction and performance was about 0.12, which is rather low. In the most recent examination by Judge *et al.* (2001) a correlation of 0.30 between satisfaction and performance was found (which is a small but meaningful association). It is probably better to assess the relationship between satisfaction and motivation, rather than satisfaction and performance. The link between motivation and performance is not a simple one, because there are many other important factors which influence employee performance besides motivational levels. These factors include job design, the functioning of machines and equipment, group norms and group co–ordination.

APPLICATION 3.1

The perils of money and other extrinsic motivators

Katherine Lawrence argued during the Conference on Promoting Markets in Creativity: Copyright in the Internet Age (2003) in Washington, DC that although money is a symbolic way of showing employees that they are valued, it might also be a dangerous motivator. She pointed out that there are three ways in which money can have serious repercussions for the creative process.

Financial rewards can distract employees from the organization's underlying goals. It is often difficult for employees within large organizations to see direct connections between their efforts and the final results. To make these connections clearer, some bonus reward systems tie individual compensation to overall firm performance. For example, stock options are thought to encourage employees to work harder as 'owners' of the firm. However, a recent study by Julia A. Welch (Good intentions gone awry: A field study of stock options in the high-tech industry, unpublished dissertation, University of Michigan, 2003) shows that stock options can become a carrot that lures employees completely off-track, causing them to be so obsessed with the hour-to-hour fluctuations in stock value that their effort and motivation fluctuate accordingly. Instead of working, employees in one firm spent hours of work time each day preoccupied with their personal stock portfolios. Rather than focusing employee effort and responsibility, stock options can be a damaging extrinsic motivator. Businesses need to consider meaningful, non-financial ways of sustaining motivation throughout the creative process.

1 Employees may not put forward their best work if they are 'bought out' for limited rewards. Often, people produce creative work in exchange for a salary or a fixed contract, resulting in the employer owning their 'copyrights'. If creativity has the

potential to produce ongoing income to the firm, individual contributions should be rewarded in kind. For example, some organizations allow individuals within the organization to hold copyrights or patents and perhaps earn royalties from them. Financial rewards aside, this simple recognition may offer a sufficient incentive. In addition, the opportunity to reap the benefits for the years that their creativity continues to be profitable may bolster existing intrinsic motivations.

2 Extrinsic rewards such as money can actually damage intrinsic motivation because employees begin to focus on the reward rather than on the work and lose interest in going the extra distance. Knowledge workers – those responsible for many of the creative products protected by copyright – typically have intrinsically motivating work, and it is important to preserve that intrinsic value as an incentive. Intrinsic motivation is encouraged through exciting opportunities, supportive work environments and recognition. As Eric Raymond, an evangelist for the open-source software movement, has said: 'You cannot motivate the best people with money . . . The best people in any field are motivated by passion . . . When are programmers happy? They're happy when they're not underutilized – when they're not bored . . . . This is a general preference in creative work. People are happiest when they're the most productive.' The open-source software movement is proof that money is not the sole motivator. Given that fact, it is important to identify what else might motivate a particular individual – whether that might be more varied projects, a chance for learning and challenge, or greater autonomy – and reward accordingly.

Extract from Lawrence, 2004.

SUMMARY

- In different definitions of motivation, the following words are often used: desires, wants, wishes, aims, goals, needs, drives, motives and incentives. Motivation in organizations is the willingness to exert high levels of effort towards organizational goals, conditioned by the effort's ability to satisfy some individual need.
- There are different theories that try to explain motivation. Recent theories and models (including self-determination theory, self-efficacy theory, the job demands–resources model, psychological empowerment theory and personal engagement theory) stress that specific antecedents (i.e. demands and resources) might affect motivation and engagement via psychological conditions, such as meaningfulness, safety, and availability and psychological need satisfaction.
- A motivating environment can be created by a) ensuring that the motives and values of the worker match those of the organization and the job; b) proper goal setting; c) facilitating subordinates' performance by creating a supportive work environment; d) appropriate use of rewards and discipline; e) providing attractive rewards; f) providing timely awards and accurate feedback; g) attending to social and group factors.

- Job satisfaction is defined as a pleasurable or positive emotional state resulting from the appraisal of one's job or job experience. The main factors influencing job satisfaction are organizational factors (pay, promotions, the work itself and working conditions), group factors (the role of the supervisor and of co-workers) and personal factors (needs and aspirations and how these are met, and how an individual views the instrumental benefits of the job). The relationship between satisfaction, motivation and performance/productivity is rather complex, and some kind of model is needed to explain it.

KEY CONCEPTS AND TERMS

- Discipline
- Engagement
- Equity theory
- Esteem need
- Expectancy theory
- Extinction
- Extrinsic motivation
- Goal
- Goal acceptance
- Goal-setting theory
- Hygiene
- Hierarchy of needs theory
- Instrumentality
- Intrinsic motivation
- Job satisfaction
- Motivation
- Need for achievement
- Need for affiliation
- Need for power
- Personal motives
- Physiological need
- Psychological empowerment
- Psychological availability
- Psychological meaningfulness
- Psychological need satisfaction
- Psychological safety
- Reward
- Safety/security needs
- Self-actualization need
- Self-determination theory
- Social need
- Two-factor theory
- Valence

SAMPLE ESSAY TITLES

- What are the differences between content and process theories of motivation?
- How can work and organizational psychologists contribute to create a motivating climate in organizations?

FURTHER READING

Books

Latham, G.P. (2007). *Work Motivation: History, Theory, Research, and Practice*. Thousand Oaks, CA: Sage.

Truss, C., Delbridge, R., Soane, E., Alfes, K. and Shantz, A. (2014). *Employee Engagement in Theory and Practice*. Abingdon: Routledge.

Journal articles

Gelfand, M.J., Erez, M. and Aycan, Z. (2007). Cross-cultural organizational behaviour. *Annual Review of Psychology*, 58, 479–514.

Rich, B.L., Lepine, J.A. and Crawford, E.R. (2010). Job engagement: Antecedents and effects on job performance. *Academy of Management Journal*, 53, 617–635.

4 Group behaviour

This chapter focuses on group dynamics and teamwork. The first section describes the importance of groups. This is followed by definitions of terms and a classification of groups. The chapter then proceeds to models of group behaviour. Factors which could explain work group behaviour are analysed next. The role of group member resources is introduced, followed by external conditions imposed on the group, group structure and group processes.

LEARNING OUTCOMES

When you have completed this chapter you should be able to:

1 Define the terms group, content, process and structure.
2 Discuss the importance of groups.
3 Distinguish between various types of groups.
4 Explain the models of group behaviour.
5 Explain group behaviour by referring to external conditions imposed on the group, group member resources, group structure and group processes.

DEFINITION OF TERMS

Next, the terms relevant to this chapter, namely group, team and group dynamics, are defined. The following elements should be considered when the term 'group' is defined (Johnson and Johnson, 2014):

* *Goals*. A group is defined as a number of individuals who share common goals. Groups are often formed because of some common goals or interests that individuals could not realize on their own. For example, a soccer team is a group that may be sustained by the mutual interests of its members in winning a championship.

- *Interdependence.* A group is defined as a collection of individuals who are interdependent in some ways. An event that affects one individual, affects all individuals.
- *Interaction.* A group is defined as a number of individuals who are in interaction with one another. The interaction may be verbal (such as giving ideas to solve a problem) or non-verbal (such as exchanging smiles in the hallway).
- *Perception of membership.* Individual members must perceive themselves as a group. Groups are composed of members who recognize each other as a member of their group and can distinguish these members from non-members. Shoppers in a checkout line are probably not recognized as members of a group.
- *Structured relationships.* A group is defined as a collection of individuals whose interactions are structured through role definitions and norms.
- *Mutual influence.* A group is a collection of individuals who influence each other.
- *Motivation.* A group is defined as a collection of individuals who try to satisfy personal needs through their association.

A *group* is defined as a collection of two or more people who are involved in face-to-face interaction, are interdependent, perceive themselves and others as part of the group, have a stable pattern of relationships between them and strive towards a common goal (Johnson and Johnson, 2014).

It seems that there are differences between a *work group* and a *work team* (Robbins and Judge, 2013). A work group is a group which interacts primarily to share information and to make decisions to help each member perform within his or her area of responsibility. Work groups have no opportunity or need to engage in collective work which requires joint effort. A work team generates positive synergy

FIGURE 4.1 A team generates positive energy through co-ordinated effort

Source: © Dragon Images/Shutterstock.com

through co-ordinated effor
which is greater than the s
a group refers to a work g

Group dynamics is an ar
group life. It includes the s
group development, and
(Johnson and Johnson, 2(

IMPORTANCE OF G

It is essential to underst
businesses and industrie
and teams to design and
work performance and
in quality circles, prob
managed work groups

Social identity theo
1989). According to
accomplishments of a
performance. People will especially

Groups can be classified on the basis of t
or informal (Johnson and Johnson, 2014)
structure, with designated assignment
airline flight crew are a formal gro
organization or a department a
neither formally structured
naturally in response to th
departments who regula

EXPLAINING

Why woul
is comple
howev

characteristics are important: similarity (e.g. regarding values an
distinctiveness (e.g. to show how they are different from others), status (e.g. linking
themselves to high-status groups) and uncertainty reduction (e.g. to help them
understand who they are and where they fit in).

When your group does well, you experience positive emotions and your self-esteem
rises. On the other hand, when your group does poorly, you feel bad about yourself.
Social identity theory helps people to reduce uncertainty about who they are and what
they should do (Hogg and Terry, 2000). Although social identities help us to
understand who we are and where we fit in, they may result in in-group favouritism
and stereotyping of other groups (Robbins and Judge, 2013).

The use of groups for the purposes described above may have advantages, but it
may also have a dark side. The use of groups may result in a waste of time and energy,
norms of low rather than high productivity, poor decision-making, destructive conflict
between groups in an organization, as well as frustration and stress (Johnson and
Johnson, 2014; Salas *et al.*, 2004).

It is crucial to promote teamwork in modern organizations using a systems approach.
Most organizations have to use their mission, business model, metrics, training,
incentives, structure, culture, decision-making and physical space arrangements to
promote collaboration and a sense of shared purpose (Castellana, 2013).

TYPES OF GROUPS

There are various types of groups such as work groups in organizations (e.g. production
groups or marketing groups), committees and informal groups. In the next few
paragraphs we will distinguish between various ways to classify groups.

...eir formality. Groups can either be formal ... *Formal groups* are defined by the organization ... establishing tasks. The members making up an ...p, so are the members of a production team in an ... a university. *Informal groups* are alliances which are ... or organizationally determined. These groups appear ... need for social contact. Three employees from different ...ly eat lunch together are an example of an informal group.

...WORK GROUP BEHAVIOUR

... some groups be more successful than others? The answer to this question ...x. A study of the variables which explain group behaviour in Figure 4.2 will, ...er, shed more light on this issue.

... Next we will focus on each of the factors that explain work group behaviour.

EXTERNAL CONDITIONS IMPOSED ON THE GROUP

External conditions imposed on the group which may affect group member behaviour include organizational culture, task design and technology.

Organizational culture

Groups are influenced by the culture of the organization. Organizational culture is defined as the internal consistent pattern of affirmations, confirmations and limitations which lead people to act, judge and justify themselves according to sanctioned ways (Johnson and Johnson, 2014; Weick, 1985). The organization culture could have an inhibiting or facilitating effect on the behaviour in a group. Group effectiveness can

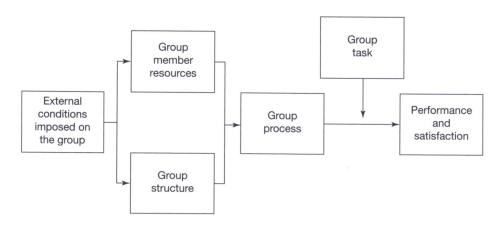

FIGURE 4.2 Variables which explain work group behaviour

be promoted if the current organization culture is supportive of innovation and shared expectations of success. It is important to enquire about social rules which may inhibit group work, and to identify existing norms for group gatherings and problem solving within the specific organization culture and the society.

Task design and technology

The effect of the nature of the task can be determined by considering the complexity of technical demands (knowledge and skills) and social demands (interaction between group members). To perform well, the group must divide the skills, inputs and strategies available in such a way that it would fit the technical and social demands of the task. The quality of group performance decreases when the task becomes too complex or too simple.

Task design and social organization depends on the technology of the organization. The mechanization of work in a coal mine may, for instance, cause those individuals to work in teams rather than on their own. Some technologies may implicate that one group member has to master all the tasks, while others are so complex that a member could only master one (e.g. a symphonic orchestra).

Optimal fit between the task, technology and social organization requires that technical processes be divided in subunits of reasonable size. Ideally spoken, each group has to be responsible for the total manufactured product, to help them to see the end results of their work. The task should be significant, challenging and require a variety of skills. The group should be responsible for the results, be interdependent and must be able to learn and get feedback. Frequent and reliable performance feedback must be built into the task.

Organization strategy

An organization's overall strategy, put into place by top management, outlines the organization's goals and the means for attaining these goals. It might direct the organization towards reducing costs, improving quality, expanding market share or shrinking the size of the total operation. The organization's strategy may influence the power of various work groups, which will determine the resources which the organization's top management is willing to allocate to it for performing the tasks. The communication of the mission of the organization is especially important for work teams, the work of which is closely related to those of other work units. Group members will be more motivated to strive for group goals if they accept them. Resistance and self-oriented behaviour arises if group members do not accept the goals.

Performance feedback

The effectiveness of a group (work team) depends on accurate and timely performance feedback. This requires reliable measurement systems, especially when the group produces quantifiable outputs and has a short work cycle (e.g. mining teams and the assembly line). It is, however, difficult to give feedback when the work cycle is long and when outputs are produced infrequently.

Reward and recognition

The nature of the reward may affect the productivity and functioning of the group. Rewards which encourage co-operation between group members have a positive effect on the motivation and interpersonal relations of group members, especially if they are interdependent. A well-structured reward system may reinforce the motivating nature of a well-designed task. Difficult, but realistic, performance objectives must be set, and the group should receive feedback about their efforts to reach these objectives. Objectives must support (rather than replace) task-based motivation. Rewards and objectives which focus on group behaviour (rather than individual behaviour) may increase the effort of group members. Conflict arises when specific individuals in the group are targeted for rewards. This problem is often experienced in organizations which rewarded individual performance in the past.

Physical environment

The seating arrangements, illumination, ventilation and physical environment where work takes place may affect the processes and results of the group. Group interaction is promoted when group members are placed near to each other. The seat taken by the group member indicates at what distance he or she feels comfortable with others. Interaction is facilitated by face-to-face seating arrangements. Although positive causal relationships have been found between productivity and group functioning on one hand, and light intensity, size of rooms, the use of music, and noise on the other hand, these effects are mediated by the attitudes (and expectations) of group members. Orienting group members positively towards environmental variables can control their effect.

Authority structures

Organizations have authority structures, which define who reports to whom, who makes decisions and what decisions individuals or groups are empowered to make. This structure determines where a given work group is placed in the organization's hierarchy, the formal leader of the group, and formal relationships between groups. While a work group might be led by someone who emerges informally from within the group, the formally designated leader – appointed by management – has authority which others in the group do not have.

The informal relationships in an organization may undermine the formal structure. For example, the personal relationship between the director of an organization and the manager of one department (of a specific division) may undermine the formal authority of the head of the division.

Intergroup relationships

The degree of interdependence between various groups in the organization varies. Organizations represent a complex structure of groups imbedded in other groups. Members try to satisfy their personal needs, as well as those of other groups to which they are affiliated to in the group (Putnam, 1988). Each group is, to an extent, dependent on other groups in an organization, because everyone contributes to the final output. Performance of one group may also be dependent on outputs of other sections or groups. Poor performance of one group may block the performance of others, which may cause frustration.

The principle of competition between groups is often used to increase the productivity of groups and individuals. Excessive competition between groups (departments and sections) may lead to a subtle application of sanctions and sabotage of other groups in the organization. Tension, frustration and conflict arising from this spreads to every individual in the group and delays the group interaction process.

Group member resources

Various group member resources (e.g. age, gender, physical characteristics and personality characteristics) may affect work group behaviour. Research showed that an increase in age is accompanied by an increase in the frequency of social contact, higher selectivity in interpersonal contact, a tendency to want to serve as leader and a decrease in conforming behaviour (Timmerman, 2000). Regarding the influence of gender on group behaviour, it can be concluded that females (compared with males) are more inclined to conform to group norms, and are more communicative in bargaining situations (Reynolds, 1984). These characteristics are, however, a function of cultural norms regarding the role of females in the society (that may change). The abilities and skills of an individual may affect his or her functioning in a group.

RESEARCH METHODS 4.1

Personality traits and group behaviour

Personality traits such as sociability and independence are related to productivity, morale and cohesion of the group. Characteristics such as dominance and unconventionality are negatively related to productivity, morale and cohesion (Robbins and Judge, 2013). Research by Barry and Stewart (1997) suggests that individual group member personality is related to the way in which groups function. Groups are most effective when group member personality characteristics are congruent with the roles they fulfil. The role of personality may be particularly important in self-managed work teams. Extroversion is the key personality-based correlate with individual impact on group performance as perceived by other group members. Groups having 20–40 per cent high extroversion members outperform groups with either fewer or more members. Barry and Stewart (1997) found no direct role for conscientiousness in group situations. It seems that conscientiousness may become less important in team-based tasks because groups are able to recognize and compensate for the lack of conscientious individuals. It may also be that conscientiousness plays a smaller role in conceptual tasks (e.g. creative tasks) and a more important role in behavioural tasks (planning, performance or competition). Group effectiveness is improved when members are socially sensitive, assertive and not too anxious.

Group structure

Work groups are not unorganized mobs. They have a structure which shapes the behaviour of members and makes it possible to explain and predict individual behaviour in the group.

Composition of the group

It is advisable to consider selecting people who are able and willing to function in a group. Two specific aspects should be mentioned in this regard, namely the heterogeneity of the group members and the compatibility of interpersonal needs of group members.

- *Heterogeneous versus homogeneous group composition.* When a group is heterogeneous in terms of gender, personalities, opinions, abilities, skills and perspectives, there is an increased probability that the group will possess the characteristics needed to complete its tasks effectively. The diversity in the group, however, increases the possibility of conflict in the group. Research showed that group productivity decreases in heterogeneous groups which are large (Cummings *et al.*, 2013).
- *Compatibility of interpersonal needs.* According to Schutz (1978), human beings have three interpersonal needs, namely inclusion, control and affection. Interaction between people could be explained by wanted and expressed behaviour in the areas of inclusion, control and affection. Heterogeneity of group members regarding inclusion, control and affection may cause conflict between group members. However, more learning and change occurs in these groups. Two individuals are compatible if each individual shows the behaviour that the other wants. Compatibility regarding affection leads to improved co-operation and productivity between group members in interpersonal learning contexts.

APPLICATION 4.1

Group cohesiveness

'High cohesiveness in groups leads to higher group productivity.' Do you agree or disagree? Explain.

Group size

The productivity of the group can increase if the group size is increased. If, however, the group size is too large, productivity may be reduced. Larger groups are more effective if it is necessary to gather facts. Smaller groups (of approximately seven members each) are, however, more able to use inputs productively (Johnson and Johnson, 2014). The optimal group size varies between four and ten members. As group size increases, communication becomes more difficult, discussions are dominated by some group members, some members feel threatened, subgroups are formed and it becomes difficult to reach consensus. Groups with an uneven number of members are preferable to those with an even number.

An important finding regarding group size is social loafing (Johnson and Johnson, 2014). Social loafing is the tendency for individuals to expend less effort when working collectively than when working individually. It challenges the logic that the productivity of the group as a whole should at least equal the sum of the productivity of each individual in that group. Social loafing develops because of the belief of some group members that others do not pull their weight. Social loafing is also caused by the belief of group members that it is impossible to measure their contributions. The implication is that where managers utilize collective work situations to enhance morale and team work, they must also provide means by which individual efforts can be identified.

Roles of group members

A role refers to a set of expected behaviour patterns attributed to someone occupying a given position in a social unit. In any group there would initially be a period of self-oriented behaviour caused by unresolved emotional issues interfering with the task (Napier and Gershenfeld, 2003). If these issues stay unresolved, the group's behaviour will be directed at self-oriented behaviour, including: a) aggressive coping, which manifests in behaviour such as arguments, interrupting other group members, ignoring others and hostile humour; b) seeking for support, which manifests in group members trying to find members who agree with them, to form a subgroup; and c) withdrawal or denial, which manifests in suppression of tension and feelings, as well as passiveness and indifference (Johnson and Johnson, 2014).

Task-orientated roles aim specifically at accomplishing a group goal. When groups gather to solve problems, make decisions, plan activities or determine policy, they are frequently hampered by group members' random behaviour. Sometimes one person monopolizes the conversation while others remain silent. Leaders in the group make use of the following behaviours to help the group reach its goals:

- *Initiating*, to get the group to begin and giving direction to the discussion.
- *Co-ordinating*, to help group members see the results of their efforts and reduce their uncertainty about the group, its problem and its solutions.
- *Summarizing*, to help move the group towards its goals.
- *Elaborating*, to explore the problem more fully and to help the group reach its goal.

Process-oriented roles help maintain a satisfactory interpersonal climate within a group, and include the following roles:

- *Tension release*, to reduce the tension in the group.
- *Gatekeeping*, to keep the communication channels in the group open.
- *Encouraging*, to increase the esteem of group members and raise their hopes, confidence and aspirations.
- *Mediating*, to resolve conflict between group members and release the tension associated with conflict.

Regarding work teams, Margerison and McCann (1990) distinguished nine team roles which people prefer to play (see Focus 4.1).

Team roles

- Creator-innovators are usually imaginative and good at initiating ideas or concepts.
- Explorer-promoters like to take new ideas and champion their cause.
- Assessor-developers have strong analytical skills. They are at their best when given several different options to analyse and evaluate before a decision is made.
- Thruster-organizers like to set up operating procedures to turn ideas into reality and get things done.
- Concluder-producers are also concerned with results. Only their role focuses on insisting that deadlines are kept and ensuring that all commitments are followed through.
- Controller-inspectors are people with a high concern for establishing and enforcing rules and regulations.
- Upholders-maintainers hold strong convictions about the way in which things should be done.
- Reporter-advisers perform an important role in encouraging the team to seek additional information before making decisions and discouraging the team from making hasty decisions.
- Linkers can play the roles played by any of the previous eight. Linkers are co-ordinators and integrators.

Work and organizational psychologists need to understand the individual strengths which each person can bring to the team, select members with this in mind and allocate work assignments which fit members' preferred styles. The researchers who developed this framework argue that unsuccessful teams have an unbalanced portfolio of individual talents, with too much energy expended in one area and not enough in other areas.

Group norms

The term 'norm' comes from the word 'normal'. Behaviour is normal if it seems to fall within the guidelines which a particular group accepts as appropriate for itself. Norms evolve only if they receive collective support. A norm can be defined as a collection of expectations held by the members of a group that specify the type of behaviour which is regarded as right or wrong, good or bad, relevant or irrelevant, permissible or impermissible in the group (Feldman, 1984). Group norms emerge from the values of a group and are standards of behaviour which are imposed on members. The group norms are the dos and don'ts that result from the interactions of group members over time. A norm, then, is a standard model or pattern of behaviour.

Norms are set regarding task and process issues, but are not always stated explicitly. There is usually an unspoken expectation that group members know the responsibilities and limitations of individual behaviour in the group. Although these implicit norms regulate group behaviour, few individuals are aware of them until they are broken.

Norms develop through communication with others. Norms develop by subtle, subliminal, beyond–awareness processes of inference from raised eyebrows or hearing supportive 'uh-hums' or watching how others gain approval. They may evolve through an interpersonal process of negotiation as we attempt to follow the rule of fitting in. Within each group there is a history of what is accepted behaviour, which has developed over time in that situation, and which members learn and understand.

According to Feldman (1984), norm enforcement which groups are likely to bring under normative control are only those behaviours that a) ensure group survival; b) increase the predictability of group members' behaviour; c) prevent embarrassing interpersonal situations; or d) express the group's central values. These group norms, though, directly affect decision-making in the group (Chen *et al.*, 2002).

Once norms are developed and agreed on, they are difficult to change. Changing group norms not only increases the forces in the direction of the desired change, but also involves holding the resistant forces constant or reducing them. Problems may arise when the values, objectives and beliefs are in conflict with group norms.

APPLICATION 4.2

Intergroup conflict and superordinate goals

Muzafer Sherif (1966), his fellow researchers, and his students organised a summer camp for twelve-year old boys in the early 1950s. The boys were strangers to one another prior to the camp. The camp was isolated from outside influences, which allowed the researchers to manipulate the conditions of interaction among the members of the camp. The researchers were interested in investigating intergroup relations, as well as the effectiveness of techniques for reducing hostility among groups. The boys were divided into groups and names like "Bull Dogs" and "Red Devils" were assigned to promote loyalty to the groups. The researchers also structured the daily activities of the boys so that interdependent, coordinated activity among group members was necessary for achieving the desired goals. Following the development of loyalty to specific groups, the researchers attempted to induce conflict between them by requiring them to undertake competing activities in which the winning group was rewarded and the losing group was not. After displaying sportsmanship for a while, the groups became hostile towards each other and started having garbage fights. The researchers next tested various methods of reducing conflict between the groups:

a. Engaging in pleasant social contact. Such contact situations had no effect in reducing intergroup conflict.
b. Establishment of a common enemy. A common enemy brought the groups together and reduced hostility between them.
c. Working together towards goals that were more important to them than continuation of the conflict (i.e. superordinate goals). For example, groups had to work together to repair a water system that was earlier sabotaged by the

researchers. After participation in activities which had superordinate goals, attitudes towards members of the other group changed, hostility disappeared and friendships were formed.

The characteristics of superordinate goals introduced by the researchers were as follows:

- A more powerful third party (i.e. the researchers) introduced the goals.
- They were perceived by the campers as natural events.
- They were not perceived by the campers as a prerequisite to solve the conflict between the groups.
- They restructured the competitive situation into a cooperative one.

Source: Sherif, M. (1966). In common predicament. Boston, MA: Houghton Mifflin.

The following learning points can be taken from the application:

- Resolving conflict through superordinate goals can lead to cooperation rather than competition between groups.
- Cooperating groups are inclined to have friendly and harmonious relationships

Group processes

Group development stages

Two approaches, namely recurring phase theories and sequential stage theories, have been taken to classify group development stages (Johnson and Johnson, 2014).

Recurring-phase theories focus on the issues that dominate group interaction again and again. For example, the group development theory of Bion (1961) states that groups function on two levels – the manifestation level (to complete the task and reaching goals) and the unconscious level (that represents underlying assumptions about the group's goal and tasks). According to this theory, groups focus again and again on three basic themes, namely dependency on the leader to tell them what to do, pairing among group members, and flight–fight, in which problems are handled by attacking or fleeing from them. The group development theory of Schutz (1978) proposed that group development occurs as members concern themselves with three issues, namely inclusion, control and affection.

Sequential-stage theories focus on the typical order of the phases of group development. One of the most famous sequential group development theories was formulated by Tuckman (Tuckman and Jensen, 1977). This theory distinguishes five stages of group development, namely forming, storming, norming, performing and adjourning.

- *Orientation stage* ('forming'). At the start of a group's life cycle the participants generally have positive expectations that something good will come from participation in their group. At the same time there is a certain amount of anxiety and concerns as individuals try to discover why they are there, what they will get out of it, and what the stated purpose of the group means. Group members are quite dependent on the situation and on whoever is in authority.

- *Dissatisfaction stage* (*'storming'*). After some time, the participants learn that what they hope for or want from the experience and what they feel is actually happening do not coincide. The earlier dependence on the authority is found unsatisfying. This leads to unpleasant feelings of frustration, sometimes anger against the task, and usually also against the authority figure. These negative feelings usually become stronger and more prominent than the earlier feelings of eagerness and hope of gaining from the experience.
- *Resolution stage* (*'norming'*). What happens at this stage is some compromise between expectations and the realities (task, leader, abilities and other members) and also some increase in skills to complete the task, either as originally construed or as redefined. Sufficient mastery of the situation and new skills allow positive feelings of increased self-esteem and pleasure in accomplishment and exceed the earlier negative feelings of frustration and anger.
- *Production stage* (*'performing'*). The production stage is characterized by the positive feelings of eagerness to be part of the experience and hope for a good outcome exceeding the negative feelings of discouragement, frustration and anger of the earlier dissatisfaction stage. This all leads to more efficient use of time, with less time spent in struggling against the leader, the other group members or the task itself. Roles become flexible and functional, and group energy is channelled into the task.
- *Termination stage* (*'adjourning'*). As the end of the experience approaches, the participants begin to concern themselves with what they have accomplished and with the impending dissolution of the group. Sometimes the feelings of loss or anticipated loss are largely denied or covered up in some way, such as joking (sometimes about death) or missing the final meeting. The work on the task during the termination stage generally decreases.

Considering the variety of relationships between work teams and organizational contexts, it seems unlikely that a single sequence can describe the development of all kinds of teams. Each team has to deal with certain developmental issues, but the order of precedence depends on the circumstances. The sequential stage model is supported by research results with training and laboratory groups, which cannot necessarily be generalized to work teams.

Studies of more than a dozen field and laboratory task-force groups confirmed that groups do not develop in a universal sequence of stages (Gersick, 1988). The timing of when groups form and change the way they work is highly consistent. It has been found that:

1   The first meeting sets the group's direction.
2   The first phase of group activity is one of passivity.
3   A transition takes place at the end of the first phase, which occurs exactly when the group has used up half its allotted time.
4   The transition initiates major changes.
5   A second phase of passivity follows the transition.
6   The group's last meeting is characterized by markedly accelerated activity.

The *punctuated equilibrium model* characterizes groups as exhibiting long periods of inertia interspersed with brief revolutionary changes triggered primarily by their members' awareness of time and deadlines. The group begins by combining the forming and norming stages, then goes through a period of low performing, followed by storming, then a period of high performing and, finally, adjourning.

Group cohesion

Group cohesion is defined as the sum of the attraction of the group for members, and the ability of the group to stay together (Bormann and Bormann, 1988). It is a result of individuals' satisfaction with the group. A cohesive group is not necessarily a more productive group. Cohesion develops even if the group has a norm of low productivity. Cohesion involves the total forces acting on members to remain in the group compared with those directing people away from the group. Group cohesion can be defined, then, in terms of both the positive rewards which you derive from being in the group and the expectancy that your outcomes would be lower if you did not belong to the group.

Highly cohesive groups are more productive, have higher morale and communicate better than low cohesive groups. Cohesive groups do more work because members take the initiative and help one another. They distribute the workload among themselves and volunteer to help one another. They pay attention to the group's problems, and spend time and effort in favour of the group. The more cohesive the group, the more effective the communication within the group. Cohesiveness encourages feedback, disagreements and questions. Members of high cohesive groups indicate when they do not understand, and disagree among themselves (Bormann and Bormann, 1988).

Members of groups with low cohesiveness are quiet, bored, apathetic, tensed and uncomfortable. They seldom disagree and there are few give-and-take discussions. Important decisions are made quickly. Members of low cohesive groups lack initiative and tend to stand around and wait for assignments. They do only what they are told to do and no more (Bormann and Bormann, 1988).

Group cohesion can be encouraged by the following factors:

1 When group members collaborate to reach a common objective and when there is a real or imagined threat in the group's environment.
2 The more satisfied group members are, the higher the group cohesion will be.
3 Cohesion is higher in a small group than in a large group.
4 More interaction between group members promotes the group cohesion.
5 The more similar the members are in terms of background and attitude, the more likely it is that group cohesion will be enhanced.
6 Group cohesion is also influenced by leadership style. A participative style will enhance cohesiveness.

Communication

Group communication can be defined as face-to-face communication among a small group of people who share a common purpose or goal, who feel a sense of belonging to the group and who exert influence on one another. Regardless of a group's size its members must be able to talk and respond to one another. They must be sensitive to the needs and feelings of other group members. Schein (1969) states that the communication process is one of the most important processes which take place in the group and is observable. He makes the following distinction of communication processes that take place within the group: a) who communicates, how often, for how long; b) who communicates to whom; c) who talks after whom, who interrupts whom; d) communication style; non-verbal communication; e) levels of communication; and f) filters.

Group decision-making

Individual and group decision-making both have strengths. Neither is ideal for all situations. Groups have the following advantages:

- *More complete information and knowledge.* By aggregating the resources of several individuals, there is more input into the decision process.
- *Increased diversity of views.* Groups can bring heterogeneity to the decision process. More approaches and alternatives could be considered.
- *Increased acceptance of a solution.* Decisions often fail because people do not accept them. If people are able to participate in a decision which affects them, they will be more likely to accept it and encourage others to accept and support it.
- *Increased legitimacy.* Group decision-making is consistent with democratic ideals and may be perceived as being more legitimate than decisions made by a single person.

Groups have the following disadvantages:

- *Time consuming.* Groups take more time to reach a decision than would be the case when an individual makes a decision. This may limit quick and decisive action.
- *Pressures to conform.* The desire by group members to be accepted and considered an asset to the group can result in conformity.
- *Domination by a few members.* One or a few members can dominate group discussions. If these members have low ability, the group's overall effectiveness would suffer.
- *Ambiguous responsibility.* It is often difficult to determine who is accountable when group decision-making is used.
- *Groupthink.* Groupthink describes situations in which group pressures for conformity deter the group from critically appraising unusual, minority or unpopular views.
- *Polarization.* In discussing a given set of alternatives and arriving at a solution, group members tend to exaggerate the initial positions they hold. In some situations, caution dominates, and there is a conservative shift. Often, however, groups tend towards a risky shift.

There are five major characteristics of an effective group decision, namely that the resources of group members are fully utilized, the time is well used, the decision is correct or of high quality, and the problem-solving ability of the group is enhanced, or at least not inhibited. A decision is effective to the extent that these five criteria are met; if all five are not met, the decision has not been made effectively. According to Johnson and Johnson (2014), consensus decision-making is the most effective method of group decision-making, but it also takes the most time. Napier and Gershenfeld

(2003) state that reaching a decision through consensus represents the ideal in terms of group participation, but it is by no means the most efficient or least tension-producing approach to decision-making. It simply indicates that each member is willing to go along with the decision.

CREATING AN EFFECTIVE GROUP

The following guidelines must be followed to create an effective group (Johnson and Johnson, 2014):

- *Goals.* Goals must be stated clearly so that all members understand the nature thereof. Goals must also be made concrete so that members can understand how to reach them. Furthermore, goals must be relevant to the needs of group members.
- *Two-way communication.* Members of a group must send and receive messages effectively to exchange information and to transmit meaning.
- *Leadership and participation.* All members should participate equally and accept responsibility for providing leadership. Participation will lead to commitment to the group and satisfaction with their membership.
- *Power and influence.* In effective groups, members' power is based on expertise, ability and access to information rather than on authority and personality characteristics.
- *Decision-making procedures.* Effective groups maintain a balance between the time and resources the group has available and the decision-making procedures.
- *Controversies.* Members of effective groups engage in constructive controversy by disagreeing and challenging one another's conclusions and arguments.
- *Conflict.* Effective groups face conflicts between group members and resolve them in constructive ways by using appropriate conflict management strategies.

SUMMARY

- Groups are defined as a collection of two or more interacting individuals with a stable pattern of relationships between them who share common goals and who perceive themselves as being a group. Various types of group, including formal and informal groups, are distinguished.
- Predictions about a work group's performance must begin by recognizing that work groups are part of a larger organization. Factors such as the organization culture, strategy, authority structures and rewards may influence the group's behaviour and results. For example, if an organization is characterized by distrust between management and workers, it is likely that the work group will restrict their efforts. Characteristics of group members may also influence the results of the group.
- Roles represent the typical pattern of behaviour in a specific social context. Roles are often differentiated into task roles and maintenance roles. In the early stages of

group development, the group may be dominated by self-oriented behaviour, which is caused by unresolved emotional issues. Norms, a set of generally agreed upon informal rules, have profound effects on organizational behaviour. Cohesiveness refers to pressures faced by group members to remain in the group and is influenced by various factors. Cohesiveness aids performance if the group's goals are consistent with management's interests. Groups develop through stages. Although different models of group development can be distinguished, one popular model classifies the stages as forming, storming, norming, performing and adjourning.

KEY CONCEPTS AND TERMS

- Communication
- Decision-making
- Group
- Group cohesiveness
- Group composition
- Group development stages
- Group member resources
- Group norms
- Group size
- Group structure
- Groupthink
- Intergroup relationships
- Interpersonal needs
- Norm
- Organizational culture
- Performance feedback
- Process
- Punctuated equilibrium
- Role
- Self-oriented behaviour
- Social loafing
- Task design
- Task-orientated role
- Team
- Team role

SAMPLE ESSAY TITLES

- Which processes occur in work groups?
- How could group effectiveness in organizations be improved?

FURTHER READING

Books

Johnson, D.W. and Johnson, F.P. (2014). *Joining Together: Group Theory and Group Skills* (5th edn). Boston, MA: Pearson.

Salas, E., Tannenbaum, S.I., Cohen, D.J. and Latham, G. (2013). *Developing and Enhancing Teamwork in Organizations: Evidence-based Best Practices and Guidelines.* San Francisco, CA: Jossey–Bass.

Journal articles

Kauffeld, S. (2006). Self-directed work groups and team competence. *Journal of Occupational and Organizational Psychology*, 79, 1–21.

Van Knippenberg, D. and Schippers, M.C. (2007). Work group diversity. *Annual Review of Psychology*, 58, 515–541.

5 Communication

This chapter introduces the reader to a number of basic issues concerned with the definition, importance, methods, nature and skills of communication. The first section gives the definition of communication and describes the importance of communication. We then look at various methods of communication, namely written, oral, downward, upward, horizontal and formal communication. The chapter then proceeds to a discussion of communication and relationship-building skills. To communicate effectively, active listening, skilful responding, good oral and written communication, assertiveness and non–verbal communication skills are required. Skilful responding can take place by using questions, minimal encouragement, paraphrasing, clarification, reflection of feelings, summarizing and confrontation. Relationship-building requires self-disclosure and feedback, co-operation, trust, intercultural sensitivity, a service orientation, self-presentation, social influence and conflict resolution. Finally, we look at how power and conflict could impact on organizations.

LEARNING OUTCOMES

When you have completed this chapter you should be able to:

1 Define communication and explain the importance of communication in organizations.
2 Distinguish between methods of communication in organizations.
3 Explain the interpersonal skills which are needed to communicate effectively and to build relationships in the work situation.
4 Identify factors which inhibit or facilitate communication in organizations.

DEFINITION OF COMMUNICATION

Communication is defined as the process by which a person, group or organization (the sender) transmits some type of information (the message) to another person, group or organization (the receiver) (Greenberg, 2011). Two or more parties exchange information and share meaning, so that a common understanding is established between them. It is only through transmitting meaning from one person to another that information and ideas can be conveyed. It is, however, important that this meaning also needs to be understood as it was intended to be understood (Robbins and Judge, 2013).

THE IMPORTANCE OF COMMUNICATION IN ORGANIZATIONS

Communication seems to play an important role in the attainment of organizational goals. Managers devote about one-third of their activities to routine communication, exchanging routine information and processing paperwork (Robbins and Judge, 2013). Communication plays an important role in managerial and organizational effectiveness. It is also one of the biggest problems that modern managers face. However, for some people communication has become an easy scapegoat on which just about every problem can be blamed – even problems of a personal, national and international nature. Communication can obviously play an important role in this regard, but it is definitely not a so-called 'cure-all' for all problems which humankind experiences.

Communication does serve certain major functions within an organization, namely those of control, motivation, emotional expression and providing information (Johnson and Johnson, 2014). The function of control is fulfilled in both a formal and an informal way. Organizations have formal guidelines which employees need to follow, for instance in the case of a grievance procedure. Communication helps to motivate employees by clarifying what they need to do and how it should be done. When they receive feedback on their efforts, it serves as a motivating mechanism. Sometimes communication is aimed at emotional expression by venting feelings of frustration or satisfaction. Communication facilitates decision-making because it provides the necessary information which is needed by the decision-maker. By providing information, communication serves the purpose of achieving co-ordinated action between different parts of an organization.

THE NATURE OF THE COMMUNICATION PROCESS

The source of the communication may be a person or an object. As an object, it may take on many forms, such as a book, a piece of paper, a radio or a television set. The message can take on many forms as well, such as an instruction, a question or even a facial expression. The characteristics of the receiver influence the way in which the message is received and interpreted (Gray and Starke, 1980).

Figure 5.1 depicts a model of the communication process (Robbins and Judge, 2013). According to Figure 5.1, there are specific processes which play a role in the feedback that the sender receives from the receiver. This feedback takes place in order to verify the message. Encoding means that the message is translated from an idea or a thought into symbols which can be transmitted. When busy with encoding, the sender should keep the receiver and his or her characteristics in mind. The sender and the receiver need to understand the symbols in the same way. The message is the physical product which the sender wishes to communicate to the receiver. It can take

FIGURE 5.1 The communication process

on different forms: speech, writing, pictures, arm movements and facial expressions. The message is effected by the code or group of symbols that is used to transfer the meaning, the content of the message itself, and the decisions regarding the selection and arrangement of codes and content. Transmission is the process through which the encoded message travels via a medium or channel or path to the receiver. These channels can be seen as pathways along which the encoded information travels. The source of the message and the way in which it is encoded play an important role in the 'type' of channel or medium which is selected. When the encoded message is delivered in a face–to–face conversation, the channel used in the transmission process is sound waves (Klikauer, 2007).

The channels (also called media) through which messages move can be of great variety. It might be an interpersonal channel, as in the case of talking and touching, to something like a fax machine, right through to something like a newspaper, a radio broadcast or a television broadcast. If one really wants to go into the technical detail, one should perhaps mention that in the case of the newspaper the way in which the message is encoded plays a particular role in the way it is perceived by the receiver. In the case of radio and television broadcasts, technical and electrical equipment are involved again, such as transmitters and receivers.

Decoding is the process by which the receiver of the message attaches meaning to it. In technical terms this means that the receiver must translate the symbols encoded in it into a form which he or she (the receiver) can understand, and then also in the way the sender intended it to be understood. If the receiver attaches different meanings to the message, the communication process can break down. Just as the sender has limited capacities to encode the message, so the receiver has limited capacities to decode the message.

It is important for the sender to keep the qualities of the receiver in mind when encoding a message and choosing the channel by which it should be transmitted. The sender should keep in mind that the receiver might be an individual, a group or an individual acting on behalf of a group. During the decoding process the receiver plays an important role in trying to understand the message as it was intended to be understood. In order to ensure that the message has been correctly understood by the receiver, it is important that the receiver gives feedback to the sender in this regard (Bundel, 2004).

Noise makes the communication process more complex. Noise refers to anything that interferes with the communication process, or which distorts the message. The message itself can also cause distortion, because of the poor choice of symbols and confusion in the content of the message. If a poor channel or medium is selected or the noise level is high, the message can become distorted. The receiver can also be a potential source of distortion. Prejudice, knowledge, perceptual skills, attention span and care in decoding are all factors which can result in distortion of the message.

METHODS OF COMMUNICATION IN ORGANIZATIONS

Written communication

Different types of written material are used in the communication process. Formal letters are usually used to communicate with someone outside the organization. Inside organizations, the so-called 'office memorandum', or 'memo', is quite prevalent. Such a memo is usually addressed to a specific person or a group of persons, and deals with a specific subject (Moorhead and Griffin, 2012).

Other types of written communication found in organizations are e-mails, reports, manuals and forms. Reports are usually used to summarize the progress or results of projects, and are thus of value in decision-making. There are different kinds of manuals in organizations. These include instruction manuals which tell employees how to operate machines, policy and procedure manuals which inform employees of organizational rules and regulations, and operations manuals which tell employees how to perform tasks and to respond to work-related problems. Information is reported on standardized documents, which are called forms. Forms are used in an attempt to make communication more efficient and information more accessible, and thus to increase the efficiency of decision-making.

Electronic communication

Electronic communication is currently one of the most important mediums of communication. This type of communication includes e-mail, text messaging, social media (e.g. Twitter and Facebook), blogs and video conferencing (Robbins and Judge, 2013).

E-mail

E-mail uses the internet to receive and transmit computer-generated text and documents. Messages sent by e-mail can be quickly written, edited, stored and distributed. E-mail is also an inexpensive medium of communication. However, e-mailing has drawbacks, including that people might misinterpret the messages in them, and it is not a good way of transmitting negative messages. It is estimated that 4.9 billion e-mail accounts will exist by the end of 2017 (www.radicati.com). According to the Radicati report, the majority of e-mail traffic in 2013 came from business e-mail. The speed of e-mail depends on the mail server of the client and software of the client, which means that it might be slow. E-mail might also be filled by spam and it might contain malware. Concerns have also been expressed regarding the limited expression of emotions in emails, as well as privacy issues which are created when emails are monitored. Given that people might have trouble keeping up with e-mail, strategies could be implemented to manage e-mail. Strategies include sending fewer e-mails, to unsubscribe from some newsletters, and to schedule e-mail for specific times during a day (Robbins and Judge, 2013). However, e-mail is the most widely used and commonly accepted form of communication.

Instant messaging and text messaging

Instant messaging (IM) and text messaging (TM) use electronic media. IMs are typically sent via computer and enable people to communicate and collaborate in real-time, while TMs are sent via handheld devices or mobile phones. IM is useful for communicating in organizations. The message is instant (i.e. it is received as soon as you send it), is brief, and promotes collaboration in real time. However, IM might be intrusive (e.g. by appearing on the screen of a device) and requires that both parties have accounts with a given instant messaging service. TM is a good way of electronic communication because the mobile phone is almost always nearby. It is a very effective method of reaching someone immediately. However, TM might be intrusive and implies costs.

Blogs

A blog is a website about a single person or organization. The blog is used to communicate opinion and ideas. Twitter (a form of blogging) is a social networking service that allows users to post information about almost any topic. It is expected that such social networking will grow to more than 4.8 billion accounts by the end of 2017 (www.radicati.com).

Oral communication

Oral communication occurs when the spoken language is used during face-to-face talks, telephone conversations, telephone messages, tape recordings and Skype meetings. Oral communication is particularly powerful because it includes not only speakers' words but also their changes in tone, pitch, speed and volume. When people listen to messages, they use all of the aforementioned cues to understand oral messages. Moreover, receivers interpret oral messages in the context of previous communications and, perhaps, the reactions of other receivers.

Downward communication

Katz and Kahn (1978) have identified five general purposes of superior–subordinate communication in an organization. They are as follows:

- To give specific task directives about job instructions.
- To give information about organizational procedures and practices.
- To provide information about the rationale of the job.
- To tell subordinates about their performance.
- To provide ideological information to facilitate the indoctrination of goals.

To a large degree, organizations in the past concentrated only on the first two of these purposes. This leads to an authoritative atmosphere, which inhibits the effectiveness of upward and horizontal communication in organizations. The media which are used in downward communication include organizational handbooks, manuals, magazines, newspapers, letters, bulletin-board items, posters, standard reports, descriptions of procedures, verbal orders and instructions from superiors, speeches, meetings, closed-circuit television sets, public address systems, telephones and electronic mail systems. The key to optimizing downward communication seems to lie in understanding the important role that the receiver of information plays in the communication process.

Upward communication

Upward communication can perhaps also be called subordinate–superior or subordinate-initiated communication. This type of communication flows from a lower level to a higher level in organizations. This type of communication provides feedback to those at higher levels, informs them of the progress which has been made towards attaining goals and is used to inform those at higher levels of the problems which are experienced at lower levels. Through this type of communication those at higher levels can also get ideas on how things can be improved in the organization. Upward communication can take on different forms. These include progress reports, suggestions placed in so-called 'suggestion boxes', information gained from employee attitude surveys, information gained from grievance procedures, discussions between superiors and subordinates, and informal 'gripe' sessions where employees have the opportunity to identify and discuss problems with their superiors or with people at higher managerial levels (Robbins and Judge, 2013).

Downward communication occurs much more frequently than upward communication. It also seems as if the duration of conversations between subordinates and their superiors tends to be much shorter than conversations between subordinates and people at the same level. Furthermore, upward communication seems to be much more inaccurate. This occurs because subordinates feel the need to highlight their accomplishments and to downplay their mistakes, so that their superiors can view their behaviour as favourable. Sometimes, subordinates are afraid to speak to their superiors for fear of being rebuked and lessening their own chances for promotion (Greenberg, 2011).

Horizontal/lateral communication

This type of communication takes place among members of the same work group, among members of work groups at the same level, or among horizontally equivalent personnel. Usually, horizontal/lateral communication tends to be easier and more friendly than downward or upward communication because the problem of status differences is not present. Horizontal communication can also become problematic, even if it is of a formal kind. People in different departments may begin to feel that they are competing for scarce resources. Informal horizontal communication can cause dysfunctional conflicts if the formal vertical channels are breached, when subordinates go above or around their superiors to get things done, or when superiors find out that actions have been taken or decisions made without their knowledge.

Formal and informal communication

Formal communication is regulated by the formal channels laid down in the structure of an organization. Informal communication refers to information shared without any formally imposed obligations or restrictions (Greenberg, 2011). Informal communication flows via informal communication networks. Informal communication networks are, of course, also found outside organizations. In this way, people are connected to each other in an informal way. Naturally, most of this communication is not necessarily work-related, but it lends itself to the very rapid flow of information. These informal channels are known as the organizational grapevine.

Information tends to flow very rapidly along the grapevine. There are mainly two reasons for this. Informal communication crosses formal organizational boundaries. Also, informal communication is mainly transmitted orally, which tends to be more rapid than written communication. Because of the oral way of communication, information tends to become distorted as it is passed along the grapevine. This does not mean that the grapevine is necessarily a bad thing. Although there are people who wish that it could be eliminated, it can sometimes be quite accurate. As long as there are people working in an organization, one will find the grapevine in operation. On the other hand, when inaccuracies enter the grapevine, it can become quite damaging. This is especially true in the case of rumours. Rumours are based on speculation, overactive imagination and wishful thinking, rather than facts (Greenberg, 2011). It is very difficult to refute a rumour. Instead, it seems to be a better strategy to concentrate on other aspects of a person or a situation, rather than directly refuting a rumour about the specific person or situation. If you directly refute a rumour, some people who did not hear it in the first place are likely to get to know about it, while others' views about it might be strengthened, perhaps only because of the rumour being denied.

For people who share in the information brought by the grapevine, it can often be beneficial. Through their access to informal information, which they would not have been able to get via formal channels and structures, people can become quite powerful in organizations. It also helps them to build informal connections with other people.

INTERPERSONAL SKILLS

A person is not born with interpersonal skills. These skills will also not appear automatically when they are needed. Interpersonal skills must be learned in the same way as other skills (e.g. to play the piano, to play tennis). In line with the structure suggested by Klein *et al.* (2006), interpersonal skills are divided into communication skills and relationship–building skills.

Communication skills

Six communication skills are distinguished, namely active listening, responding skills, oral communication, written communication, assertive communication and non–verbal communication (Theobald and Cooper, 2004).

Active listening

Active listening is the conscious attempt to attend to verbal and non–verbal nuances in another person's message (Johnson, 2014). Listening is an intellectual and emotional process which integrates physical, emotional and intellectual inputs to understand the meaning of the message. It also revolves around the meaning behind the words. However, it is difficult to listen actively. It is estimated that people generally comprehend about 25 per cent of a typical verbal message (Barker *et al.*, 1995). To listen effectively, the listener postpones his or her judgement and values, eliminates interruptions and disturbances, focuses on the contents of the message, rephrases what the speaker says in his or her own words, and looks for the important themes in what he or she says. Recurring themes must be noted. The listener tries to understand the person's message and determines what it means to him or her personally.

Responding skills

Responding skills are used to explore issues and problems in interpersonal situations. Responding skills include questioning, minimal encouragement, paraphrasing, summarizing, reflecting and confrontation (Ivey, 1988).

- *Questioning.* Open and closed questions can be used in a communication session. Open questions can be used to start a conversation, to encourage the individual to elaborate, to get specific examples of ideas, behaviour and feelings and to motivate him or her to communicate. Closed questions can be used to define the subject of discussion, to get specific information, to determine borders of a problem and to focus the session by interrupting the person who talks a lot.
- *Minimal encouragement.* Minimal encouragement refers to a direct quotation of what the individual has said, or short comments like 'uh, huh' or 'Tell me more . . .'. Silences can also be used.
- *Paraphrasing.* By paraphrasing, the content of the person's messages is reflected. It is a summarized repetition of what the other person says. An appropriate format for the response is: 'You say. . .', 'In other words. . .', 'It seems that. . .', 'It appears as if . . .'.
- *Clarification.* Clarification brings vague and ambiguous information into focus, encourages the person to elaborate and can be used to find meta–messages. Clarification is often put in the form of a question, such as 'Are you saying that . . .?' or 'Do you mean that . . .?'
- *Reflecting feeling.* By reflecting feeling the listener demonstrates his or her understanding of the feeling of the person, whether it was expressed directly or indirectly. The feelings of the speaker can be identified by listening for feeling words and by observing the person's non-verbal behaviour. The format of a reflection of feeling is: 'You feel . . .' but it must fit the person's feeling words. Add the context or situation to which the feelings are connected (e.g. 'You feel tense when you write exams').
- *Summarizing.* Summarizing refers to the shortened reflection of the speaker's behaviour. The key ideas, themes and emotions in the discussion should be summarized without adding new ideas. Summarizing can be seen as a more detailed paraphrasing and is aimed at changing the direction of the discussion, reducing the tempo, or to end the conversation and revise progress. Summarizing is used when themes are repeated and progress is not apparent.
- *Confrontation.* A confrontation is a verbal response used to describe contradictions, conflicts and meta–messages that are apparent in the speaker's feelings, ideas and actions. The objective of confrontation is to help the speaker see other ways of observing a situation, and to help him or her to become more aware of the incongruence in thoughts, feelings and actions.

Oral communication

It is possible that the listener will understand if the speaker's message is clear, concrete, direct and authentic. The sending of clear, concrete messages demands a conscious effort. The person who communicates effectively has a clear picture in his or her head of what he or she wants to say. He or she can clarify the message and elaborate on it.

He or she is receptive to feedback, and uses it to direct his or her thoughts. Complete and specific messages, which fit the frame of reference of the person to whom the message is sent, must therefore be conveyed. A person must also accept ownership and responsibility for his/her ideas, opinions, feelings and needs by making personal statements. This is made by using personal pronouns when communicating ('I', 'my', 'mine') rather than talking for nobody ('some people', 'one') or to speak for somebody else ('you', 'we', 'our').

Written communication

It is important to phrase written messages effectively. Written communication skills include the clarity of writing as well as the appropriateness of the content, tone and format (Klein *et al.*, 2006). It is important to attend to these aspects in electronic communication. Misunderstandings occur often in mail messages because they lack the non-verbal cues which are given in oral communication.

Assertive communication

Assertive communication entails that a person describes his or her feelings, thoughts, opinions and preferences in an appropriate way. To be assertive, one must be aware of the difference between three concepts, namely, assertiveness, aggression and passiveness. An aggressive person believes that his or her rights are more important than those of others. The passive style is characterized by timid and self-denying behaviour and rests on a person's assumption that his or her rights are less important than those of others. The style of an assertive person is expressive and self-enhancing, and rests on the assumption that his or her rights as well as the other person's rights are equally important.

Studies have shown that assertiveness is more effective than aggressiveness in both work-related and consumer contexts (Infante and Gorden, 1985; Raudsepp, 1992). Individuals should learn to be less aggressive and passive, and to be more assertive. Assertive behaviour is characterized by good eye contact, a strong, steady and audible voice, and selective interruptions. Assertive people should avoid glaring or little eye contact, threatening gestures and a weak voice. Appropriate verbal behaviours include direct and unambiguous language and the use of 'I' messages (Johnson, 2014).

Non-verbal communication

Non-verbal communication refers to messages sent independent of the written or spoken word. Non-verbal behaviour has been studied extensively and it was found that socially inadequate people make less use of non-verbal indicators or use them in the wrong way (Trower, 1990). It has been estimated that non-verbal communication is responsible for up to 60 per cent of the message being communicated (Arthur, 1995). Non-verbal communication has a significant impact on behaviour in organizations, including perceptions of others, hiring decisions, work attitudes and turnover (Liden *et al.*, 1993; Wright and Multon, 1995). A person communicates by means of his or her eyes, facial movement and expressions, tone of voice, posture and body movements (Hall, 1985). Non-verbal communication is subjective, easily misinterpreted, and dependent on cross-cultural differences (Axtell, 1991). The belief that there is only one 'correct' interpretation of a non-verbal message does not promote interpersonal communication.

Relationship-building skills

Self-disclosure and feedback

Self-disclosure involves the individual sharing his or her self, thoughts, feelings and experiences with another individual and is necessary for effective communication and interpersonal relationships. A healthy relationship is built on self-disclosure. If a person hides his or her feelings from others, the tension in the relationship rises and his or her awareness of the inner experience fades. Self-disclosure leads to higher self-awareness (Johnson, 2014).

Feedback can be defined as a verbal and non-verbal process where one individual reveals to another how he or she sees the other's behaviour and how he or she feels about it. It is difficult to give feedback in such a way that the person receiving it accepts it. It is, however, a skill that is learned and for which certain guidelines exist. It is possible to reduce a person's defence against receiving of feedback and to maximize his or her ability to use it for personal growth by giving feedback in an objective way, without disturbance (Johnson, 2014).

The effects of self-disclosure and feedback in interpersonal situations can be illustrated by the Johari window model (see Figure 5.2).

	Known to self	Not known to self
Known to others	Public area	Blind area
Not known to others	Hidden area	Unknown area

FIGURE 5.2 The Johari window

Source: J. Luft (1984: 72). Reproduced with permission from McGraw Hill.

According to the Johari window, there are certain things a person knows about him- or herself, certain things about him- or herself that he or she does not know, certain things others know about him or her, and certain things others do not know about him or her. The more information known to a person and to other persons, the clearer communication could be. The public area can be enlarged and the blind area can be decreased through feedback from others. The hidden area can be decreased by means of self-disclosure (Luft, 1984).

Co-operation

Co-operation is defined as the offering of assistance to team members who need it, pacing activities to fit the needs of the team, and behaving in ways that are not misinterpreted by team members (Klein *et al.*, 2006). Co-operation means that individuals engage in joint action to accomplish a goal that both want. Studies support the notion that co-operation contributes to teamwork in organizations.

Trust

Trust is defined as 'the willingness of a party to be vulnerable to the actions of another party based on the expectation that the other party will perform a particular action important to the trustor, irrespective of the ability to monitor or control that other party' (Mayer *et al.*, 1995). Trust is constantly changing as individuals interact, and it is something that is hard to build and easy to destroy. The key to building trust is being trustworthy, by self-disclosing and by being accepting and supportive of others (Johnson, 2014). Individuals who lack trust will tend to overprotect themselves and their work environment, withhold information and avoid risk-taking.

Intercultural sensitivity

Intercultural sensitivity is defined as the ability to recognize multiple perspectives on an event or behaviour, to recognize one's own cultural values and those of others, and to pick up on verbal and non-verbal signals. Intercultural sensitivity is necessary in order to understand that one's own preferred way of doing things is but one of several possible approaches, and that other cultures may have different perspectives and preferences. The ability to recognize the needs of listeners through verbal and non-verbal signals in communication helps to empathize with culturally different others and to adjust to different ways of communicating.

Intercultural sensitivity requires that an individual demonstrates comfort with other cultures, positive evaluation of other cultures, understanding of cultural differences, empathy for individuals from other cultures, open-mindedness, sharing of cultural differences with others, seeking feedback on how he or she is received in other cultures and adaptability (Dunbar, 1993).

Service orientation

Employees should have the necessary customer service skills to interact effectively with clients. Four factors underlie service orientation, namely active customer relations, polite customer relations, helpful customer relations and personalized customer relations (Fogli and Whitney, 1991).

Self-presentation

Self-presentation is the process by which a person tries to shape what others think of him or her (Johnson, 2014). An individual must establish and maintain impressions that are congruent with the perceptions he or she wants to convey to others (Goffman, 1959; Baumeister, 1982). The goal is for one to present him- or herself the way in which he or she would like to be thought of by the individual or group he or she is interacting with.

Social influence

Persuasion and politicking can be used to change others' attitudes and behaviours. Persuasion is a process that is used to guide people towards the adoption of an idea, attitude or action by rational and symbolic means. It is a problem-solving strategy, and relies on 'appeals' rather than force. Three strategies of persuasion are distinguished, namely persuasion through credibility, persuasion through logical reasoning and persuasion through emotional appeal.

Power bases

- *Reward power.* Individuals with the capacity to control the rewards workers will receive are said to have reward power over them.
- *Coercive power.* A person has coercive power when he or she controls the punishment of others.
- *Legitimate power.* Legitimate power refers to the recognized right of individuals to exercise authority over others because of their position in an organizational hierarchy.
- *Referent power.* Individuals who are liked and respected by others can get them to alter their actions in accordance with their directives – a type of influence known as referent power.
- *Expert power.* To the extent that a person recognizes another person's advanced knowledge and skills, and follows orders because that person knows best, that person is said to have expert power.

Power is the capacity to change the behaviour or attitudes of another in a desired manner (Greenberg, 2011). One can have power but not impose it. It is therefore a capacity or potential. Power is a function of dependency. The greater B's dependence on A, the greater is A's power in the relationship. Dependence is based on alternatives that B perceives and the importance which B places on the alternatives which A controls. A person has power over you when he or she controls something you desire. French and Raven (1959) identified five bases of power derived from the characteristics which individuals possess and the nature of the relationship between individuals with and without power (see Focus 5.1).

The extent to which organizational participants have a sense of personal power and control over their work has become recognized as critical to their performance and well-being. This is known as empowerment. The following strategies could empower employees: a) expressing confidence in employees' abilities and holding high expectations concerning their abilities; b) allowing employees to participate in the decision-making process; c) allowing employees freedom and autonomy in how they perform their jobs; d) setting inspirational goals for employees; e) using legitimate power in a sensible and positive way, and limiting the use of coercive power (Robbins and Judge, 2013).

Organizational politics refer to actions not officially sanctioned (approved) by an organization taken to influence others in order to meet one's personal goals (Greenberg, 2011). Organizational politics involves placing one's self-interests above the interests of the organization. This element of using power to foster one's own interests distinguishes organizational politics from uses of power which are approved and accepted by organizations. Political activity is likely to occur in the face of ambiguity. When there are clear-cut rules about what to do, it is unlikely that people will abuse their power by taking political action. Organizational politics will be more active at higher levels in the organization. The following political tactics are used most often in organizations (Greenberg, 2011):

- *Blaming and attacking others*. Blaming and attacking others is one of the popular political tactics in organizations. This manifests in looking for a scapegoat (someone who could take the blame for some failure).
- *Controlling access to information*. Controlling who knows and does not know certain things is one of the most important ways of exercising power in organizations.
- *Cultivating a favourable impression*. Another way to enhance organizational control is to ensure that the impression you make will be favourable.
- *Developing a base of support*. To be successful in influencing others, individuals sometimes gain the support of others in the organization. This includes lobbying for ideas before they are officially presented and ensuring that others are committed to them in advance.
- *Aligning oneself with other persons who are powerful*. One way of dealing with power is by connecting oneself with other persons who are powerful.

The following techniques may be helpful for dealing with organizational politics:

1 *Clarify job expectations*. Assignments should be well defined and the way work will be evaluated should be clarified.
2 *Open the communication process*. Decisions which are likely to be monitored by all are unlikely to allow any one individual to gain excessive control over desired resources.
3 *Be a good role model*. Managers must set an example of honest and reasonable treatment.
4 *Do not ignore game players*.

Conflict resolution

Conflict is defined as a process which begins when one party perceives that another party has negatively affected, or is about to negatively affect, something the first party cares about. Conflict is common in most modern organizations. Its effects are too costly to ignore. Managers report that they spend almost 20 per cent of their time dealing with conflict and its consequences. Destructive conflict may cause resentment and broken relationships. Conflict is therefore a very important topic for work and organizational psychologists.

Opposing (incompatible) interests lie at the bottom of organizational conflict. Yet conflict involves more than this. Disputes sometimes erupt in situations where the interests of the two sides are not clearly opposed, while in other cases conflict fails to develop despite the existence of deep divisions between opposing parties. The parties to it must perceive conflict; whether or not conflict exists is a perception issue. There must also be some form of interaction for conflict to exist.

ACTIVITY 5.1

Coping with organization politics

In which places and conditions is political behaviour likely to occur in organizations? How can a manager cope with organization politics?

Functional conflict is a constructive form of conflict which supports the goals of the group and improves its performance. Dysfunctional conflict is a destructive form of conflict which hinders group performance. The criterion which differentiates functional conflict from dysfunctional conflict is group or organizational performance. Conflict would be functional if it furthered the objectives of the group. The conflict process has five stages, namely potential opposition, cognition and personalization, intentions, behaviour and outcomes (Robbins and Judge, 2013).

- *Stage 1: Potential opposition or incompatibility.* The first step in the conflict process is the presence of conditions which create opportunities for conflict to arise. These conditions include communication, structure and personal variables. Semantic differences and misunderstandings may create opportunities for conflict. Structure includes variables such as size, degree of specialization of group members, member–goal compatibility, leadership style, reward systems and the degree of dependence between groups. Differences between individual value systems and personality characteristics may be sources of conflict. Individuals who are highly authoritarian and dogmatic, and who demonstrate low self-esteem lead to potential conflict.
- *Stage 2: Cognition and personalization.* If the conditions in Stage 1 negatively affect something that one party cares about, then the potential for opposition becomes actualized in the second stage. The conditions can only lead to conflict when one or more of the parties are affected by and are aware of the conflict. A conflict which is perceived is not necessarily personalized. A may be aware that B and A are in serious conflict, but it may not make A tense. It is at the felt level, when individuals become emotionally involved, that parties experience anxiety, tension, frustration and hostility.
- *Stage 3: Intentions.* Intentions intervene between people's perceptions and emotions and their overt behaviour. These intentions are decisions to act in a given way. This stage is important because individuals have to infer the other's intent in order to know how to respond to their behaviour. Conflicts are often escalated because one party attributes the wrong intentions to the other.
- *Stage 4: Behaviour.* Conflict becomes visible during this stage. This stage includes the statements, actions and reactions made by the conflicting parties. These conflict behaviours are usually overt attempts to implement each party's intentions. The following techniques can be used to manage the conflict during this stage: a) problem-solving meetings between conflicting parties; b) goal-setting where the co-operation of everyone is needed; c) expanding the resources which create the conflict; d) withdrawing or avoiding the conflict; e) playing down the differences while emphasizing common interests; f) compromising; g) using formal authority to solve the conflict; h) training people to alter their attitudes and behaviour; i) altering the structural variables.
- *Stage 5: Outcomes.* Outcomes of conflict may be functional, in that the conflict results in an improvement in performance. It may also be dysfunctional, in that it hinders performance. Functional conflict improves the quality of decisions, stimulates creativity and innovation, encourages interest among group members and provides the medium through which problems can be aired and tension released. Better and more innovative decisions will result from situations where there is some conflict. Conflict may also have dysfunctional and destructive

outcomes. Uncontrolled opposition breeds discontent, which acts to dissolve common ties and eventually leads to the destruction of the group. Conflict may retard communication, reduce group cohesiveness and cause subordination of group goals to the primacy of infighting between members.

FACTORS WHICH FACILITATE OR INHIBIT COMMUNICATION IN ORGANIZATIONS

Various factors – previous life experience, individual differences and situational factors – might impact on the effectiveness of communication and interpersonal relationships of workers (Klein *et al.*, 2006).

Previous experience

The experiences of workers during childhood and adulthood might affect their communication with others. These experiences include family relationships, peer relationships and social relationships at work (Klein *et al.*, 2006).

Individual differences

Individual differences could impact on the effectiveness of communication and interpersonal relationships. Three individual difference variables, namely emotional intelligence, personality traits and collective orientation can influence the nature of interpersonal relations at work (Klein *et al.*, 2006).

Emotional intelligence

Salovey and Mayer (1990), who coined the term 'emotional intelligence', defined it as 'a form of intelligence that involves the ability to monitor one's own and others' feelings and emotions, to discriminate among them and to use this information to guide one's thinking and actions'. Salovey and Mayer initiated a research programme to develop measures of emotional significance and to assess its significance. Widespread interest in the topic of emotional intelligence arose following the publication of Goleman's (1995) book, *Emotional Intelligence*.

Emotional intelligence seems to be a controversial subject. One of the reasons for this is because differences exist over whether emotional intelligence is an ability (Mayer *et al.*, 2000) or a personality trait (Goleman, 1995; Bar-On, 1997). Goleman (1995) and Bar-On (1997) conceived emotional intelligence as a personality trait, which implies that it involves attitudes, preferences and values. According to Goleman (1995), emotional intelligence entails a) knowing what you are feeling and being able to handle those feelings without having them swamp you; b) being able to motivate yourself to get jobs done, be creative and perform at your peak; and c) sensing what others are feeling, and handling relationships effectively. Bar-On's (1997) definition states that it is an array of non-cognitive capabilities, competencies and skills. Critics of the trait approach (Landy, 2005; Locke, 2005) pointed out that the definition of emotional intelligence is constantly changing, that it has no clear measurement, that it is little more than a loose conglomeration of extant personality traits, and that research on emotional intelligence did not demonstrate incremental validity over traditional personality models. The trait approach has led to assessment devices that are based upon self-report, yielding self- and other perceptions of these traits rather than an estimate of a person's actual emotional ability.

The ability–based conceptualization (e.g. Mayer *et al.*, 1999) is not subjected to the same criticism as the trait approach. The ability approach suggests that a skill–based or behavioural measurement (preferably not based on self-report), which focuses narrowly and specifically on emotional skills and abilities only, has demonstrated construct distinctiveness and has demonstrated that good psychometric properties should be used. Emotional intelligence (according to the ability approach) includes four dimensions, namely a) Emotional Perception, which involves such abilities as identifying emotions in faces, music and stories; b) Emotional Facilitation of Thought, which involves such abilities as relating emotions to other mental sensations such as taste and colour, and using emotion in reasoning and problem solving; c) Emotional Understanding, which involves solving emotional problems such as knowing which emotions are similar, or opposites, and what relations they convey; and d) Emotional Management, which involves understanding the implications of social acts on emotions and the regulation of emotion in self and others.

Personality traits

Certain personality traits are regarded as predictors of interpersonal incompetence and communication difficulties. Examples of such traits are arrogance, selfishness, aloofness, emotional instability and compulsiveness (Klein *et al.*, 2006). Klein *et al.* showed that personality dimensions (extroversion, emotional stability, openness, agreeableness and conscientiousness) accounted for 20 per cent of the variance in interpersonal skills. Agreeableness is regarded as an important dimension which predicts interpersonal skills, while extroversion is an important predictor when a task requires social interaction.

Collective orientation

Individuals with a collective orientation will tend to display better interpersonal skills, and will be more willing to work with others than individuals who do not have a collective orientation (Klein *et al.*, 2006).

APPLICATION 5.1

Too much of a good thing . . . ?

The Anonymous Employee website (www.anonymousemployee.com) was created to fill the communication gap that exists in most workplaces.

It provides employees and employers with an opportunity to discuss issues that affect productivity and morale. Read the ensuing case study posted by an anonymous employee under the poor communication section of the website and consider solutions to their problem:

> I feel weird writing a question in the 'poor communication' section of this website, but that's really what my situation is about. My company is all about

communication. We offer phone and Internet services. We all have blackberries and desktop computers for use at work. The management takes communication extremely seriously and whenever there is an issue, a memo is sent out to keep everybody on top of things. The problem is that I feel overwhelmed by the amount of communication. We each easily receive over a dozen email memos every day. When I arrive at work in the morning, I'm faced with at least five or six new memos. As much as it's well intended, I simply cannot remember everything that is sent to me in all of these memos. Policies are always changing, new services are being added, new staff members are entering, old ones are leaving, and lots of other 'issues' are always being brought to everybody's attention. There's no way to keep up. I'm a very organized person, but I don't know how to stay on top of things.

- Consider the communication process and identify the underlying cause of this employee's problem.
- Which strategies would you implement to enhance the effectiveness of the communication process in this organization?

SUMMARY

- Communication is defined as the process by which a person, group or organization (the sender) transmits some type of information (the message) to another person, group or organization (the receiver).
- Communication seems to play an important role in the attainment of organizational goals. Communication does serve certain major functions within an organization, namely those of control, motivation, emotional expression and providing information.
- The source of the communication may be a person or an object. The characteristics of the receiver influence the way in which the message is received and interpreted.
- Various communication methods exist in organizations, namely written communi-cation, oral communication, downward communication, upward communication, horizontal/lateral communication and formal/informal communication.
- Interpersonal skills include communication skills (i.e. active listening, responding, oral communication, written communication, assertive communication and non-verbal communication) and relationship-building skills (i.e. self-disclosure and feedback, co-operation, trust, intercultural sensitivity, service orientation, self-presentation, social influence and conflict resolution).
- Various factors might impact on the effectiveness of communication and interpersonal relationships of workers. These include previous life experience, individual differences (e.g. emotional intelligence, personality traits and collective orientation) and situational factors.

KEY CONCEPTS AND TERMS

- Active listening
- Assertive communication
- Clarification
- Conflict
- Confrontation
- Co-operation
- Decoding
- Downward communication
- Emotional intelligence
- Encoding
- Feedback
- Formal communication
- Horizontal communication
- Intercultural sensitivity
- Minimal encouragement
- Non-verbal communication
- Oral communication
- Organizational politics
- Paraphrasing
- Power
- Questioning
- Receiver
- Responding skills
- Self-disclosure
- Self-presentation
- Service orientation
- Social influence
- Source
- Summarizing
- Trust
- Written communication

SAMPLE ESSAY TITLES

- How can effective communication in organizations be ensured?
- What is the role of emotional intelligence in effective communication in organizations?

FURTHER READING

Books

Johnson, D.W. (2014). *Reaching Out: Interpersonal Effectiveness and Self-Actualisation* (11th edn). Boston, MA: Pearson.

Van der Molen, H. and Gramsbergen–Hoogland, Y.H. (2005). *Communication in Organization: Basic Skills and Conversation Models.* New York: Psychology Press.

Journal articles

Keyton, J., Caputo, J.M., Ford, E.A., Fu, R., Leibowitz, S.A., Liu, T., Polasik, S., Ghosh, P. and Wu, C. (2013). Investigating verbal workplace communication behaviors. *Journal of Business Communication*, 50(2), 152–169.

Mishra, K., Boynton, L. and Mishra, A. (2014). Driving employee engagement: The expanded role of internal communications. *Journal of Business Communication*, 51(2), 183–202.

6 Leadership

This chapter introduces the reader to the nature and theories of leadership. The first section focuses on the definition of leadership. We then look at reasons why leadership is important for organizations. The chapter then proceeds to a discussion of theories of leadership. We look at various approaches to leadership, including the trait approach, the behavioural approach, the contingency approach and a few recent approaches. A major breakthrough in our understanding of leadership came when researchers recognized the need to include situational factors. In addition, the study of leadership has expanded to include visionary approaches to leadership. As we learn more about the personal characteristics which followers attribute to charismatic and transformational leaders, and about the conditions that facilitate their emergence, we should be better able to predict when followers will exhibit extraordinary commitment and loyalty to their leaders and their goals.

LEARNING OUTCOMES

When you have completed this chapter you should be able to:

1 Define leadership.
2 Discuss the importance of leadership.
3 Evaluate the different leadership theories (including *trait theories*, behavioural theories, contingency theories and recent developments).

Definition of leadership

In terms of the number of printed pages devoted to the subject, leadership appears to be one of the most important issues in work and organizational psychology. It is not easy to define leadership. There are almost as many different definitions of leadership as there are persons who attempted to define the concept (Bass, 1981). Bass (1997: 17) states that 'leadership has been conceived as the focus of group processes, as a matter of personality, as a matter of inducing compliance, as the exercise of influence, as particular behaviours, as a form of persuasion, as a power relation, as an instrument to achieve goals, as an effect of interaction, as a differentiated role, as an initiation of structure, and as many combinations of these definitions'.

Leadership is the ability to influence a group towards the achievement of goals (Robbins and Judge, 2013). The source of this influence may be formal, such as that provided by the possession of managerial rank in an organization. A person may assume a leadership role because of the position he or she holds in the organization. However, not all managers are leaders and not all leaders are managers. In general, leadership refers to non-coercive influence techniques. This implies that leadership rests in part on positive feelings between leaders and their subordinates.

Four common themes have been emphasized in the definition of leadership, namely that it is a process that involves influencing others, that it occurs within a group context, and that it involves goal attainment (Northouse, 2001). Leadership involves an influence process and only occurs when individuals willingly adopt the goals of the group as their own. Thus, leadership concerns building cohesive and goal-oriented teams. Leadership is persuasion, not domination.

Many people struggle with the differences between management and leadership (Cooper, 2005). Most experts agree that leadership and management are different. However, the terms 'leader' and 'manager' are often used interchangeably. A manager is a person who takes on a management role, which comprises activities such as planning, processing information, organizing, controlling and communicating with customers or suppliers. Managers will be leaders when they exert influence over their subordinates in order to attain organizational goals. Many persons who are leaders are not managers. They operate in contexts outside the world of business and do not perform activities associated with managerial roles (e.g. organizing, controlling and planning).

Importance of leadership

There are various reasons why leadership is important. Leadership matters because of the following reasons (Lewis, 2011):

- Leadership solves the problem of organizing collective effort. Good leadership leads to organizational success, as well as financial and social well-being of people.
- Bad leaders cause misery for people who are subject to their domain.
- Several patterns of leadership behaviour are associated with subordinates' performance and satisfaction. Reactions to inept leadership include turnover, insubordination, industrial sabotage and malingering. Studies from the mid-1950s show that 60–75 per cent of the employees in any organization report that the worst or most stressful aspect of their job is their immediate supervisor. Good leaders may put pressure on their people, but abusive and incompetent leaders cost management millions in lost productivity. The most common complaints from direct reports concern: a) managers' unwillingness to exercise authority; b) managers tyrannizing their subordinates.
- Top managers account for 14 per cent of the variance in organizational performance.

LEADERSHIP THEORIES

Various theories have been developed to explain leadership. These theories can roughly be studied in terms of four approaches, namely trait theories, behavioural theories, contingency theories and recent theories (including the attribution perspective, charismatic leadership, and transactional and transformational leadership).

Trait theories

Trait theories focus on discovering the leadership personality and examining what it is about the character, underlying motivations and behavioural styles that make an individual a leader. The tendency to describe people in terms of traits has a long history. Throughout history many people believed that leaders are born, not made, and that great leaders are discovered, not developed. In the early twentieth century there were many strong advocates of the trait theories of leadership. Wiggam (1931), for example, concluded that the survival of the fittest and marriage among them produces an aristocratic class that differs biologically from the lower classes.

RESEARCH METHODS 6.1

Researching trait theories of leadership

Hundreds of studies have been conducted to identify the personal attributes of leaders. The typical research studies on trait theories have compared the characteristics of a leader (defined as an individual holding a position of authority) with the characteristics of a follower (defined as an individual not holding a position of authority). The findings of these studies are somewhat contradictory and inconclusive. Mann (1959) reviewed 125 studies of leadership and personality characteristics representing over 700 findings. He concluded that intelligence and personal adjustment seem to be correlated with leadership (Wright, 1996).

Leaders were found to score higher on tests of a wide variety of characteristics, including intelligence, personality, task motivation and performance, and social competence. These tests have, however, not proved to be reliably useful in the selection of leaders. The safest conclusion which can be drawn from trait studies of leadership is that individuals who have the energy, drive, self-confidence and determination to succeed will become leaders, because they work hard to get leadership positions (Bass, 1981). The best predictor of leadership success is prior success in leadership roles, but a previously successful leader may fail when placed in a situation which imposes demands incompatible with his or her personality. Research has shown that leaders differ from non-leaders regarding ambition and energy, honesty and integrity, self-confidence and job relevant knowledge. None of these traits will, however, guarantee success as a leader.

The implication of trait theories is that it is possible to select the right person to assume formal positions in groups and organizations. Traits of leaders may act as a moderating variable in determining leadership behaviour (Zaleznik, 1993). In certain combinations, personality traits may account for about 35 per cent of the variance in leadership behaviour (Bass, 1998). However, the trait approach is not very successful in explaining leadership because it: a) overlooks the needs of followers; b) fails to clarify the relative importance of various traits; c) does not separate cause from effect, (for example are leaders self-confident or does success as a leader build self-confidence?); d) ignores situational factors.

Behavioural theories

The behavioural theories focus on specific behaviour which effective leaders exhibit that might differentiate them from ineffective leaders (Burke and Cooper, 2004). The difference between trait and behavioural theories lies in the underlying assumptions. If trait theories were valid, then leadership would be inborn. On the other hand, if there were specific behaviours which identified leaders, then it would be possible to train and develop individuals to become leaders. The implication of behavioural theories is that the behaviour of individuals should be studied in order to identify leaders and that it is possible to train leaders. Although the behavioural theories are criticized for the fact that they do not consider the situation in which leadership occurs, they added valuable insights to the field. The following behavioural theories can be distinguished: a) Harvard studies; b) University of Michigan studies; c) Ohio State studies; d) the Managerial Grid.

Harvard studies

Bales (1953) at Harvard University conducted research on behaviour in small groups. The research showed two types of leader behaviour in small groups, namely task leadership and socio-emotional leadership. The task leader will keep reminding the group of its aims and bringing the group back to them whenever they stray from their problem-solving purpose, coming up with new ideas when they get stuck. The social-emotional leader is particularly sensitive to other people's needs, uses praise and other forms of feedback and is more inclined to ask for suggestions than to give them. According to Bales (1953), a group member could only be a task leader or a socio-emotional leader.

Michigan studies

Studies which were done at the University of Michigan's Survey Research Center by Tannenbaum and Schmidt (1958) also tried to locate the behavioural characteristics of leaders. The researchers at this university focused on two dimensions of leadership behaviour, namely employee orientation and production orientation (see Focus 6.1).

The results of the Michigan researchers strongly favoured employee-oriented leaders. Employee-oriented behaviour causes high productivity and high job satisfaction, while production-oriented behaviour causes low productivity and low job satisfaction.

Dimensions of leadership behaviour (Michigan studies)

- *Employee-oriented leaders* emphasize interpersonal relations, take interest in the needs of their subordinates and accept individual differences among members.
- *Production-oriented leaders* emphasize the task aspects of the job. Their main concern is the accomplishment of the group's tasks, and group members are seen as a means to an end.

Ohio State studies

The most comprehensive of the behavioural theories resulted from the research which began at the Ohio State University in the late 1940s (Halpin and Winer, 1957). The researchers found that two independent dimensions, namely initiating structure and consideration, accounted for most of the leadership behaviour described by subordinates (Hersey *et al.*, 2013; see Focus 6.2).

Leaders high in initiating structure and consideration achieve high subordinate performance and satisfaction more frequently than those who rate low on consideration, initiating structure or both. High scores on both these dimensions do not, however, always result in positive consequences.

The Managerial Grid

According to Blake and Mouton (1964), leadership styles are influenced by two variables, namely concern for production and concern for people. These two variables can be represented on a scale of different intensities from one to nine. Although a wide variety of leadership styles are possible, Blake and Mouton concentrate mainly on five leadership styles, i.e. 9,1; 1,9; 1,1; 5,5 and 9,9.

- The *9,1 style* emphasizes concern for production to a large degree (9), while there is little concern for the human factor (1). The basic assumption is that there is an unavoidable contradiction between the needs of the organization and those of its

Dimensions of leadership behaviour (Ohio State studies)

- *Initiating structure* refers to the extent to which a leader is likely to define and structure his or her role and those of subordinates in the search for goal attainment.
- *Consideration* refers to the extent to which a person is likely to have job relationships which are characterized by mutual trust, respect for subordinates and regard for their feelings.

members. The leader regards people as instruments who must be bent to perform work. Strict control is exercised, while little opportunity is given for responsibility and own initiative.

- The *1,9 style* emphasizes concern for people (9), while production must adapt to man and his or her social needs (1). Leaders give considerable attention to the attitudes and feelings of persons. People are not driven, but merely encouraged.
- The *1,1 style* emphasizes low concern for people (1) and for production (1). The leader leaves followers to work as they prefer. The leader has a messenger function and does not accept responsibility for followers.
- The *5,5 style* is a compromise style where both production and people factors receive equal attention. The assumption of this style is that people will be willing to work and obey orders if the reasons are explained to them.
- The *9,9 style* emphasizes high concern for production (9) and high concern for people. The objective of the 9,9 style is to promote the conditions which integrate creativity and high morale through concerned action.

Leaders were found to perform best under a 9,9 style, as contrasted with the other styles. There is little substantial evidence to support the conclusion that a 9,9 style is most effective in all situations (Robbins and Judge, 2013).

Contingency theories

The predicting of leadership success is more complex than isolating a few traits or preferable behaviour. In organizations, contingency theory emphasizes the fit between organizational processes and the characteristics of the situation. Leadership effectiveness is also dependent on the situation. Therefore, there is no best way to lead people. The best way to lead people depends on the situation. Situational variables include the degree of structure in the task performed, the quality of leader–member relations and the maturity of followers (Robbins and Judge, 2013).

The contingency theory of Fiedler

Fiedler (1967) developed the first comprehensive contingency theory of leadership. Fiedler's contingency theory suggests that leadership performance can only be understood in relation to the context in which it occurs and that success is achieved when there is a good leader–situation match. The model of Fiedler proposes that effective group performance depends on the match between the leader's style of interacting with subordinates and the degree to which the situation allows control.

According to Fiedler, an individual's basic leadership style is a key factor in leadership success. Therefore, he begins by trying to find out what the basic style is. Fiedler developed a personality measure, the least preferred co-worker (LPC) scale, which measures whether a person is task- or relationship- oriented. The LPC scale contains sixteen contrasting adjectives (such as efficient–inefficient, supportive–hostile). The respondent is asked to think of all the co-workers he or she has ever had and to describe the one person he or she least enjoyed working with by rating him or her on a scale of 1 to 8 on each of the adjectives. An individual's basic leadership style is determined by analysing their responses on the scale. If the least preferred co-worker is described in relatively positive terms (a high LPC score), then the person is primarily interested in good personal relations with this co-worker. High LPC leaders seem mainly concerned with establishing good relationships with subordinates. In contrast, leaders who perceive the least preferred co-worker in negative terms (a low LPC score) seem primarily concerned with attaining successful task performance and would be labelled task oriented. About 16 per cent of respondents score in the middle range. Such persons cannot be classified as either relationship- or task-oriented and thus fall outside the theory's predictions. Fiedler believes that an individual's leadership style is fixed. This means that if a situation requires a task-oriented leader and the person in that leadership position is relationship-oriented, either the situation has to be modified or the leader removed and replaced if optimum effectiveness is to be achieved.

After an individual's basic leadership style has been assessed through the LPC, it is necessary to match the leader with the situation. The effectiveness of low or high LPC leaders depends on situational factors, such as the degree to which the situation is favourable for leaders (provides them with control over subordinates). Fiedler identifies three situational criteria which can be manipulated to create the proper match with the behavioural orientation of the leader, namely a) the degree to which the leader enjoys the loyalty of group members; b) the extent to which task goals and subordinates' roles are clearly defined; and c) the leader's ability to enforce compliance by subordinates. The next step is to evaluate the situation in terms of these three contingency variables. The better the leader–member relations, the more highly structured the job, and the stronger the position power, the more control or influence the leader has.

With knowledge of an individual's LPC and an assessment of the three contingency variables, Fiedler's theory proposes matching them up to achieve maximum leadership effectiveness. The leader's situational control can range from very high (positive relations with group members, a highly structured task, high position power) to very low (negative relations, an unstructured task, low position power). Low LPC leaders (who are task oriented) are superior to high LPC leaders (who are people oriented) when situational control is either very low or high. High LPC leaders have an edge when situational control falls within the moderate range. Under conditions of low situational control, groups need guidance and direction to accomplish their tasks. Since low LPC leaders are more likely to provide such structure than high LPC leaders, they will be superior in such cases. Low LPC leaders also have an edge under conditions which offer the leaders a high degree of situational control. Here, low LPC leaders realize that conditions are good and that successful task performance is almost assured. As a result, they turn their attention to improving relations with subordinates and often adopt a 'hands-off' style. High LPC leaders, feeling that they already enjoy good relations with their subordinates, may shift their attention to task performance. Their attempts to provide guidance in this respect may be regarded as interference by subordinates, with the result that performance is impaired.

If the situation offers the leader moderate control, conditions are mixed and attention to good interpersonal relations is often needed. High LPC leaders, with their interest in people, have an advantage in such situations. Low LPC leaders may in such situations continue to focus on task performance and become even more autocratic and directive. The negative reactions of subordinates to such behaviour may have detrimental effects upon performance.

Fiedler's theory implies that leaders and situations should be matched. Individuals' LPC scores indicate the type of situation for which they are best suited. According to the theory there are two ways to improve leader effectiveness: a) change the leader to fit the situation; b) change the situation to fit the leader. This could be done by restructuring tasks or increasing or decreasing the power of the leader to control factors such as salary increases, promotions or disciplinary actions. Fiedler's model goes significantly beyond trait and behavioural approaches by attempting to isolate situations, relating his personality measure to his situational classification, and then predicting leadership effectiveness as a function of the two (Robbins and Judge, 2013).

Hersey's Situational Leadership® Model

The Situational Leadership® Model of Hersey (1982) is a contingency theory which focuses on the readiness levels of followers to determine the most appropriate leadership style. Successful leadership is achieved by selecting the correct leadership style, which is contingent on followers' readiness. Regardless of what the leader does, effectiveness depends on the actions of their followers. This is an important dimension which has been overlooked in most leadership theories. The term 'readiness' refers to the extent to which people have the ability and willingness to accomplish a certain task.

Hersey's model uses two distinct leadership dimensions, namely task and relationship behaviour. Based on combinations of task and relationship behaviour, four leadership styles, namely telling, selling, participating and delegating are distinguished (Hersey *et al.*, 2013):

- *Telling* (*high task–low relationship*). The leader defines roles and tells people what, how, when and where to do various tasks.
- *Selling* (*high task–high relationship*). The leader provides both directive behaviour and supportive behaviour.
- *Participating* (*low task–high relationship*). The leader and follower share in decision-making with the main role of the leader being facilitating and communicating.
- *Delegating* (*low task–low relationship*). The leader provides little direction or support.

Hersey identifies the following four stages of follower readiness:

- *R1*: Individuals are both unable and unwilling to take responsibility to do something.
- *R2*: Individuals are unable but willing to do tasks. They are motivated but lacking skills.

- *R3*: Individuals are able but insecure or unwilling to do what the leader wants.
- *R4*: Individuals are able and willing to do what is expected from them.

As followers reach high levels of readiness the leader responds by decreasing control over activities and by decreasing relationship behaviour. At stage R1, followers need clear and specific directions. At stage R2, both high-task and high-relationship behaviour is needed. The high-task behaviour compensates for the followers' lack of ability, while the high-relationship behaviour tries to get the followers to buy into the leader's desires. R3 creates motivational problems which are best solved by a supportive, non-directive leadership style. At stage R4, the leader does not have to do much because followers are both willing and able to take responsibility.

Leader–member exchange theory

Leader–member exchange (LMX) theory (Dienesch and Liden, 1986) advocates recognition of individual differences and an emphasis on dyadic relationships between a leader and each of his or her subordinates. Research focused on the quality of leader–subordinate interaction. A high quality relationship is characterized by the member having high levels of responsibility, decision influence and access to resources. Members who enjoy a high quality LMX relationship are said to be in the in-group. A low quality LMX relationship is characterized by the leader offering low levels of support to the member, and the member having low levels of responsibility and decision influence. Members who have a low quality LMX relationship are said to be in the out-group (Graen and Uhl-Bien, 1995).

Leader–member relationships emerge as the result of a series of exchanges or interactions during which leader and member roles develop. This role-formation process involves three phases, namely:

- *Role taking.* The member enters the organization and the leader assesses his or her abilities and talents. Based on this assessment, the leader provides opportunities for the member to 'take' a specific role. Mutual respect is essential in this stage. Leaders and members must each understand how the other views and desires respect. This might be difficult in mixed-gender relationships because men and women may interpret or define respect differently. The leader–member relationship will not develop and progress to the next stage if there is a lack of respect.
- *Role making.* The leader and the member engage in unstructured and informal negotiation. During this phase the member begins to 'make' a role. In this stage trust must be developed in order for leaders and members to further develop the relationship and influence each other's attitudes and behaviours. If trust is violated even a single time in diverse dyadic relationships, the relationship may be destroyed.
- *Role routinization.* An ongoing social exchange pattern emerges or becomes 'routinized'. Mutual obligation is formed in this phase. Role making has been established at this point and leaders and members have shared meanings.

The role formation process develops through a mechanism referred to as 'negotiating latitude'. This negotiation is hypothesized to occur through the series of exchanges or interactions between the leader and the member. Work-related variables and the leader's and the member's affective responses to their initial interaction may be important components in the development of the LMX relationship. The affective responses are influenced by the perceived similarity between the leader and the member. The more the leader and the member perceive that they are similar, the more they will like each other and the more likely they are to develop a high quality LMX relationship. Additionally, attraction might be affected by the amount of interaction that occurs between the leader and the member. Leaders and members who share a high quality LMX relationship tend to interact more about personal topics than about work-related topics, which may result in higher levels of trust. Leaders tend to trust in-group subordinates and therefore empower them with decision-making authority.

RECENT APPROACHES TO LEADERSHIP

More recent approaches to leadership are discussed next. These approaches include the attribution theory of leadership, charismatic leadership, transactional versus transformational leadership. In these approaches, leaders are seen as managers of meaning, rather than merely in terms of their influence on subordinates.

Attribution theory of leadership

Attribution theory deals with people trying to make sense from cause–effect relationships. When something happens, they want to attribute it to something. According to attribution theory, leadership is merely an attribution which people make about other individuals. Using the attribution framework, researchers have found that people characterize leaders as having traits such as intelligence, outgoing personality, strong verbal skills, aggressiveness and understanding. The high-consideration, high-structure leader was found to be consistent with attributions of what makes a good leader (Robbins and Judge, 2013).

Charismatic leadership

The model of Conger and Kanungo (1987) proposes that charismatic leadership is an attributional phenomenon founded on subordinate perceptions of the leader's behaviour. The process begins by the leader articulating an appealing vision. The leader then communicates the vision and high performance expectations and expresses confidence that the followers can attain them. Next, the leader conveys a new set of values, and by his or her behaviour sets an example for followers to imitate. Finally, the leader demonstrates how to achieve the mission using empowerment, modelling and unconventional tactics. Some examples of individuals cited to be charismatic leaders include Nelson Mandela and Martin Luther King (see Application 6.1).

Experts believe that people can be trained to exhibit charismatic behaviour (Robbins and Judge, 2013). Charismatic leadership may not always be needed to achieve high levels of employee performance. It may be most appropriate when the follower's task has an ideological component. That is probably the reason why charismatic leaders are likely to surface in politics, wartime, religion and when a business firm is transforming.

APPLICATION 6.1

Profile of Nelson Rolihlahla Mandela

Richard Sengel (*Time*, 9 May 1994) interviewed Nelson Mandela and noted the following story, which indicates his perspective on leadership.

> 'When you want to get a herd to move in a certain direction,' he said, 'you stand at the back . . . A few of the more energetic cattle move to the front and the rest of the cattle follow. You are really guiding them from behind.' With a smile he added: 'This is how a leader should do his work.'
>
> Source: R. Sengel (9 May 1994). The making of a leader. www.time.com/time/time100/ leaders/profile/mandela_related.html

FIGURE 6.1 Nelson Mandela

Source: © Paul Velasco; Gallow Images/ CORBIS.

Nelson Rolihlahla Mandela is the most inspirational leader of the second half of the twentieth century. He was born in a village near Umtata in the Transkei on the 18 July 1918. His father was the principal councillor to the Acting Paramount Chief of Thembuland. After his father's death, the young Rolihlahla became the Paramount Chief's ward to be groomed to assume high office. After receiving a primary education at a local mission school, Nelson Mandela was sent to Healdtown, a Wesleyan secondary school of some repute where he matriculated. He completed his BA by correspondence, took articles of clerkship and commenced study for his LLB. He entered politics in earnest by joining the African National Congress in 1942. During the 1950s, Mandela was the victim of various forms of repression. After the Sharpeville Massacre in 1960, the ANC was outlawed, and Mandela, still on trial, was detained. In 1962 he left the country unlawfully and travelled abroad for several months. Not long after his return to South Africa Mandela was arrested and charged with illegal exit from the country, and incitement to strike. Mandela was convicted and sentenced to five years' imprisonment. While serving his sentence he was charged, in the Rivonia Trial, with sabotage. Mandela was sentenced to life imprisonment and started his prison years in the notorious Robben Island Prison. In 1988 he was moved to the Victor Verster Prison near Paarl from where he was eventually released. In the early 1990s, with great magnanimity and force of character, Mandela was able to help negotiate an end to the system of apartheid leading to his election as president of a free and democratic society in 1994. Although Nelson Mandela died on 5 December 2013, people across the globe still respect him for his leadership.

Transactional versus transformational leadership

Bass (1985, 1990) defined transformational leadership in terms of how the leader affects followers, who are intended to trust, admire and respect the transformational leader. He identified three ways in which leaders transform followers, namely a) increasing their awareness of task importance and value; b) getting them to focus first on team or organizational goals, rather than their own interests; and c) activating their higher-order needs. Charisma is seen as necessary, but not sufficient, for leadership. Two key charismatic effects that transformational leaders achieve are to evoke strong emotions and to cause identification of the followers with the leader. This may be through stirring appeals. It may also occur through quieter methods such as coaching and mentoring.

Transformational leadership is grounded in moral foundations that are based on four components, namely idealized influence, inspirational motivation, intellectual stimulation and individualized consideration (Bass, 1998). Transformational leadership is not seen as being sufficient for effective organizations. It must be accompanied by effective management (transactional leadership). Transactional leaders guide or motivate their followers in the direction of the established goal by clarifying role and task requirements. The Ohio State studies and Fiedler's model have concerned transactional leaders. Transformational leaders inspire followers to transcend their own self-interests for the good of the organization, and are capable of having a profound and extra-ordinary effect on their followers. They pay attention to the concerns and development needs of individual followers, they change followers' awareness of issues by helping them look at old problems in new ways, and they are able to excite, arouse and inspire followers to put out extra effort to achieve group goals.

Research indicates that transformational leadership is more strongly correlated than transactional leadership with lower turnover rates, higher productivity rates and higher employee satisfaction (Bass, 1998). The criticism against transformational leadership is that it has poorly defined parameters, and that it treats leadership as a personal predisposition rather than as a behaviour that can be learned.

APPLICATION 6.2

A good leader does the right things right!

Managing a vision and purpose is one of the big challenges facing leaders. Leaders need certain skills to achieve this successfully and to create trust in their ability to lead. Nelson Mandela is regarded as a symbol of visionary and charismatic leadership because he was so innately skilled to present and manage vision and purpose. Lombardo and Eichinger (2000) profiled the skills necessary to manage vision and purpose (see below). Assess your own ability (or skills gaps), and that of a leader in your environment, to manage vision and purpose according to the skills profile.

Unskilled

☐ Can't communicate or sell a vision
☐ Not a good presenter

- ☐ Can't turn a good phrase or create compelling one liners
- ☐ Uncomfortable speculating on the unknown future
- ☐ Isn't charismatic or passionate enough to excite and energize others
- ☐ Can't simplify enough to help people understand complex strategy
- ☐ May not understand how change happens
- ☐ Doesn't act like he/she really believes in the vision
- ☐ More comfortable in the here and now

Skilled

- ☐ Communicates a compelling and inspired vision or sense of core purpose
- ☐ Talks about possibilities
- ☐ Is optimistic
- ☐ Creates mileposts and symbols to rally support behind the vision
- ☐ Makes the vision sharable by everyone (inclusive approach)
- ☐ Can inspire and motivate entire unit or organizations

Overused skill

- ☐ May leave people behind
- ☐ May lack patience with those who don't understand or share his/her vision and sense of purpose
- ☐ May lack appropriate detail-orientation and concern for administrative routine
- ☐ May lack follow-through on the day-to-day tasks
- ☐ Lombardo and Eichinger (2000) provide remedies for skills gaps and it might be beneficial to consult their book if you lack certain skills.

Source: M.M. Lombardo and R.W. Eichinger (2000). *For your Development: A Development and Coaching Guide* (3rd edn) p. 389 (ISBN 0-9655712-3-8)

Ethical leadership

Ethical leadership is defined as 'the demonstration of normatively appropriate conduct through personal actions and interpersonal relationships, and the promotion of such conduct to followers through two–way communication, reinforcement, and decision making' (Brown *et al.*, 2005: 120). An ethical leader possesses specific traits (e.g. integrity, honesty and trustworthiness), exhibits specific behaviours (doing the right thing, showing concern for people and being open), and makes decisions in a prescribed way (e.g. holds to values and follows ethical rules). Furthermore, the ethical leader actively promotes ethical behaviour in organizations through his or her actions and communications.

Spiritual leadership

Spiritual leadership comprises the values, attitudes and behaviours that are necessary to intrinsically motivate one's self and others so that they have a sense of spiritual survival through calling and membership (Fry, 2003). Spiritual leadership entails creating a vision wherein organization members experience a sense of calling in that their life has meaning, and establishing a culture based on altruistic love whereby leaders and followers have genuine care, concern and appreciation for both the self and others, thereby producing a sense of membership (Fry and Cohen, 2009). Altruistic love incorporates a wide variety of positively oriented traits, processes, intentional behaviours and performance outcomes such as kindness, forgiveness, integrity, compassion, honesty, patience, trust and loyalty. Spiritual leadership elevates processes, behaviours and outcomes for leaders, followers and organizations.

Authentic leadership

Authentic leadership is defined as 'owning one's personal experiences, be they thoughts, emotions, needs, preferences, or beliefs, processes captured by the injunction to know one-self' and behaving in accordance with the true self (Harter, 2002: 382). Authentic leadership has four components (Illies *et al.*, 2005; Walumbwa *et al.*, 2010; Zamahani *et al.*, 2011): self-awareness, self-regulation, relational transparency and balanced processing (paying attention to both positive and negative interpretations about themselves and their leadership style). Authentic leaders may possess the ability to enhance follower commitment and citizenship behaviours, which might affect performance in a positive way (Walumbwa *et al.*, 2010).

Recent research in state-owned enterprises showed that authentic leadership affected psychological capital, i.e. the hope, optimism, self-efficacy and resilience of subordinates as well as their job satisfaction (Amunkete and Rothmann, in press). Authentic leadership and psychological capital played an important role in the retention of employees in state-owned enterprises.

Positive leadership

Positive leadership refers to the facilitation of extraordinarily positive performance by focusing on the strengths and capabilities of people (Cameron, 2008). It adds four strategies to the competencies often expected from leaders, namely the cultivation of a positive climate in the organization, positive relationships, positive communication and positive meaning.

- *Positive climate* refers to a condition in which positive emotions predominate over negative emotions in the work environment. A positive climate is characterized by optimistic attitudes and cheerful outlooks. A negative climate is character-ized by stress, anxiety and distrust. Conditions that foster positive emotions lead to optimal individual and organizational functioning (i.e. positive deviance). A positive climate can be promoted by fostering compassion, forgiveness and gratitude.
- *Positive relationships* can be promoted by building energy networks and reinforcing strengths.
- *Positive communication* is established by obtaining best-self feedback and using supportive communication.
- *Positive meaning* can be built by affecting human well-being, connecting to personal values, highlighting extended impact and building community.

SUMMARY

- Leadership is the process whereby one individual influences other group members towards the attainment of defined group or organizational goals. Leaders generally use non-coercive forms of influence and are influenced, in turn, by their followers. Not all managers function as leaders. Conversely, not all leaders are managers. The two terms should therefore not be treated as synonyms.

- Leadership plays an important role in understanding individual, group and organizational behaviour, for it is the leader who usually provides the direction towards goal attainment. In this study unit, different approaches to the study of leadership were described, distinguishing between the trait approach, the behavioural approach, the contingency approach and a few recent approaches.

- Various theories have been developed to explain leadership. These can roughly be studied in terms of four approaches, namely trait theories, behavioural theories, contingency theories and recent theories (including the attribution perspective, charismatic leadership, and transactional and transformational leadership).

- A major breakthrough in our understanding of leadership came when researchers recognized the need to include situational factors.

- The study of leadership has expanded to include visionary approaches to leadership. As we learn more about the personal characteristics which followers attribute to charismatic and transformational leaders, and about the conditions that facilitate their emergence, we should be better able to predict when followers will exhibit extraordinary commitment and loyalty to their leaders and their goals.

- In line with the developments in positive organizational behaviour, research showed that positive leadership (i.e. positive climate, positive relationships, positive communication and positive meaning) and authenticity from the leaders play an important role in job performance and retention of employees.

KEY CONCEPTS AND TERMS

- Attribution theory
- Behavioural theories
- Charismatic leadership
- Consideration
- Contingency theories
- Employee orientation
- Follower maturity
- Harvard studies

- Leadership
- Leader–member exchange
- Managerial grid
- Michigan studies
- Negotiating latitude
- Positive leadership
- Production orientation
- Role making

- Role routinization
- Role taking
- Structure
- Trait theories
- Transactional leadership
- Transformational leadership
- Vision

SAMPLE ESSAY TITLES

- Do you think there is one best leadership theory? Evaluate the different leadership theories.
- What are the differences between transactional and transformational leadership?

FURTHER READING

Books

Burke, R. and Cooper, C. (2006). *Inspiring Leaders*. London: Routledge.

Cameron, K. (2013). *Practicing Positive Leadership: Tools and Techniques that Create Extraordinary Results*. San Francisco, CA: Berrett-Koehler Publishers.

Hersey, P.H., Blanchard, K.H. and Johnson, D.E. (2013). *Management of Organizational Behavior: Leading Human Resources* (10th edn). Boston, MA: Pearson.

Journal articles

Cameron, K. and Plews, E. (2012). Positive leadership in action: Applications of POS by Jim Mallozzi, CEO, Prudential Real Estate and Relocation. *Organizational Dynamics*, 41, 99–105.

Wang, H., Sui, Y., Luthans, F., Wang, D. and Wu, Y. (2014). Impact of authentic leadership on performance: Role of followers' positive psychological capital and relational processes. *Journal of Organizational Behavior*, 35(1), 5–21.

2 | Work psychology

7 Human resource planning and job analysis

This chapter introduces the reader to human resource planning and job analysis. The first section focuses on human resource planning. We look at the definition of human resource planning. The chapter then proceeds to the reasons for human resource planning and the human resource planning process. Regarding the human resource planning process, various phases are discussed, including analysing the situation, determining the characteristics of the present workforce, analysing the demand for and the supply of human resources, determining the human resource goals, designing and implementing human resource plans, and gathering/analysing information that can be used as feedback to update the human resource planning process. The second section focuses on job analysis. We look at the definition of job analysis, the steps in job analysis, the uses of job analysis information and methods of job analysis. Lastly, we discuss job descriptions and job specifications.

LEARNING OUTCOMES

When you have completed this chapter you should be able to:

1 Define human resource planning and discuss the rationale for and process of human resource planning.
2 Describe the steps that have to be carried out when doing human resource planning.
3 Describe job analysis and distinguish between job analysis, job description and job specifications.

HUMAN RESOURCE PLANNING

Definition of human resource planning

Human resource planning is a planned analysis of the present and future (quantitative and qualitative) human resource needs of an organization and the implementation of action plans in order to ensure the adequate supply of human resources. It is an ongoing process that it is linked to many other activities that take place inside an organization, especially human resource management activities, such as recruitment, performance appraisal and training (Coyle-Shapiro *et al.*, 2004).

Reasons for human resource planning

The reasons for human resource planning can be summarized as follows:

- Through human resource planning it is possible to put human resources to strategic use. This means that the strategic planning of an organization can be done on a much surer base than before. Through sound human resource planning unnecessary risks can be avoided when strategic organizational planning is done. In this way, human resource planning is necessary in order for an organization to adapt to (expected) changes in the environment. These changes can be of a great variety, such as changes in legislation, in markets, in products or services, in the opening up of new markets, in technology and in competition from other organizations.
- Because organizations usually make use of a visual model of their human resource system when doing human resource planning, it is easy to see when problems will be encountered. In this way the necessary adjustments in plans can be made as soon as these problems are visualized. These problems might be in the form of an over- or an under-supply of particular workers at a given stage in the future.
- Through human resource planning more effective use over the short term and over the longer term can be made of an organization's available human resources. When the human resource is utilized effectively, it also means that other resources, such as time, machines and money, can also be utilized more effectively.
- Human resource planning gives organizations the opportunity to develop high-level personnel to take up the positions of those that leave senior level and management jobs. Organizations that make use of a large number of technical or professional workers or highly skilled managers need to know when these types of workers are to be replaced in future, because these workers are frequently in short supply. Human resource planning allows an organization to continually upgrade the skills and abilities of its entire workforce by concentrating on activities such as recruitment, selection, placement, training and development, and career management.
- Human resource planning activities ensure that the top management team of an organization is able to gain a scientific view of, and also the necessary insight into, the interaction between the organization's strategic planning, and its complex and expensive human resource. Human resource planning places the management of

an organization in a position to manage the human resource in a way that complies with all the legal requirements and to effectively counter any actions instituted by workers or labour unions.

- Human resource planning has a direct influence on the quality of work life that workers experience. It gives the workers a sense of security and builds a sense of trust in an organization as an employer. This usually leads to workers being less absent from work, being involved in fewer accidents, doing better quality work and being less prone to leave the organization (Schabracq, 2005).

THE HUMAN RESOURCE PLANNING PROCESS

Next, an overview will be given of the main steps that should be followed in doing human resource planning.

Situational analysis/scanning the environment

The first phase in human resource planning is linking the human resource function in an organization with its strategic plan. The strategic plan should be in line with the current environmental conditions, as well as with the long-term changes in these conditions. The human resources of an organization are one of the mechanisms that can be used to adjust the organization to changing environmental conditions. That is why the human resource manager should preferably be a member of the team that does the strategic planning for an organization.

An organization should gather as much relevant information about its environment as possible. It should set (or adjust) its goals in terms of marketing, production and finances on the basis of this environmental scanning. The goal of human resource planning is to make a contribution towards the efficiency of an organization. For that reason it should be integrated with the organization's short- and long-range business goals and plans.

The length of the planning period should also be considered. Organizations tend to do short-range human resource planning, perhaps because there is less danger of being wrong about one's prediction if one sticks to a planning period of not more than one year, or at least not more than two years. A planning period of up to two years is usually called a short-range period. A planning period of two to five years is usually called a medium- or intermediate-range period. When one goes beyond the five-year period, one is thinking about long-range planning. The longer the time frame being used, the more difficult it becomes to anticipate the different factors that will influence the planning process.

It is of the utmost importance that human resource managers and line managers work together to develop business plans and to determine the need for human resources. They should also determine what the characteristics of the workforce should be if it is to fit in with the (future) business strategies. It will most probably also be necessary to develop programmes in order to ensure that the strategies can be carried out.

An analysis of the current human resource situation

Usually the next step in the human resource planning process is to determine the characteristics of the workers employed by the organization at the present time. This means that an inventory of present personnel must be developed. Sometimes such an inventory is also called a skills inventory or a human resource information system. To be useful, the human resource information system should be computerized. Sometimes organizations might ask a computer programmer to develop a human resource information system or a personnel inventory that suits the purposes of the specific organization.

The type of information that is found in a human resource information system depends on the needs of the specific organization. At the least, it should contain basic information about each employee. When one thinks of it as a skills inventory, it should contain personal information (e.g. names and ages of workers), employment history, present job or position and job grade, present salary and salary scale, skills, education, job experience, and training, special qualifications or achievements, results of performance appraisals or other indicators of potential, and personal career goals. From the information found in a skills inventory, the skill levels of the present employees and the extent to which they can be developed can be assessed.

An analysis of the demand for and the supply of human resources

The second step in human resource planning is to analyse the future demand for and the supply of human resources. Demand in the case of human resource planning refers to the number of workers needed at a specific time and place, and the characteristics that they need to possess. 'Characteristics' refers to the abilities, skills and experience that the workers need to fill the particular positions. 'Supply', in the case of human resource planning, refers to the number of workers and their characteristics that are available to fill the particular positions. The following questions should be answered to determine the demand and supply of human resources:

- What are the positions that will need to be filled during the period for which human resource planning is being done? The human resource planner has to forecast how many workers will probably resign, how many positions will be made redundant and how many new positions will be created. Past tendencies concerning resignations, redundancies and the forming of new positions can be analysed. Previous attitude surveys can be linked to labour turnover to get an idea of the number of vacancies that might occur. Business plans can be used to get an idea of the number of positions that will be made redundant or be created.
- How and where will we find the human resources needed to fill the positions that we have identified? Here it is important to determine what the characteristics of those human resources should be. After this, the characteristics of the present workforce, and also of those that might be recruited from outside the organization can be considered. The organization should have up-to-date records of retirements, advancements and appointments that have taken place in the past. When looking at the characteristics of the present workforce, it is important to develop a skills

inventory. When determining the demand for and the supply of human resources, different quantitative methods can be used, but the forecasting methods that are usually used depend a great deal on human judgement. Various techniques that can be used during this forecasting process are the following: an expert can do the forecasting; sometimes a panel of experts is used for this purpose; tendencies noticed in the past can be used to make projections into the future. Sophisticated modelling techniques and multiple forecasting techniques can be used, where different factors (such as sales volumes or the gross national product) can be correlated with employment figures. These more sophisticated techniques include mathematical models, simulations and the statistical technique of regression analysis.

Human resource planning takes place on two levels, namely on the quantitative level and the qualitative level. The *quantitative level* has to do with ensuring that the right number of people having the right qualifications are available at the right time. The factors that influence an organization's future human resources needs include the staff turnover rate, the absence rate, retirements, changes in statutory working hours and women employees that get married or who become pregnant. This means that the factors that influence personnel turnover and absences should be studied very closely when one does human resource planning. The *qualitative level* has to do with having the right kind of people available, that is, the people who are able to communicate on an individual and group level, who are suitably motivated, are reasonably satisfied and loyal employees.

The motivation of workers should also be considered. This can be accomplished by ensuring that the work is performed in such a way and the work environment is of such a nature that people are able to utilize their skills and abilities. People should be trained to communicate effectively. Organizations should determine whether the employees are reasonably satisfied with their work. When selecting employees, organizations should determine whether candidates possess the qualities needed to do the work and fit into the 'culture' of the organization (Hough and Furnham, 2003).

Determining human resource goals

Once the supply of, and the demand for, human resources for a specified period of time has been determined, it is possible to compare the demand with the supply. If there is a difference between the forecasts of the demand and the supply, an organization needs to decide on the action steps needed to eliminate this difference or discrepancy. If an organization engages in short-term planning, it may be possible to quantify the goals. The following are examples of short–term human resource goals: a) increasing the number of the possible job applicants by means of a recruitment campaign; b) attracting candidates that have the necessary qualifications; c) upgrading the qualifications of people who are selected and appointed; and d) making sure that those who are appointed remain in the employ of the organization as long as possible.

The design and implementation of human resource plans

It is during this phase that the plans that can lead to the organization reaching its human resource goals must be designed and implemented. In the case of the forecasted demand being greater than the forecasted supply of human resources, these plans could include recruitment, selection, performance appraisal, training, paying attention to remuneration (salaries and wages), advancement, and career development activities and instituting a system of overtime work. It is here that it is very important that all the activities of the human resources function/department should take place in a co-ordinated and integrated fashion. In the case of the forecasted demand being smaller than the forecasted supply of human resources, the following are possible strategies that can be implemented: early retirements, retrenchments, making use of a process called work-sharing (for instance, where two employees each perform half of a job), working shorter work weeks and not filling positions that are vacated by people who retire or who resign.

Gathering and analysing information that can be used as feedback

Human resource planning does not stop with the implementation of strategies to reach the human resource goals. Previously it was stated that human resource planning is an ongoing process. This means that human resource planning must not be seen as something that is perhaps done once a year and is then filed away and forgotten. Throughout the period for which human resource planning was done, the human resource planning function will have to seek feedback on the progress towards the goals that were set. On the basis of the feedback received, adjustments need to be made to the human resource plan. Because short-term human resource goals are usually set in a quantitative manner (for example, the number of artisans needed to be recruited by the end of a certain period), it is usually quite easy to determine the degree to which these goals have been reached.

Factors in the environment may change during the period planning was done for. The skills inventory should also be updated. It may be that the training programmes did not bring about the necessary changes in the skill levels that were forecasted. It may also happen that because of tough economic times fewer workers opted for earlier retirement. From what has just been said, it is clear why human resource planning should be carried out on a continual basis.

JOB ANALYSIS

Definition of job analysis

Job analysis is defined as the process of gathering job information by breaking the job down into its component elements in order to identify what tasks and responsibilities a job consists of, what skills, knowledge and abilities are required to do the job, and what environmental conditions surround the job. A job description is a written summary of the key performance areas (tasks, duties and/or responsibilities) of a specific job. The job description includes a clear presentation of what is done, how it is done and why it is done. A job specification is a written explanation of the minimum requirements needed for effective performance on a given job. It includes knowledge, skills, abilities, traits and other characteristics needed for effective job performance.

Steps in job analysis

The job analysis process involves a number of steps:

- *Step 1: Decide who should conduct the job analysis.* If an organization only has an occasional need for job analysis information, it may hire a temporary job analyst from outside. Other organizations will have job analysis experts employed on a full-time basis. Still other organizations will use supervisors, job incumbents or some combination of these to collect job-analysis information. Regardless of who collects the information, the individual should thoroughly understand people, jobs and the total organization system.
- *Step 2: Examine the total organization and the fit of each job.* This step provides a broad view of how each job fits into the total structure of the organization. Organization charts and process charts are used to complete this step.
- *Step 3: Determine how the job analysis information will be used.* Different uses of job analysis information call for different approaches. For example, if management's purpose is to ensure that a selection test is valid by proving that the content of the test reflects the content of the job, then job analysis will focus on the job's work activities. On the other hand, the objective of developing a performance evaluation system that will be defensible in court may require the gathering of information about behaviour that results in more and less successful performance.
- *Step 4: Select the jobs to be analysed.* Since it is usually too costly and time-consuming to analyse every job, a representative sample of jobs needs to be selected. The manager of the specific department must be contacted and the objectives of the process discussed with him or her. It is essential to get his or her co-operation. Since job analysis plays a central role in the management of people, it should be conducted when a new job is introduced in the organization, and when the job's major tasks and thus worker performance requirements change.
- *Step 5: Collect data by using acceptable job analysis techniques.* Techniques like interviews, observation and questionnaires are used to collect data on the characteristics of the job, the required behaviour and the employee characteristics needed to perform the job.
- *Step 6: Prepare the job description and job specification.*

The knowledge and data collected in steps 1–6 are used as the foundation for other human resource activities.

Uses of job analysis

Job analysis is the foundation of human resource management. Job analysis can be used in each of the following human resource activities:

- Job analysis can be used to prepare *job descriptions*. A complete job description contains a job summary, the job duties and responsibilities, and an indication of working conditions.
- Job analysis is used to write *job specifications*. The job specification describes the individual traits and characteristics required to do the job well.

- Job analysis makes it possible to *organize* and integrate the total workforce based on duties and responsibilities.
- The *staffing* programme of an organization rests on the information supplied by the job analysis. Job analysis information can be used to help recruiters to seek and find the type of people that will fit into the organization, to supply information about the nature of the job, to set standards that applicants must reach, to determine which selection techniques can be used, and to establish criteria for the selection process.
- The analyst can use the information gathered through job analysis for *training and development* purposes (e.g. the training needs of employees, the content of training courses, and relevant training methods).
- Job analysis supplies the basic data needed to do a *job evaluation*. Job evaluation is a systematic process to determine the value of a job relative to all other jobs in an organization.
- Job analysis is used to determine the criteria and requirements for *performance appraisal* of a job holder. Without an adequate job analysis, it is possible that the success of a given employee will be judged in terms of behaviours that may appear important, but in fact have little bearing on whether the worker is successful.
- Job analysis can be used in *career development*. The movement of individuals into and out of positions, jobs and occupations is a common procedure in organizations.
- Working conditions and *safety* can be improved based on the results of a job analysis. The safety of a job depends on a proper layout, standards, equipment and other physical conditions.

Job analysis methods

There are five basic methods, which can be used separately or in combination, of collecting job analysis data. These methods are observation, interviews, questionnaires, critical incident technique and job incumbents' diaries.

Observation

Direct observation is used for jobs that require manual, standardized and short job-cycle activities. Observation will be especially useful in jobs that demand few skills, where work is controlled mechanically, which involve physical activities and where the work cycle is short. The job of an automobile assembly-line worker, an insurance company filing clerk and an inventory stockroom employee are examples of jobs which can be analysed by using observation. In contrast, observation is not appropriate for jobs that involve significant amounts of mental activity, such as a research scientist, lawyer or mathematician. Jobs involving intangible factors such as judgement, computations and decision-making present few opportunities for supplying information to the observer.

The job analyst observes what the employee does, why he or she does it, how he or she does it, which skills are used and what physical demands are placed on the employee. In order for observations to be maximally useful, an adequate, representative sample of employees needs to be observed at various times during the work period. It is useful to be as unobtrusive as possible when observation is used. Employees must not be disturbed in the execution of their duties. The job analyst must also remember that employees might change their behaviour when they are observed. The employee must have the opportunity to study the job analysis notes, and to modify incorrect observations.

The interview

The interview is probably the most widely used data- collection technique. It permits the job analyst to talk face to face with job incumbents. The job incumbent can ask questions, and this interview serves as an opportunity for the analyst to explain how the job analysis knowledge and information will be used. Reliable, accurate and comprehensive information can be gathered by interviewing employees and supervisors. Interviews can be conducted with a single job incumbent, a group of individuals or with a supervisor who is knowledgeable about the job. Usually a structured set of questions will be used in interviews so that answers from individuals or groups can be compared.

The interview has the following *advantages*:

- It allows the job analyst to gather complete and accurate work information, provided care is taken that the job is not deliberately inflated. The job analyst should also confirm the information with other job incumbents and their immediate supervisor.
- Interviewing the employee saves him or her from providing a written description of his or her work – something that usually causes headaches for employees.
- The interview gives the employee the opportunity to receive first-hand information regarding the reasons for job analysis from the job analyst.

Interviewing a person to analyse a job has the following *disadvantages*:

- It requires much time if many jobs need to be analysed.
- It is an expensive method, because the organization must pay the salary of the job analyst and the working time of the interviewee is lost.
- It is impossible to involve all the workers. If questionnaires are used it is possible to involve many employees.
- Inaccurate information may be collected. For example, if a job incumbent believes that the job analysis interview will be used to set the job's compensation level, he or she may provide inaccurate information. It is necessary to interview more than one person, to plan the interview carefully, to use relevant questions and to establish rapport with the interviewee.

The questionnaire

The job analyst can construct a questionnaire to send to employees and supervisors. The information gathered by using the questionnaires is checked to ensure that it is accurate and complete. The job holder and his or her supervisor are usually asked to complete the questionnaire. The questionnaire includes specific questions about the job, job requirements, working conditions and equipment. The format and degree of structure that a questionnaire should have are debatable issues. There is really no best format for a questionnaire. It should be kept as short and simple as possible, its objectives should be explained, what it is being used for – people want to know why it must be completed, and it should be tested before it is used.

The questionnaire has the following advantages: a) It makes provision for maximum participation because each employee and supervisor can complete a questionnaire; b) it prepares employees for follow–up interviews (if interviews are used), because it gives them time to think about the different aspects of their jobs; c) it saves time and money if questionnaires are completed accurately. However, questionnaires have the following disadvantages: a) It is difficult to construct a good questionnaire; b) it is difficult and time-consuming to interpret the answers to the questions; c) employees sometimes are irritated by questionnaires. This may lead to carelessness in the completion of questionnaires.

The motivation of employees to complete questionnaires is usually a problem. Many job analysts use a combination of interviews and questionnaires to analyse jobs. The combination of the questionnaire and the interview will supply more accurate information, give the employee the opportunity to elaborate on the answers given on the questionnaire, and give the job analyst the opportunity to receive first-hand information regarding the reasons for job analysis.

The critical incident technique

In this method employees and supervisors are asked to report critical incidents in their work behaviour that are effective or ineffective in reaching their job objectives. The elements, the situation in which it took place, what the employee did that was effective or ineffective and the effects of the behaviour are indicated for each incident. The advantage of this method is that real behaviour, rather than opinions or subjective impressions, is used as the yardstick of how the job must be done. The disadvantage is that it takes much time to gather, analyse and classify incidents. Using the critical incidents method, 'average' worker behaviour is often difficult to discern and it may not be possible to compile a complete job description.

Job incumbent diary

The diary is a recording by job incumbents of job duties, frequency of the duties and when the duties were carried out. This technique requires the job incumbent to keep a diary on a daily basis. Unfortunately, many individuals are not disciplined enough to keep such a diary. If a diary is kept up to date, it can provide good information about the job. Comparisons on a daily, weekly or monthly basis can be made. The diary is especially useful when attempting to analyse jobs that are difficult to observe, such as those performed by engineers, scientists and senior executives.

JOB DESCRIPTIONS

The job description is one of the primary outputs provided by a systematic job analysis. It is a written description of what the job entails. While there is no standard format for a job description, it will include information regarding the following aspects:

- *Job title.* A title of the job and other identifying information such as its wage and benefits classification.

- *Summary*. A brief two-sentence statement describing the purpose of the job and what outputs are expected from job incumbents.
- *Key performance areas*. A description of the primary job duties and responsibilities in terms of what is done, how it is done and why it is done.
- *Equipment*. A clear statement of the tools, equipment and information required for effectively performing the job.
- *Environment*. A description of the working conditions of the job, the location of the job and other relevant characteristics of the immediate work environment such as hazards and noise levels.

The guidelines for writing job descriptions are given in Focus 7.1.

FOCUS 7.1

Guidelines for writing job descriptions

1 Write about the job, not the person.
2 Describe only what is required of the incumbent.
3 Describe the what and the how of each task.
4 Begin each sentence with a present tense active verb. Try not to use adjectives.
5 Be concise, do not give irrelevant details, subjective statements or opinions.
6 Use concrete examples to explain unfamiliar or broad responsibilities.
7 Present the tasks in a logical sequence.

JOB SPECIFICATION

The job specification evolves from the job description. It indicates the competencies (qualifications, personal traits and experience) needed to perform the job effectively. The job specification is especially useful for offering guidance for recruitment and selection.

Job specifications can be compiled in three ways:

1 The job analyst judges which competencies are important for good performance. This approach saves time, but is subjective. Although this method indicates which competencies are essential for work success, it does not indicate the relative importance of these competencies for work success.
2 A group of specialists who know the job determine the competencies needed for the job in behavioural terms. This approach starts with a list of competencies (knowledge, aptitudes, skills and personality characteristics) that are defined and judged by specialists after they have studied the job description. In this way one will get a profile for each job. This approach is more objective, but requires more time.

3   Psychometric tests are used to determine job specifications. First, current employees are tested with a range of psychometric tests. Second, their work performance is assessed to determine who is more successful and less successful on the job. Next, the differences between the psychometric tests of successful and less successful groups are analysed to determine the job specifications.

Regardless of the method used to determine job specifications, two aspects should be considered, namely that a) minimum acceptable standards should be specified, and b) flexibility should be shown in the application of job specifications. It serves as a guideline and may be adapted if there is a limited supply of candidates for a vacant job. Job specifications include the following aspects: a) educational and training required; b) experience needed; c) special skills required; d) physical and mental abilities required; e) emotional characteristics required.

An example of a job description and job specifications is set out in Application 7.1.

APPLICATION 7.1

A job description and job specifications

Job identification

Job title	HR Manager
Company	Company X
Location/workplace	Head Office
Job title of immediate supervisor	HR Executive
Job title(s) of subordinate(s)	Organizational Development Manager, Training Manager, Personal Assistant
Job level	7

Job summary

Primary output: to ensure the HR needs of company X are met

Job duties and responsibilities

Key performance areas	Accountabilities
Implement HR strategies	An annual HR tactical plan in support of the strategic goals of the company.
	Ensure sound employee support systems that enhance the culture of the company.
	Ensure the implementation of proactive organizational development strategies.
	Ensure effective management and quality assurance of processes in the HR department, i.e. administrative processes, recruitment and selection, policies and procedures, leave management, communication and performance management.

Job specifications

Qualifications   Master's degree in either Human Resource Management or Work and Organizational Psychology

Experience   At least five years' experience in HR development and management

Job specific behavioural dimensions

1 *Quality orientation*: Accomplishing tasks by considering all areas involved, no matter how small; showing concern for all aspects of the job; accurately checking processes and tasks; being watchful over a period of time.

2 *Work standards*: Setting high standards of performance for self and others; assuming responsibility and accountability for successfully completing assignment or tasks; self-imposing standards of excellence rather than having standards imposed.

3 *Technical professional knowledge*: Having achieved a satisfactory level of technical and professional skill or knowledge in position-related areas; keeping up with current developments and trends in areas of expertise.

SUMMARY

Human resource planning was defined as ensuring that an organization has the right number of suitably qualified workers available at the right time. In order to achieve this, human resource planning has to be linked to the strategic planning process and to the business plan of an organization. The reasons for human resource planning were described. The human resource planning process may take on many forms, one of which was described. It consists of analysing the situation (scanning the environment), determining the characteristics of the present work force, analysing the demand for and the supply of human resources, and determining the human resource goals. It further consists of designing and implementing human resource plans to reach these goals, and gathering and analysing information that can be used as feedback to update the human resource planning process.

• Job analysis is defined as the process of gathering job information by breaking the job down into its component elements in order to identify what tasks and responsibilities a job consists of, what skills, knowledge and abilities are required to do the job, and what environmental conditions surround the job. There are six steps in job analysis, starting with examining the total organization and the fit of jobs, and concluding with the preparation of the job specification. The uses of job analysis include strategic planning, recruitment, selection, training, compensation and job design. It is clear from the above discussion that amateurs should not conduct job analysis. Training is essential before a person can analyse a job. Before conducting a job analysis, organization charts should be studied to acquire an overview of the organization. The techniques that can be used to analyse a job include observation, interviews, questionnaires, diaries or a combination of these.

- A job description concentrates on the job. It explains what the job is and what the duties, responsibilities and general working conditions are. A job specification concentrates on the characteristics needed to perform the job. It describes the qualifications that the incumbent must possess to perform the job. Recruitment has been defined as the process of attracting suitable candidates to apply for vacancies that exist in an organization.

KEY CONCEPTS AND TERMS

- Critical incident technique
- Demand
- Human resource information system
- Human resource planning

- Interview
- Job
- Job analysis
- Job description
- Job incumbent diary
- Job specification
- Observation

- Occupation
- Position
- Questionnaire
- Situational analysis
- Strategic plan
- Supply
- Task

SAMPLE ESSAY TITLES

- Is there a link between human resource planning, strategic planning and the business plan? Motivate your answer.
- Do you agree with the following statement? 'Job analysis is the cornerstone of human resource management.' Motivate your answer.
- Which techniques can be used to analyse the job of a financial manager in an organization?

FURTHER READING

Books

Armstrong, M. and Taylor, T. (2014). *Armstrong's Handbook of Human Resource Management Practice* (13th edn). London: Kogan Page.

Whetzel, D.L. and Wheaton, G.R. (2007). *Applied Measurement: Industrial Psychology in Human Resources Management*. Mahwah, NJ: Lawrence Erlbaum.

Journal articles

Hawkes, C.L. and Weathington, B.L. (2014). Competency-based versus task-based job descriptions: Effects on applicant attraction. *Journal of Behavioral and Applied Management*, 15(3), 190–211.

Pató, B.S.G. (2014). The 7 most important criterions of job descriptions. *International Journal of Business Insights and Transformation*, 7(1), 68–73.

8 Recruitment and selection

This chapter introduces the reader to recruitment and selection. The first section focuses on recruitment. We look at the definition of recruitment and describe recruitment planning and the development of a recruitment strategy. In developing a recruitment strategy it is necessary to determine who will do the recruiting, what kind of recruiting will be used, where it will be done, and what sources and methods of recruitment will be used. The chapter then proceeds to the actual recruitment process, preliminary screening and evaluation of the recruitment efforts. The second section focuses on the selection of staff. We define selection and describe the factors that should be considered before making selection decisions. Then we look at the selection procedure (including the preliminary screening interview, completion of the applicant blank, psychometric tests, the selection interview, reference checks and physical examinations) and requirements for selection predictors. We describe the factors that should be considered when rejecting applications and auditing the selection process.

LEARNING OUTCOMES

When you have completed this chapter you should be able to:

1 Define recruitment and describe recruitment planning.
2 Develop a recruitment strategy by considering the type of recruiters needed, kind of recruitment, place of recruitment, and sources and methods of recruitment.
3 Identify the factors that should be considered during the actual recruitment process.
4 Define selection and motivate why selection is important for organizations.
5 Describe the factors which affect selection decisions and explain the requirements for selection predictors.
6 Evaluate the suitability of different selection predictors for different jobs.
7 Discuss the considerations when applicants are rejected and develop a strategy to audit the selection process.

RECRUITMENT

Definition of recruitment

Recruitment is defined as a process of seeking and attracting suitable candidates from within the organization or from outside the organization for job vacancies that exist. 'Suitable candidates' means those who possess the required characteristics that will enable them to perform satisfactorily in the specific job.

Recruitment planning

Before any recruitment can be done, an organization needs to decide what the nature and number of job vacancies are. This information comes from human resource planning and job analysis. In recruitment planning that information is used to decide on the number and characteristics of potential candidates that need to be attracted. Organizations try to recruit more candidates than the number they wish to employ. Some candidates will most probably be overqualified for the specific positions, while some might not really be interested in obtaining a position.

An organization needs to keep a balance between setting recruitment standards that are too high or too low. When an organization is operating in a so-called 'tight labour market' (where there are few candidates for the number of job openings), it might be tempted to lower standards regarding the candidates' qualifications. This might lead to other undesirable outcomes. An organization might decide to retain high standards and to spend much time and money to attract suitable candidates. It seems that when organizations retain higher standards, fewer candidates apply for jobs, but then these candidates are also better qualified (Kepes and Delery, 2006).

From past experience, organizations usually know how many potential candidates they need to reach through their recruitment efforts in order to have a sufficient number of applicants from which to choose. The number will most probably vary with the type of vacancy or job. The type of recruitment source and the recruitment method will also have to be taken into consideration when deciding on the number of candidates that have to be reached.

Developing a recruitment strategy

When developing a recruitment strategy, an organization must answer the following questions:

- Who will be doing the recruiting and how should they be prepared?
- What kind of recruiting will be used?
- Where will the recruiting be done?
- What sources and methods of recruitment will be used?

Recruiters and their preparation/characteristics

In most organizations the human resource department is responsible for the co-ordination of the recruitment process. Because recruiters come into direct contact with possible candidates, it is of great importance that they should be knowledgeable about the organization in general and about the specific jobs that are vacant. Often, recruiters are the main source of information that potential candidates make use of in deciding to apply for a position. The reason for this is that potential applicants know so little about the organization. They have to make use of the information supplied by recruiters when deciding to apply for a position. The ideal recruiter is someone who can make potential applicants enthusiastic about the organization. A recruiter should have very good interpersonal skills and should be able to supply realistic information to possible applicants. He or she should be a likeable person, be enthusiastic and must show personal interest in applicants (Rosenfeld *et al.*, 2002).

Kind of recruitment

Both positive and negative aspects about the organization and job should be provided to applicants. When an organization (through its recruiting efforts) gives applicants both positive and negative information about the organization and job in a balanced and objective way, it is called realistic job previews. One of the main reasons for giving a realistic job preview is to reduce the 'reality shock' and disappointment when a newcomer eventually joins an organization and finds that his or her expectations are not being met and/or that circumstances are quite different from those which were envisaged. Unless the applicant has no other option than to take the job offered to him or her, a realistic job preview gives the applicant the chance to 'opt out', without losing face, because the decision to 'opt out' is based on realistic information. It also seems that if an applicant, in the face of a realistic job preview, still decides to join an organization, such a person will most probably be a more committed employee.

Place of recruitment

Organizations tend to recruit managerial and professional employees on a countrywide or a regional basis, technical employees/artisans on a regional or a local basis, and clerical and manual workers on a local basis. Generally speaking, organizations make use of past experience to decide where to concentrate their recruitment efforts, and to get the best return on the money invested in recruitment.

The basis of recruiting will also depend on the job-seeking behaviour of applicants. One aspect of job-seeking behaviour is, for instance, the distance a person will travel to look for a job. Another aspect might be the media a potential candidate might use when searching for a job. The state of the labour market will also play a role. If, for instance, there are very few qualified clerical workers available locally, an organization will concentrate its recruitment efforts on a regional basis.

Sources and methods of recruitment

Sources refer to the segment(s) of the labour market where applicants can be found, such as schools, colleges, universities, other organizations and sources of unemployed people. Methods refer to the specific way(s) of obtaining applicants. Here one can think of something like direct applications or so-called 'write-ins' or 'walk-ins', referrals by present employees, advertising using different media, private and public employment agencies and so-called 'executive search agencies/firms'. It seems safe to say that sources do influence the methods used.

Internal recruitment

Internal recruitment has various advantages:

1   Most people, at one time or another, expect to be appointed to some higher position, having a greater status and paying a higher salary. If an organization appoints from within, it can lead to an increase in the morale of employees because their expectations are being met.
2   It is possible to more accurately assess the knowledge, skill and personality characteristics of an organization's present employees than those of outside applicants who have to go through a selection process.
3   The recruitment and selection process is simplified because, with a few exceptions, candidates from outside sources are only needed for entry-level jobs.
4   The career development of employees can be planned far more systematically and suitable career paths for them to follow can be more easily identified.
5   The candidates already know how the organization operates.
6   The investment already made in present employees is continued.

Recruiting and subsequent appointing from within also has some disadvantages:

1   It leads to inbreeding that can prevent the development of new ideas and much needed creativity.
2   An organization needs to have very good training programmes in place through which the knowledge and skills of employees can be upgraded in order for them to be promoted to the vacant positions.
3   If an organization wants to appoint from within, it needs to ensure that when candidates are first employed, they have the potential to be promoted, otherwise, people might be promoted to a point where they are unable to carry out the duties of the job successfully.
4   It might lead to 'infighting' among colleagues, which does the morale of employees no good.

There are different internal recruitment methods that an organization can use:

- An informal search for a suitable candidate can be conducted. This method is not recommended because it does not give everybody that might be interested or qualified a fair chance to apply for the specific job.
- A system of job posting and job bidding can be used. Job posting simply means that vacancies are advertised internally in such a way that everyone that is eligible is able to take notice of the vacancy.
- When vacancies occur, the human resource information system can also be searched. Such a system contains up-to-date information on each employee's skills, abilities and personal characteristics. When vacancies do occur, use will also have to be made of the human resource plan. If career paths are in place for employees, it will also be clear which employees could be promoted to the vacant positions.

External recruitment

An organization makes use of a number of different recruitment methods to attract suitable candidates from outside the organization. It might be cheaper to hire certain categories of employees from outside than to train present employees, the pool from which one can select is much greater, and people appointed from outside bring in new ideas. On the negative side recruiting from outside sources might be quite costly. Candidates from outside sources need more time to become orientated and adjusted to their new surroundings. Resentment can also develop in present employees when candidates from outside rather than themselves are appointed.

The following external recruitment methods can be used:

- *Advertisements*. Many organizations make use of advertisements in newspapers, magazines and professional journals/periodicals and over the radio and television to attract suitable candidates. When recruitment advertisements are used, the following goals should be kept in mind: first, to reach the 'right' audience (target population) and, second, to attract sufficient suitable candidates and as few (unqualified) candidates as possible. This means that one has to understand the characteristics of the target population and what motivates them to apply for a vacancy. If one receives too many applications for a specific vacancy, then it shows that there is something wrong with the communication process. An effective recruitment advertisement appear to require the following conditions:

  - It should be based on a thorough job description and must provide details about the job and about the job specification.
  - In order to ensure that a realistic job preview is given, it is important that the necessary unfavourable information about the job is also provided.
  - One should be specific in describing tasks and the remuneration package.
  - The facts should be presented in a positive way.

- *Private employment agencies*. These agencies have information of a large number of possible candidates on computer which can be matched against the job specifications of vacant jobs. If they do not have suitable candidates on file or on computer, they do the necessary advertising to attract the required candidates. A private employment agency is able to do a lot of the administrative work associated with recruitment, but they tend to charge large fees for their services.
- *'Walk-ins' or 'write-ins'*. This simply means that sometimes applicants write in to the organization to apply for jobs, even though no such jobs have been advertised. Sometimes applicants come in person to apply for jobs which have not been advertised.
- *Referrals by employees*. It often happens that the information that a vacancy exists is passed along by means of word of mouth among colleagues and their friends. The advantage of this recruitment method is that it is very time- and cost-effective. Unfortunately, it might lead to inbreeding and the forming of cliques.
- *Educational institutions*. Organizations can let recruiters visit different educational institutions to recruit suitable candidates. Sometimes an organization is looking for candidates who possess specific scholastic, academic or professional qualifications. In order to reach these candidates, it is important for organizations to build

up relationships with these educational institutions, which will be more than willing to supply information on suitable candidates.

- *Executive search firms.* These concentrate on the recruiting of middle and top managers. In order for them to attract suitable candidates, these executive search firms take much care to ensure that the job specifications are clearly stated. Middle and top managers recruited by means of this method are often drawn away from other organizations. That is why this method of recruiting is often called 'head-hunting'. It is nothing out of the ordinary for them to ask a fee that amounts to one-third of a successful candidate's annual salary.
- *Other methods.* There are a variety of other methods an organization can use to recruit suitable candidates:

  - An organization may make use of direct-mail recruiting, by obtaining mailing lists from different professional bodies or societies, and sending the specific advertisements to all the people on these mailing lists.
  - Recruiters may set up stands at job fairs or career exhibitions.
  - Many organizations also make use of the services of temporary help agencies.

The actual recruitment process

Once an organization has decided on a recruitment plan and a recruitment strategy, the following two broad steps have to be carried out: the potential sources of recruitment must be activated and the 'sales' message must be communicated to qualified applicants.

Activating the sources of recruitment

The following tasks have to be performed:

- Preliminary screening of applicants has to be done to eliminate those candidates who are clearly unsuitable.
- Candidates have to be transported to the organization and will have to be housed for the duration of the selection process.
- Line managers must be ready to interview candidates.
- Candidates who have been unsuccessful must be notified to that effect.
- Formal employment offers must be sent to successful candidates.
- The acceptance or rejection of such offers must be processed.
- A well-functioning record system which can be utilized at any moment to check what progress has been made in the recruitment process needs to be in place.

Communicating the 'sales' message to potential applicants

An organization should not 'oversell' itself to potential candidates. The organization should take note of the factors that influence a person's decision to apply for a job and to join an organization. It appears that the message and the medium through which it is communicated play a significant role in this regard.

- *The message.* A potential candidate is likely to apply for a job and to keep on working at that job, if there is something in the remuneration package that attracts him or her. This has implications for the nature of the message that has to be communicated to the potential applicant. Although there is no clear-cut answer as to what should be included in this message, the following can be used as pointers:

- Salary and the nature of the work play a role in most candidates' decision to apply for a job.
- The geographical area in which the organization is located and the possibilities for advancement are important for people who apply for managerial or professional positions.
- Job security is an important factor for unschooled or lower-schooled workers.
- Working conditions, hours of work and the nature of supervisors and co-workers are often of no great concern when applying for a job.

- *The medium.* The effectiveness of a recruitment message also largely depends on the medium through which the message is delivered. It seems that the credibility or 'believability' of the medium plays an important role in getting the message across. Credibility of media is based on trust, perceived expertise and personal liking. Therefore, media such as personnel agencies and recruitment advertisements have the least credibility, while the smaller and more intensive media, such as friends and personal contacts, have the most credibility.

Preliminary screening

There are several ways to go about doing preliminary screening. It might consist of doing a quick check on the application blanks that were returned by applicants. One can also do a check on curricula vitae and testimonials that were sent in by applicants. It might even consist of doing some reference checking on applicants. In the case of 'walk-ins' the screening might consist of an interview with the applicant.

Evaluation of recruitment

Several methods can be used to evaluate the recruitment effort of an organization. For instance, the outcomes of the recruitment effort could be studied. The following questions should be answered:

- Have all the vacancies been filled?
- What is the nature of the work performance and labour turnover of applicants that have been accepted?
- What is the average cost incurred for every candidate that has been appointed?
- Is this cost in accordance with what has been planned for?
- Did everything in the recruitment process go according to plan?

These are the type of questions usually asked when doing a utility analysis of the recruitment effort. A utility analysis of the different recruitment methods or media that were used can be done to get an indication of the relative costs and benefits of the different methods or media.

SELECTION

Definition of selection

Selection involves the sorting out of applicants for a vacant job and the elimination of those applicants who do not fit the requirements of the job and/or the organization. The content of different jobs differs, as do the abilities and skills required. For example, the abilities and skills that are required of a telephone operator differ from those required of the manager of a retail store. Applicants also differ regarding their abilities, aptitudes, skills, experience, age and education. Therefore, the objective of selection is to assess which applicant will best fit a specific job (Cooper *et al.*, 2003).

The importance of selection

Selection is a major expense for organizations. A lot of money is spent on recruitment, selection and training. In addition to these costs, there is the cost incurred by the new employee's inability to meet performance requirements while learning the job. Often, it takes a year before the employee actually deserves the salary for the position. The costs are even greater if the wrong person is hired.

Despite the high costs of selection, research has shown conclusively that good selection pays off. Sometimes good selection methods are expensive to develop and refine, which can discourage organizations from investing in them. Selection, however, affects the quality of personnel and their task performance. Training will also be more successful if you select the right quality people. Poor selection causes a poor fit between the job and the individual, which contributes to job dissatisfaction, poor performance and high labour turnover.

Factors that influence the selection decision

Three factors may influence the selection decision: the job description and job specification, the organization and social environment, and the successive hurdles or the multiple correlation approach.

Job description and job specification

If a selection programme is to be successful, the employee characteristics stated in the job specification must accurately summarize what is necessary for effective performance on the job. An accurate list of characteristics can only be generated after the organization has conducted a thorough job analysis. Job specifications which are important for selection purposes include education and training, experience, physical characteristics, and personal characteristics and competencies.

Organization and social environment

The organization and social environment refer to the values of the organization, the way things are done, social cliques, openness to new employees and the personality of the manager. The objective of selection will be to assess whether the applicant would adapt to these values and conditions. A match between the values of the employee and those of the organization contributes to his or her commitment.

The selection approach

Three approaches – the successive hurdles approach, the compensatory approach and the combined approach – can be used during selection.

- *The successive hurdles approach.* Using the successive hurdles approach, the candidate must fit the requirement of each step in the selection process (for example, the application form, psychometric testing or medical examination) to be considered for appointment. This approach saves time and money because it prevents unsuitable applicants going through the whole selection process.
- *The compensatory approach.* The compensatory approach allows very high performance on one selection procedure to compensate for low performance on another.
- *The combined approach.* It is possible to combine the successive hurdles approach and the compensatory approach. In this case the abilities and motivation that are critical for success are first assessed. If the applicant does not fit these requirements, his or her application is rejected. If he or she fits the critical requirements, he or she goes through the whole selection process, and then the selection decision is made.

Selection procedure

A systematic selection procedure must be followed to make selection decisions. Selection procedures refer to procedures or actions that can be used to acquire and integrate information to make a recommendation and/or final human resource decision. The assumption of a selection procedure is that the procedures used predict an important and relevant behavioural requirement or job performance.

The selection procedure is given in Figure 8.1. The procedure may be adapted depending on the job requirements. If physical requirements (for example, eyesight,

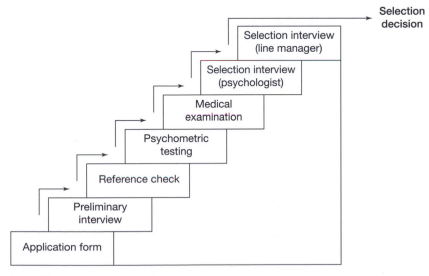

FIGURE 8.1 The selection procedure

fitness and hearing) are important requirements, then the medical examination may take place earlier. Another important consideration is that the application form and psychometric tests must be administered prior to the selection interview to verify the results obtained during the interview.

The next section focuses on the predictors that can be used as part of the selection procedure.

REQUIREMENTS FOR SELECTION PREDICTORS

Personnel selection is based on individual differences between people. The work performance of different individuals also differs. This stresses the importance of individual differences in the selection of the right person for the right job. Before a selection predictor is used, it must be valid, reliable and fair.

Validity

The term 'validity' refers to how well a measure assesses the attribute it is being used to assess. An intelligence test is valid if it measures intelligence as it is defined.

The validity of a predictor is not absolute but is relative to its intended use. It is valid as long as it successfully measures the attribute that the user intends it to measure. In other words, a measure that is valid for one purpose may not be valid for another. An aptitude test that is used for the selection of university students may not be valid for the selection of managers. The term 'validation' refers to the process of assessing the validity of a measure. Validation indicates whether it is justifiable to make a particular inference from a score obtained on the predictor. A validity coefficient is a correlation coefficient between a predictor measure (e.g. a psychometric test) and a criterion measure (e.g. work performance) applied to the same group of individuals. The correlation coefficient expresses the degree to which two sets of numbers are in agreement, or correlated, with each other.

The following types of validity are distinguished:

- *Criterion-related validity*. Criterion-related validity measures scores on a predictor, which is usually a selection device. It also measures scores on a criterion (or a set of criteria), which is usually job behaviour such as performance, absenteeism and training success. A predictor score and criterion score are obtained for each person in a sample, and the statistical relationship between the two sets of scores is computed. Predictors in validation are usually chosen because they are similar to the actual selection techniques the organization is considering. A good predictor distinguishes applicants from each other and does it reliably. Good criteria should be: a) affected by individuals, not determined largely by others or by technology; b) relevant to the goals of key constituents in the organization; c) measurable at reasonable cost, with adequate quality and in practical ways; d) affected by the individual differences reflected in the predictors; and e) remain stable over time. Sales performance might seem a complete criterion for the validation of a selection battery for sales personnel. However, sales may be contaminated by unrelated factors (e.g. the territory assigned to individuals). Sales performance may also be deficient by failing to reflect important factors (e.g. working as part of a team and completing paperwork). Two types of criterion-related validity – concurrent validity and predictive validity – can be computed (see Focus 8.1).

- *Content validity.* A predictor has content validity if its items are representative of important aspects of a dimension or the job. (For example, are the items of an IQ test representative of what can be defined as intelligence? Does the application form include questions about the most important aspects of the applicant in relation to the job?)

- *Construct validity.* A predictor (e.g. an intelligence test) has construct validity if it correlates with a specific construct (e.g. intelligence). It takes time to assess the construct validity of a test because the relationship between a predictor and other measuring instruments must be determined.

- *Face validity.* Face validity is a non-statistical type of validity, which indicates what the test measures on face value. It refers to the judgement of the validity of a predictor by the person on whom it is administered. An engineer who is tested

---

FOCUS 8.1

Types of criterion-related validity

- *Concurrent validity.* In the case of concurrent validity the predictor scores (e.g. scores on IQ tests) of current employees are correlated with their job performance (e.g. quantity and quality of work). The predictor and criterion data are gathered at the same time (which is why it is called concurrent validity). The correlation coefficient between the predictor and criterion is called the concurrent validity of the predictor (in this case the IQ test). Organizations use this method because time and cost considerations make it impossible to determine the predictive validity of a predictor. The disadvantage of the concurrent validity design is that poor performers are not included in the study and employees may perform better on the predictor (because of their experience).

- *Predictive validity.* Predictive validity indicates if a predictor (e.g. an IQ test) can be used to predict future behaviour. Predictor scores are gathered from a sample of applicants (not current employees). Next, selection decisions are made regarding these applicants, without considering their scores on the predictor. (The applicants are selected by using methods used in the past, excluding the predictor that you want to validate.) Criterion scores (e.g. quality and quantity of work, ratings of supervisors) are gathered after the employees have been working for a while (e.g. six months). After that, the correlation between the predictor and criterion is calculated. Predictive validity is indicated if the employee who scored high on the predictor performs well on the job. This method eliminates the disadvantages of the concurrent validity design, but requires more time and administration. The results are also not immediately available.

may easily assess the material used in the predictor and identify irrelevant aspects. High face validity is necessary to create a positive attitude towards the predictor.

Reliability

The reliability of a predictor refers to the consistency of performance of the same individual on the predictor at different times. For example, if you test a person's blood pressure with a device today, and you test it again after two weeks, the device must give the same results (if there was no change in the person's blood pressure). A predictor must be reliable. Statistical procedures are used to obtain a numerical estimate of a measure's reliability. The most common numerical estimate is called a reliability coefficient. Basically, the reliability coefficient measures the extent of agreement among two or more applications of the same measurement device to the same group of individuals. To be reliable, the test must have a reliability coefficient (r) higher than 0.95.

The reliability of a measurement device (predictor) is not a guarantee of its validity. Reliability only indicates the consistency of measurement and not the extent to which it measures what it is supposed to measure. However, a predictor cannot be valid if it is unreliable. Reliability of a predictor is essential, but not adequate for its validity. The reliability of a predictor must be indicated in its manual.

Different types of reliability are defined in Focus 8.2.

Fairness

Fairness is a perceptual variable along which people will differ. There are several variables that affect perceptions of fairness and some potential outcomes associated with these perceptions (Arvey and Faley, 1988).

- *The processes and procedures used.* A selection procedure will be perceived as fair when:
  - Subjective decision-making by the employer is minimized.

FOCUS 8.2

Types of reliability

- *Test–retest reliability* indicates the relationship between scores of the same people on the same predictor on different occasions.
- *Parallel forms reliability* indicates the correlation between predictor scores of the same people in equivalent forms of the test on different occasions.
- *Inter-rater reliability* is assessed by calculating the correlation between the ratings of answers on a predictor by different assessors (e.g. in projective personality tests). This type of reliability gives an indication of the objectivity of scoring procedures.
- *Internal consistency reliability* indicates the homogeneity of the items of the predictor. Although items are independent, it must focus on the same content area. High internal consistency is the result of high correlation coefficients between items and equal difficulty of items.

- The selection process is consistent across applicants, e.g. interview questions should be the same for males and females.
- The selection process is not subject to manipulation. Applicants should be examined against a common set of standards.
- The selection process is developed and managed by professionals. Professionals often rely on sets of selection standards that help to ensure fairness.
- The organization maintains the confidentiality of data supplied by the candidate.
- The review of applicant information is made by several individuals who represent different perspectives and constituents.

- *The nature of information used.* Variables that are explicitly illegal would be perceived as unfair by most candidates. Variables based on merit (e.g. talent, abilities, experience) are considered more fair than variables that are not (e.g. family connection or political loyalty). Variables that are job-related are considered more fair than variables that are not. Variables that seem related to the job (content validity), show empirical relationships to important aspects of the job (empirical validity) or reflect central psychological constructs important to the job (construct validity) are perceived as more fair than variables that bear no direct relationship to the job. Information that invades the privacy of a candidate will be considered less fair than information that does not. The use of selection instruments that probe candidates' personal lives, explore sexual habits or invade these emotional components believed to be private may be perceived as unfair.
- *The relative outcomes achieved.* Perceptions of fairness have to do with whether the 'right' number of disadvantaged people (e.g. blacks, women) were selected compared with a majority group (usually white males). If these people are disadvantaged in the selection process, the organization must show the job-relatedness of the selection device. This component of selection fairness emphasizes the outcomes of prediction and test use, instead of the selection procedures and information used.
- *Different constituents.* Different constituents may have different perceptions of fairness even when the procedures used, the information gathered and the relative outcomes achieved are kept constant. What might be perceived as fair by one constituent might not be perceived as fair by another. These perceptions will differ according to whether the applicant was hired or not.
- *Situational factors.* Perceptions of selection fairness might depend on situational factors, for instance whether an organization has a history of hiring minorities and whether the organization has enjoyed high profits and could therefore afford to hire protected group members.

Types of selection predictors

The most important selection predictors will be discussed next.

The application form

The application form consists of questions designed to provide information on the general suitability of applicants for jobs they are seeking. The questions address the applicant's educational background, previous job experience, physical health and other areas that may be useful in judging a candidate's ability to perform a job. The application form serves as a means for deciding if the applicant meets the minimum requirements of a position, and assessing the candidate's strengths and weaknesses. It serves as a basis for the selection interview and supplies information for human resource information systems.

A problem with application forms is the possibility that the applicant will provide inaccurate information. When people are competing for a job, they may distort information that they give in order to 'look good'. Distortion can range from inflation of school and university grades to outright lies involving types of jobs held, companies for whom they worked or educational degrees earned. This happens especially when it is difficult, timely and costly to verify the information. If the candidate supplies false/misleading information, the organization may terminate his or her application.

Psychometric testing

A psychometric test is a systematic, standardized and objective procedure to observe a sample of an individual's behaviour and to quantify it on a scale. A score, which indicates the individual's score on a continuum, is awarded on the basis of his or her performance on the test. Each item is an observation of the individual's behaviour. The test of n items is a representative sample of the total spectrum of the concept measured. For example, a test that measures the ability to solve arithmetic problems represents a sample of a universe of arithmetic problems. It measures a representative sample of an individual's arithmetic ability. Psychometric tests are subject to mistakes because a sample of observations (which may not be representative of the universe) is used.

Psychometric tests can be classified in different ways, namely administrative considerations and test content. The following classification of psychometric tests can be made on the basis of administrative considerations:

- *Speed tests versus power tests.* Speed tests usually have demanding time limits. The amount of work completed per time unit is manifested in the scores on these tests. Speed tests are used when individuals must solve problems in a short time–span. Speed is also a factor in certain skills (e.g. typing). Power tests have no rigid time limits. The individual gets sufficient time to complete the test, and if a time limit is used, it is usually for the convenience of the tester.
- *Group tests versus individual tests.* Group tests are administered at the same time on a group of people. These tests are especially used for selection and placement purposes because they allow many candidates to be tested on one day. Individual tests are administered on an individual basis and are expensive. Individual tests are used for high–level selection and when interpersonal rapport with the candidate is important.
- *Paper and pencil tests versus performance tests.* Paper and pencil tests are used for selection purposes. The individual's scores on these tests are not related to the manipulation of physical objects or equipment. Examples of these tests include the verbal comprehension test and a mechanical insight test. These tests are increasingly being replaced by computers. Performance tests require that the individual responds by manipulating specific physical objects or equipment. The individual's scores on a performance test are related to the quantity and quality of manipulation of the objects or equipment (e.g. a practical driving test).

- *Aptitude versus proficiency tests.* An aptitude test measures an individual's future potential for a specific activity. The objective of a proficiency test is to assess the applicant's level of proficiency at the time of the testing (for example, a knowledge test).

The following classification of psychometric tests can be made on the basis of test content (Hough and Oswald, 2000):

- *Ability tests.* Ability tests measure individual characteristics that could lead to learning specific skills. They indicate which tasks the individual will be able to perform if he or she receives the necessary training, and which tasks he or she is able to perform currently. Ability tests include cognitive tests, mechanical and spatial tests, perceptual accuracy tests, motor tests and physical tests (see Focus 8.3).
- *Personality tests.* Personality tests include objective tests and projective tests. Objective tests (personality questionnaires) are paper and pencil tests with a clear stimulus (e.g. statements regarding preferences for different lifestyles) and clear responses that may be selected. Personality questionnaires are concerned with measures of emotional adjustment and tendencies towards extroversion or introversion. The five-factor model of personality enjoys considerable support in personnel selection (Clarke and Robertson, 2005).
- *Interest questionnaires.* Interest questionnaires can be used to determine likes and dislikes for various activities. Some people would rather work indoors than outdoors; some like to deal with people, others prefer working with machinery; some crave responsibility, others strive to avoid it. By matching interests and vocations, it is quite apparent that job satisfaction and motivation, at least, can be increased. As in other questionnaires, the respondents can fake the results if motivated to do so.
- *Work sample tests.* Work sample tests are samples of tasks that are performed in a specific job. The assumption of these tests is that performance results acquired from realistic simulations of the job are the best predictor of work performance. Most studies in which work samples were used report validity coefficients higher than 0.50.

References

References can be used as a predictor for selection purposes because this method is not as expensive and time-consuming as other methods. It is based on the assumption that past behaviour is a good predictor of future behaviour. The following references can supply information about applicants:

- *Educational institutions.* Schools, colleges and universities can be visited or contacted to enquire about the candidate's marks, position in the class, extracurricular activities, motivation and emotional adaptability.
- *Previous employers.* Previous employers can supply information about the applicant's quality and quantity of work, participation, personality characteristics, initiative and interpersonal relationships. The accuracy of the information supplied by the candidate can be verified, as well as jobs held, salary and reason for quitting.

Types of ability tests

Cognitive tests include intelligence tests and aptitude tests. Intelligence tests measure abilities that can be used in different situations and jobs. Most items measure some combination of vocabulary, symbol manipulation, mathematics, reading comprehension and reasoning. Aptitude tests measure abilities that are more situation and job specific (e.g. verbal comprehension, word fluency, general reasoning, perceptual speed and memory).

In *perceptual accuracy tests* (which are especially important in clerical jobs) it is expected from the individual to compare a standard stimulus with a test stimulus to determine the differences.

Mechanical tests measure the individual's comprehension of mechanical principles.

Spatial tests measure the ability to manage concrete material through visualization (that is, the ability to determine the appearance of an object if it is rotated).

Motor tests measure physical abilities (e.g. finger dexterity, speed of arm movement, arm–hand stability, finger speed and reaction time).

Physical tests include fitness tests (cardiovascular power, muscle power) and physical ability (for jobs that are physical demanding).

RESEARCH METHODS 8.1

Validity of selection predictors

Research shows that ability tests are supported by favourable validity data. Ability tests (including intelligence and aptitude tests) are valid predictors of work performance and success in training programmes (in various jobs and occupations). Personality tests and interest questionnaires have lower validity for selection purposes. Few studies indicated significant correlation coefficients between personality tests and interest questionnaires, and job performance. However, it seems that these tests are very useful for the selection of management and sales personnel.

- *Testimonials.* The candidate can be asked to nominate friends as references. Friends are usually not able to assess a candidate's job behaviour. Few validation studies were done on references and testimonials, which makes it difficult to judge the validity thereof. These reports are usually favourable and do not discriminate between good and poor candidates. The problem may be overcome by informing the suppliers of the reports about the information needed, and by giving feedback to them regarding the usefulness of their information.

Physical examinations

Some organizations require that those most likely to be selected for a position complete a medical questionnaire or take a physical examination. According to Armstrong and Taylor (2014), the reasons for such a requirement include:

1   In case of later workers' compensation claims, physical condition at the time of hiring should be known.
2   It is important to prevent the hiring of those with serious communicable diseases. This is especially so in hospitals, but it applies to other organizations as well.
3   It may be necessary to determine whether the applicant is physically capable of performing the job under question.

These purposes can be served by the completion of a medical questionnaire, a physical examination or a work physiology analysis. The last of these is neither a physical examination nor a psychomotor test. It is used for the selection of manual workers who will be doing hard labour. The purpose of work physiology analysis is to determine, by physiological indexes (heart rate and oxygen consumption), the true fatigue engendered by the work.

Physical examinations have not been shown to be very reliable as a predictor of future medical problems. This is at least partially due to the state of the art of medicine. Different physicians emphasize different factors in the exam, based on their training and specialities. There is evidence that correlating the presence of certain past medical problems (as learned from a medical questionnaire) can be as reliable as a physical examination performed by a physician and probably less costly.

Interviews

Interviewing is probably the most popular – and most criticized – method of employee selection. This popularity seems to prevail at all job levels, from unskilled to executive. Despite its popularity, the interview has been criticized as unreliable and invalid. The lack of reliability and validity raises potential legal hazards; if an interview appears to discriminate unfairly, management may face an uphill battle in court because of the generally low validity of most interviewing approaches. Besides, the interview is often a subjective process that allows the intrusion of personal biases, and this factor arouses the suspicion of courts.

A selection interview can be defined as a conversation with three objectives, namely: a) to provide information about an applicant's suitability for a job and organization to the interviewer; b) to provide information about the job and organization to the applicant; and c) to treat the applicant in such a way that a positive attitude towards the organization is maintained.

Structured versus unstructured interviews

A *structured interview* is an interviewing method in which the content, format and evaluation of the interview are specified in advance and followed by the interviewer. The structured interview is generally more reliable and valid than the unstructured interview, perhaps because more attention is paid to the purpose of the interview and more time is spent in planning it.

An *unstructured interview* is an interviewing method in which the content, format and evaluation of the interview are not specified in advance. Unstructured interviews may lead to a hasty evaluation of the candidate. The advantage of the unstructured interview over the structured interview is that it yields more detailed information about the applicant's experiences, feelings and values. This format allows interviewers to consider factors and initiate discussions that they might not have planned in advance.

Interviews may be unreliable and invalid, partly because they are often done in a haphazard way. Therefore specialists are urging employers to use structured rather than unstructured interviews (see Focus 8.4).

The following recommendations can be made regarding selection interviews (Heneman *et al.*, 1989):

- Restrict the use of interviews to characteristics and behaviour that interviews can assess most effectively. The interview is appropriate to measure personal relations characteristics (e.g. sociability and verbal fluency) and good citizenship characteristics (e.g. dependability, conscientiousness and stability). A third characteristic, job knowledge, has also been evaluated in interviews, but other predictors may be more suitable for this purpose.
- *Incorporate more structure in the interview format.* The reason for structure is to ensure that the interviewer consistently gathers information about all relevant requirements from each applicant. Because the interviewer has information from each applicant on the same characteristics, it is easier to choose among the applicants.
- *Use job-related questions.* The most useful questions provide direct, specific information about characteristics required on the job – detailed questions about the applicant's participation in work, training or educational activities relevant to the job.
- *Make the scoring formal.* The most commonly used formal systems require the interviewer to rate the interviewee on a series of characteristics. The rating scales have a number at each point, each with an adjective (for example, not acceptable, marginal, minimal, good and superior) or a brief description.
- *Use a panel interview.* In a panel interview, several interviewers meet as a group with the applicant. Panel interviews are frequently used to hire technical or highly

FIGURE 8.2 Interviewers should be well trained before they conduct selection interviews

Source: © Adam Gregor/Shutterstock.com

skilled personnel. Planning is essential to the success of the panel interview. One interviewer should be the chairperson, and each interviewer should question the applicant in turn. There should be assigned areas for each interviewer to question, and evaluations should be completed separately by each interviewer.

- *Train the interviewer.* The main skills of an interviewer include accurately receiving information, critically evaluating the information received, and regulating his or her own behaviour in asking questions.

Assessment centres

An assessment centre is defined as a multimethod, multitrait and even multimedia technique. It is a series of individual and group exercises in which a number of candidates participate while being observed by several specially trained judges (Kraut, 1976). Assessment centres are designed to provide a view of individuals performing critical work behaviours. The candidates are asked to complete a series of evaluative tests and exercises, and to attend feedback sessions. The popularity of the assessment centre can be attributed to its capacity for increasing an organization's ability to select employees who will perform successfully in management positions. In assessment centres a wide array of methods, including several interviews, work samples and simulations, and many kinds of paper-and-pencil tests of abilities and attitudes, are used.

Most assessment centres are similar in a number of areas:

- Groups of approximately twelve individuals are evaluated. Individual and group activities are observed and evaluated.

- Multiple methods of assessment are used. These include interviewing, objective testing, projective testing, games, role plays and other methods.
- Assessors doing the evaluation are usually a panel of line managers from the organization. They can, however, be consultants or outsiders trained to conduct assessments.
- Assessment centres are relevant to the job and have higher appeal because of this relevance.

As a result of candidates participating as part of a group and as individuals, completing exercises, interviews and tests, the assessors have a large volume of data on each individual. Individuals are evaluated on a number of dimensions, such as organization and planning ability, judgement, analysis, decisiveness, flexibility and resistance to stress. The rater judgements are consolidated and developed into a final report. Each candidate's performance in the centre can be described if the organization wants this type of report. Portions of the individual reports are fed back to each candidate, usually by one or more members of the assessment team.

The assessment centre report can be used to determine the suitability of individuals for particular positions, the promotability of individuals, individuals' functioning in a group, and the training and development needs of candidates. Research on assessment centres has indicated that they are a valid way to select managers. Assessment centres can predict future success with some accuracy. The disadvantages of assessment centres are that they are a relatively expensive managerial selection technique. In some circumstances less costly and complicated techniques may sometimes be just as effective.

Making the final selection decision

The final step in the selection process is choosing one individual for the job. If there is more than one qualified person, a value judgement based on all of the information gathered in the previous steps must be made to select the best candidate. In many organizations, the human resource department handles the completion of application forms, testing, interviewing and reference checking, and arranges physical examinations. The final selection decision is usually left to the manager of the department with the job opening.

Rejecting applicants

Interviewers, being no different from other people in this respect, frequently find it difficult to inform an applicant, directly to his or her face, that he or she does not measure up to the organization's standards.

A person may feel rejected when his or her application is rejected. If those responsible for making the employment decision are sure in their own minds that the applicant should not be hired, there is no justification in holding out vague hopes. If it is a well-qualified individual but there are no openings at present for his or her talents, but it is expected that there will be openings in the near future, it makes sense to inform him or her.

The interviewer has the threefold objectives of maintaining the person's ego and self-concept, maintaining goodwill towards the organization, and definitely letting the applicant know that he or she is rejected. There are a number of ways of communicating to the person that he or she is being rejected. If the applicant can clearly see that his or her vocational aptitudes and interests or wage level needs are totally incompatible with the situation, he or she may withdraw. If the individual possesses certain skills and abilities that might be appropriate in another job situation, he or she may be informed that while the pattern of his or her skills, interests and abilities is good, he or she does not match the particular job for which the organization is hiring.

If the person possesses all the required technical abilities but is rejected because of personality, this presents a difficult challenge to the interviewer. Since personality traits cannot be measured objectively, there is a danger of creating the feeling that the candidate is discriminated against if he or she is told that his or her personality is unsuitable. This situation demands real skill on the part of the interviewer to diplomatically convey the message that the interviewee is being rejected. At times it is best to imply that the organization is going to pick just one or a very few out of a number of good candidates. The competitive situation will mean that just the top few will be hired.

Auditing the selection effort

In order to ensure that the selection process accomplishes the results expected, a comprehensive audit should be conducted. The following issues can be examined in such an audit:

- Does the selection programme meet affirmative action standards?
- Is there a delay in filling job openings?
- What percentage of those who apply are hired?
- What percentage of those hired resign or are discharged during the probation period?
- What is the cost of the selection per person hired?
- How well do the predictions derived from each of the selection techniques correlate with job performance?
- How well do those hired perform at the job?
- Has feedback been obtained from applicants regarding treatment received throughout the selection process?

SUMMARY

- Recruitment has been defined as the process of attracting suitable candidates to apply for vacancies that exist in an organization. Recruitment forms a crucial part of the overall human resource provisioning or employment process. It is thus very important to carefully plan the recruitment process. An organization needs to decide whether it will primarily use inside or outside sources when doing recruiting. It is therefore also important to develop a recruitment strategy. When developing such a strategy, one has to look into the characteristics of recruiters, the kind of recruiting to be done, where recruiting will be done and what sources and methods of recruiting will be used.

- The objective of selection is to obtain the employees who are most likely to meet the organization's standards of performance and who will be staffed and developed on the job.

The following points were stressed:

- Selection is influenced by job and organization factors.
- Reasonable criteria for the choice must be set prior to prediction.
- The selection procedure includes the preliminary screening interview, completion of the applicant blank, psychometric tests, the selection interview, reference checks and physical examinations.
- The predictors used must be valid, reliable and fair.
- Using a greater number of accepted methods to gather data for selection decisions increases the number of successful candidates selected.
- Larger organizations are more likely to use sophisticated selection techniques.
- Even if the most able applicant is chosen, there is no guarantee of successful performance on the job.

KEY CONCEPTS AND TERMS

- Ability test
- Application form
- Assessment centre
- Combined approach
- Compensatory approach
- Concurrent validity
- Construct validity
- Content validity
- Criterion-related validity
- External recruitment
- Executive search firm
- Face validity
- Fairness
- Interest questionnaire
- Internal consistency
- Internal recruitment
- Inter-rater reliability
- Interview
- Parallel forms reliability
- Personality test
- Predictive validity
- Preliminary screening
- Private employment agency
- Psychometric test
- Recruitment
- Recruitment planning
- Recruitment strategy
- Reference
- Reliability
- Selection
- Selection procedure
- Successive hurdles approach
- Test–retest reliability
- Utility analysis
- Validity
- Walk-ins
- Work sample test

SAMPLE ESSAY TITLES

- Which factors should be taken into account when trying to give realistic job previews?
- What factors influence an organization's choice of selection methods?
- How can an organization improve the validity of its interviews?
- What is an assessment centre? How will you develop an assessment centre?
- What can be done to promote fair selection in organizations?

FURTHER READING

Books

Chamorro-Premuzic, T. and Furnham, A. (2010). *The Psychology of Personnel Selection*. Cambridge: Cambridge University Press.

Povah, N. and Thornton, G.C. (2011). *Assessment Centres and Global Talent Management*. Surrey: Gower.

Journal articles

Roth, P.L., Oh, I., Buster, M.A., Campion, M.A., Le, H., Van Iddekinge, C.H. and Robbins, S.B. (2014). Differential validity for cognitive ability tests in employment and educational settings: Not much more than range restriction? *Journal of Applied Psychology*, 99(1), 1–20.

Schmidt, F.L. (2012). Cognitive tests used in selection can have content validity as well as criterion validity: A broader research review and implications for practice. *International Journal of Selection and Assessment*, 20(1), 1–13.

Walker, H.J., Bauer, T.N., Cole, M.S., Bernerth, J.B., Field, H.S. and Short, J.C. (2013). Is this how I will be treated? Reducing uncertainty through recruitment interactions. *Academy of Management Journal*, 56(5), 1325–1347.

9 Induction, training and development

This chapter introduces the reader to induction, learning and development in organizations. The first section focuses on the definition of terms. The chapter then proceeds to induction (i.e. the introduction of new employees to an organization). We look at the objectives of induction, investigate who should be responsible for induction, focus on the content of an induction programme, and describe how induction programmes can be evaluated. The third section focuses on training and development of employees. We focus on the goals of training and the training cycle (i.e. needs assessment, the development and presentation of training programmes, and the evaluation of training programmes).

LEARNING OUTCOMES

When you have completed this chapter you should be able to:

1 Define induction, learning and development.
2 Discuss the content of an induction programme.
3 Discuss the follow-up and evaluation of an induction programme.
4 Discuss the goal and objectives of training.
5 Explain the training cycle.
6 Discuss the identification of training needs.
7 Explain learning principles and evaluate different training methods.
8 Distinguish between the four levels of evaluation of training programmes.

DEFINITION OF TERMS

Induction is the process of receiving and welcoming employees when they first join an organization. Induction includes relinquishing certain attitudes, values and behaviours

The components of training and development

Learning is the act by which the individual acquires knowledge, skills and attitudes that result in relatively permanent changes in behaviour. Knowledge is divided into declarative and procedural knowledge. Declarative knowledge refers to factual information about a specific topic, while procedural knowledge refers to routines on how to do something. An individual should have declarative knowledge before he or she can have procedural knowledge. Any behaviour that has been learned is a skill. Attitudes are evaluative tendencies towards an object.

Development is defined as the growth of a person's ability and potential through the provision of leaning and educational experiences.

Training is the systematic application of formal processes that involves the acquisition of knowledge, skills and attitudes to increase the performance of employees. Training is directed at the improvement of skills, including motor skills, cognitive skills and interpersonal skills.

Education refers to the development of the knowledge, values and understanding required in all aspects of life, rather than knowledge and skills relating to a particular activity.

as the new recruit learns the organization's goals, the means of attaining those goals, basic job responsibilities, effective job behaviour and work rules (Armstrong and Taylor, 2014). Much of this is learned on the job from co-workers and work teams. Induction is geared towards the 'fitting in' of the new employee with the way in which an organization operates. It is a learning process which starts during recruitment and continues after the new employee is placed in the job.

Training and development is the process of ensuring that the workforce of an organization has the knowledge, skills and engagement it needs. The components of training and development are described in Focus 9.1 (Armstrong and Taylor, 2014; Warr, 2002).

INDUCTION

The objectives of induction

Induction has various objectives (Armstrong and Taylor, 2014; Byars and Rue, 2011). First, it helps to create realistic employee expectations, especially in the case of new employees who have a long professional training period which provides much practical work experience. During their training period people such as attorneys and general practitioners learn to a large extent what to expect in the actual work situation. Second, it makes the new employee become productive sooner. Third, it reduces the fear, anxiety and insecurity experienced by the new employee. New employees are unsure whether they will succeed on the job. A well-organized induction programme will tend to put these fears at rest. Fourth, it reduces the possibility that the new employee may leave soon after joining the organization. Staff turnover tends to be rather high during the first few months after new employees join an organization. If a new employee can see that he or she can make a positive contribution towards the activities of the organization, this tendency to leave will be reduced. Fifth, it creates job satisfaction and a positive attitude towards the organization. Last, it saves the time of superiors and co-workers, because during a well-planned and well-executed induction programme the new employee is taught what is expected of him or her and how his or her tasks have to be carried out.

Who is responsible for induction?

The decision about who should be responsible for induction depends on the particular circumstances, for instance, the size of the organization, the size of the human resource department, the role that a labour union and its officials play in the induction process and the general policy of the organization regarding induction. In bigger organizations it appears to be a shared responsibility. In this case the responsibility is shared between the human resource department and the managers or supervisors. The responsibility of the human resource department is for the general orientation of new employees, while that of the managers or supervisors may be termed departmental and job orientation. Byars and Rue (2011) also refer to the so-called 'buddy system' in which the job orientation is conducted by one of the new employee's fellow workers.

The content of induction programmes

The content of an induction programme depends on the particular circumstances. Besides providing new employees with a well-structured orientation programme, it is also advisable to issue them with written material that they can always refer back to. It is desirable for each new employee to receive an orientation kit, or packet of information, to supplement the verbal orientation programme. This kit is normally prepared by the human resource department and can provide a wide variety of materials. Care should be taken in the design not only to ensure that essential information is provided but also that too much information is not given.

Some orientation materials that might be included in an orientation kit include the company organization chart, a map of the company's facilities, a copy of the policy and procedures handbook, a list of holiday and fringe benefits, copies of performance appraisal forms, dates and procedures, copies of other required forms (e.g. expense reimbursement form), emergency and accident prevention procedures, sample copy of a company newsletter or magazine, telephone numbers and locations of key company personnel, and copies of insurance plans. Many organizations require new employees to sign a form indicating that they have received and read the orientation kit (Byars and Rue, 2011). This is done to protect the organization if a grievance should arise and the employee should allege that he or she had not been aware of certain organizational policies and procedures.

Follow-up and evaluation of induction programmes

It is important to follow up any induction activities. It is of very little use if the human resources manager tells the new employee that he or she 'should drop by if any problems occur'. The human resource department should have a scheduled follow-up one month after the new employee has been placed. The supervisor/manager should also check how well the new employee is doing. The supervisor/manager should also answer any questions that the new employee has to ask about aspects that have arisen since he or she attended the orientation programme.

The human resource department should also evaluate on an annual basis the total induction programme. This should be done to determine whether the programme is meeting the needs of the organization, as well as the needs of new employees. Data gathered during such an evaluation can be used to improve the present programme.

Feedback from new employees can be used to evaluate the effectiveness of a programme (Byars and Rue, 2011). Various methods can be used to obtain feedback, namely a) unsigned questionnaires that are completed by all employees; b) in-depth interviews with randomly selected new employees; c) group discussion sessions with new employees who have settled into their jobs. From the above-mentioned feedback that is received, an organization can adapt its induction programme. An organization should make use of the suggestions that employees made during the feedback sessions. This is important, because the induction process has a definitive impact on the performance of the new employee.

TRAINING AND DEVELOPMENT

The goals of training and development

Training is only one component of the learning and development process that includes all of the experiences that enhance and build employees' employment-related characteristics (Sonnentag et al., 2004). The problem is, however, that a training programme frequently occurs because a few people decide it is needed, or because the latest fad can be sold to top management. They find the money to get it started and measure success by how many people participate. Effectiveness is seldom measured.

The best companies integrate training within a systematic set of human resource activities, including selection, rewards and job design. Training can be used as a strategic tool for attaining the goals of the organization and the employees. The link between training and strategic goals seems obvious, but it is often lost in the day-to-day struggle to implement programmes and deal with crises. In that case, training becomes an activity, rather than a strategy.

Training as activity is characterized by no client, no business need, no assessment of performance effectiveness, no effort to prepare the work environment to support training and no measurement of results. Training as a strategy is characterized by a partnership with the client, link to a business need, assessment of performance effectiveness, preparation of the work environment to support training and measurement of results.

The reasons for training can be summarized as follows (Armstrong and Taylor, 2014; Byars and Rue, 2011):

- To give employees direction in their jobs and acquaint them with their working environment so that they can become productive quickly.
- To provide the human resources that are necessary for commerce and industry to be effective.
- To increase the loyalty and morale of employees.
- To improve the quality and quantity of an organization's output and to reduce costs.

The training and development cycle

The training and development cycle consists of three phases (see Figure 9.1). These phases include the following (Wexley and Latham, 2002):

- Identification of training and development needs.
- Training and development.
- Evaluating the training and development programme.

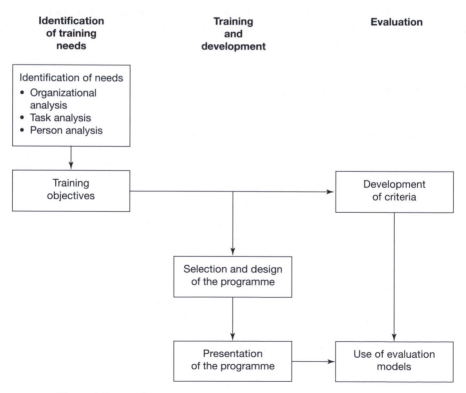

FIGURE 9.1 The training cycle

Identification of training and development needs

Training must be directed towards the accomplishment of some organizational objective, such as more efficient production methods, improved quality of products and services or reduced operating costs. The organization should commit its resources only to those training activities that can best help in achieving its objectives.

Needs assessment is a systematic analysis of the specific training activities required by job holders and an organization to achieve the objectives of the job and the organization. The organizational needs assessment requires an examination of the long-term and short-term objectives of the organization. The organization's financial, social, human resource, growth and market objectives need to be matched with its human talent, structure, climate and efficiency. The knowledge, skills and abilities needed to perform the job are carefully considered. What are the tasks? What skills are needed to perform well? What does performing well mean? Data from current employees, supervisors and experts need to be collected to complete this part of the needs assessment.

The employee's needs must also be considered: ask the employee what he or she needs to competently perform the tasks. This will provide useful information. Evaluate the employee's performance against a standard or the outputs of co-workers to help identify strengths, weaknesses and needs.

Training can improve the individual's performance only when a) the employee does not have the knowledge and skills to do the job; b) the low performance is not due to a lack of practice; and c) the low performance is not due to other causes.

Wexley and Latham (2002) identified five methods that can be used to gather needs assessment information: interviews, questionnaires, observation, focus groups and document examination (see Focus 9.2).

By observation, asking and listening, the manager can conduct a performance analysis. The specific steps in performance analysis include the following:

1 Appraise the performance of employees in order to determine how they are doing, in comparison with how they should be doing, and determine behavioural discrepancies.
2 Assess the cost and value of correcting a behavioural discrepancy.
3 Determine if it is a can't do or won't do situation. It is important to determine if the employee could do the expected job if he or she wanted to.
4 Set standards, because under-performance might result if an employee does not know what the standards are.
5 Remove obstacles relating to time, equipment and people, which result in behaviour discrepancies.
6 Allow the employee time to practise, so that he or she can perform the job better.
7 Provide training if the performance analysis indicates that knowledge, skills or attitudes need to be altered.
8 Redesign the job through job enrichment, job simplification or enlargement if necessary to improve performance.
9 Transfer or terminate the employee's services if all else has failed.
10 Create a motivational climate. Sometimes a skilled employee does not want to perform the job because of motivational problems. Rewards, punishment,

Methods to assess training needs

- *Interviews*. Interviews with employees can be conducted by human resource specialists or by external consultants. The following questions should be investigated: a) What problems does the employee experience in the job? b) What knowledge and/or skills does the employee need to improve performance on the job? c) What training does the employee feel is needed? If interviews are to provide useful information, employees must feel that their input will be valued and not be used against them.
- *Questionnaires*. Questionnaires can be used to assess training needs. This involves developing a list of skills required to perform a particular job effectively and asking employees to check those skills in which they believe they need training. Attitude surveys and customer surveys can also be used to determine training needs.
- *Observation*. A specialist can observe the behaviour of employees in their jobs and translate these observations into training needs.
- *Focus groups*. Focus groups are composed of employees from various departments and levels in the organization. Each group investigates the following questions with the help of a facilitator: a) What knowledge/skills will employees need in order for the organization to stay competitive over the next five years? b) What problems does the organization experience that can be solved through training?
- *Document examination*. Document examination is concerned with examining organizational records on absenteeism, turnover and accident rates to determine if problems exist and whether they can be solved through training. Performance appraisal information can also be studied in order to determine training needs.

discipline or some combination may be needed to create a positive climate for the optimal use of skills.

Presenting training programmes

After training needs have been determined, specific and measurable objectives must be established for meeting these needs. Effective training objectives should state what the organization, department or individual should achieve once training is completed, for example to improve listening and feedback skills for use in the performance appraisal programme.

Training objectives can be categorized as:

- *Instructional objectives*. What facts, principles and concepts are to be learned in the training programme? Who is to be taught? When are they to be taught?

- *Organizational and departmental objectives*. What impact will the training have on organizational and departmental outcomes, such as absenteeism, turnover, costs and productivity?
- *Individual performance and growth objectives*. What impact will the training programme have on the attitudes, behaviour and personal growth of the trainee? (What should he or she be able to do after the training?) Under what conditions should the trainee be able to perform the trained behaviour? How well should the trainee perform the trained behaviour? Explicit objectives serve a number of purposes. They assist in developing the criteria to be used in evaluating the training outcome. Together training objectives and evaluation criteria also help in choosing relevant instructional material. During training, objectives help motivate trainees to organize their efforts in a way that will help them accomplish those objectives. Before a training programme is presented, the presenter should ensure that sound learning principles are followed (to maximize learning). Then, the training methods that are most applicable for the specific situation must be selected (Wexley and Latham, 2002; Warr, 2002).
- *Maximization of learning*. For training to have any effect at all, trainees must learn something from it. When training is effectively designed and trainees are motivated, learning can occur. The use of sound learning principles during the development and implementation of training programmes contributes to its success.
- *Ability to learn*. Individuals enter training with different experiences, different levels of familiarity with the material, and different mental and physical abilities. The training demands should match the abilities of trainees. Training that is too difficult or too easy is likely to be less effective. Testing trainees prior to beginning training can help ensure a good match.
- *Motivation to learn*. In order to learn, a person must want to learn. Perhaps the most important motivation trainees bring to training is their desire to change their behaviour and results on the job. In the context of training, motivation influences a person's enthusiasm for training, keeps attention focused on training activities and reinforces what is learned. People strive to achieve objectives they have set for themselves. The objectives of employees include job security, financially and intellectually rewarding work, recognition, status, responsibility and achievement. The learning process is facilitated when the training programme helps employees to achieve these objectives. Supportive supervisors and the expectation that training results will be assessed later on the job contribute to higher trainee motivation.
- *Goal setting*. Individuals' conscious goals may regulate their behaviour. The trainer's job is to get the trainees to adopt or internalize the goals of the programme in the following ways:

  - Convey the learning objectives at the outset and at various strategic points throughout the training programme.
  - Make goals difficult enough to be a challenge.
  - Supplement the overall goals with subgoals to maintain feelings of accomplishment.

- *Reinforcement.* The idea behind reinforcement is that behaviour appearing to lead to a positive consequence tends to be repeated, while behaviour leading to a negative consequence tends not to be repeated. Learners must be rewarded for new behaviour in ways that satisfy needs, such as pay, praise, recognition and promotion. For example, a trainee who is praised for good performance is likely to continue to strive for additional praise. According to the expectancy theory, individuals are motivated to choose behaviour that has the greatest chance of producing desired consequences. Trainees must believe that acquiring the knowledge and skills from training will lead to desired outcomes and that training can provide that knowledge or skill.
- *Flow of the training programme.* Each segment of the training should be organized so that the individual can see not only its purpose, but also how it fits in with the other parts of the programme. Later segments should build on those presented earlier.
- *Modelling and self-efficacy.* The trainer can build trainees' skills by allowing them to see models of good and poor performance, and by giving trainees confidence in their abilities to apply their skills. Confidence building includes providing trainees with encouragement, guidance and feedback on how well they are doing, and providing the opportunity for practice (Bandura, 1977).
- *Practice and repetition.* Learning requires time to assimilate what has been learned, to accept it, internalize it and to build confidence in what has been learned. This requires practice and repetition of the material. After sufficient practice the skills may become automatic, requiring little conscious thought. Trainees should be given opportunities to continue practising even after they have achieved proficiency the first time. 'Overlearning' leads to a relative permanent change in behaviour and automatic responses to the learned task.
- *Spacing of sessions.* Training spread out over a period of time facilitates the learning process. The interval most conducive to learning depends on the type of training.
- *Material must be meaningful.* Appropriate material for sequential learning (for example, cases, problems, discussion outlines and reading lists) must be provided. The learning methods used should be as varied as possible. Boredom destroys learning. Any method that is overused will begin to bore learners.
- *Small training units.* The learning material should be presented in small segments or units. This format allows quick feedback to the trainee on how well he or she is doing.
- *Whole or part training.* Learning is facilitated when an overview is given to trainees, and it is then divided into portions for in–depth instruction. Whether to use whole or part learning depends also on the difficulty of the task, and the degree of relationship between subtasks.
- *Transfer of learning.* The trainer must do his or her best to make the training as close to the reality of the job as possible to ensure that the newly learned behaviour is transferred to the work environment.
- *Knowledge of results.* Knowledge of results (feedback) influences the learning process. Keeping employees informed of their progress as measured against some standard helps in setting goals for what remains to be learned. The process of analysing progress and establishing new objectives enhances learning. Precautions

should be taken that goals are not so difficult to achieve that employees become discouraged.

- *The characteristics of the instructional environment and instructors.* The instructional environment can be designed around events such as gaining attention, informing learners of objectives, presenting the training stimulus material, providing feedback, assessing performance and enhancing retention and transfer. The instructor should have informed everyone, arranged the facilities, checked the physical requirements, secured the necessary equipment, established training objectives, and studied the lesson plan to anticipate group responses and to prepare experiences.

Training methods that can be used can be classified as on-site methods and off-site methods. On-site training methods include the following (Wexley and Latham, 2002; Warr, 2002):

- *On-the-job training.* On-the-job training is probably the most widely used method of training. The employee is placed into the real work situation and shown the job and the tricks of the trade by an experienced employee or the supervisor. Although this programme is simple and relatively inexpensive, if it is not handled properly the costs can be high in damaged machinery, unsatisfied customers and poorly trained employees. To prevent these problems, trainers must be carefully selected and trained. The trainee should be placed with a trainer who is similar in background and personality. The trainer should be motivated by training and be rewarded for doing it well.
- *Apprentice training.* Apprentice training is a combination of on-site and off-site training. It requires the co-operation of the employer, trainers at the workplace and technical training institutions. The apprentice commits to a period of training and learning that involves both formal classroom learning and practical on-the-job experience.
- *Vestibule training.* In vestibule training, the trainee learns the job in an environment that simulates the real working environment as closely as possible (for example, training of pilots in a simulated cockpit of an aeroplane). A machine operator trainee might run a machine under the supervision of a trainer until he or she learns how to use it properly. Only then is the trainee sent to the shop floor. This procedure can be quite expensive if the number of trainees supervised is not large.
- *Coaching.* Coaching is defined as 'a collaborative relationship formed between a coach and a coachee for the purpose of attaining professional or personal development outcomes which are valued by the coachee' (Grant *et al.*, 2010: 3). Coaching aims to help individuals to identify desired outcomes, establish specific goals, enhance motivation by identifying strengths and building self-efficacy, identify resources and formulate specific action plans, monitor and evaluate progress towards goals, and modify action plans based on feedback. Coaching fails when inadequate time is set aside for it, when the coachee is not allowed to make mistakes if rivalry develops, or if the dependency needs of the coachee are not recognized and accepted by the coach.
- *Computer-based training.* Computer-based training permits self-paced learning and immediate feedback. This type of training works as follows. A trainee sits at a

FIGURE 9.2 Computer-based training permits self-paced learning

Source: © Goodluz/Shutterstock.com

terminal with a monitor. The computer is programmed with the training materials. The trainee communicates by programming or using the keyboard to input commands or requests. The advantages of computer-based training include availability, self-paced features, distribution and adaptability, and work simulation.

- *Job rotation.* Trainees can be rotated through a series of jobs to broaden their managerial experience. Organizations often have developed career plans that include a mix of functional and geographic transfers.

Because of the perceived relevance of on-the-job experience, on-site training methods should be used in training programmes. Off-the-job development programmes should, however, supplement them where expertise is not readily available. Off-site training methods include:

- *Lectures.* In a lecture an instructor presents material to a group of learners. Lectures are relatively inexpensive to develop and deliver. They can impart factual knowledge quickly and efficiently. Lectures, however, lead to one-way communication, are insensitive towards learner differences and do not allow feedback to the trainer. Many of these difficulties can be overcome by a competent lecturer who makes use of discussions during the lecture.
- *Conference.* The conference is a participative method that emphasizes small group discussion in which the instructor guides rather than instructs trainees through a process of questions, answers and discussion to a desired outcome. The objectives of the conference method are to develop problem-solving and decision-making

skills, present new and complex material, and modify attitudes. Topics for the discussion can be chosen by the instructor or by trainees. The leader of the session prepares for the topic in advance of the session. The training group may be given an agenda for the meeting or may develop it on their own. The conference method requires a high degree of participation from the trainees and provides immediate feedback and the opportunity to assess own learning by listening to the comments made by the instructor and other group participants. The conference method is limited in the amount of substantive material that can be covered in one session. It also requires trainees with good verbal skills and self-images so that they are not threatened by group participation.

- *Audio, video and teleconferencing*. Recordings, films and slides can be distributed to learners and used independently or in conjunction with other training methods. It is possible to produce effective videos at low cost. The advantage of audio–visual techniques is their ability to quickly distribute a consistent training experience to a large number of individuals without being constrained by the time limits of instructors or logistical requirements. With video teleconferencing, learners are in remote classrooms equipped with televisions and microphones. The instructor provides the training from a video studio, often linked to learners via satellite. Learners can see the instructor and ask questions via audio links to the studio. Audio teleconferencing provides a similar arrangement but uses only audio connections.
- *Programmed instruction*. Programmed instruction presents the learner with a series of tasks, allows evaluation of success at intervals throughout the training, and provides feedback about correct and incorrect responses as the learner advances through the training. Programmed instruction can be incorporated into books, machines and computers. Careful attention must be given to learning sequences and objectives. Learners progress faster with programmed instruction than with lectures. Other advantages of programmed instruction are that materials can be packaged and distributed, and learners can use the material at their convenience and when they are ready. It also makes provision for self-paced learning, which allows flexibility according to different abilities.
- *Learning-by-doing*. Learning-by-doing training techniques copy the essential elements of real world situations: they allow learners to play a role or make decisions about the situation and then receive feedback about their effectiveness. Business games allow learners to make decisions about business variables, often competing against other individuals or teams. The case study presents learners with a written report of a realistic situation. The learners analyse the information and prepare solutions for discussion. Role-playing involves having trainers act out simulated roles. Interpersonal skills can be learned by using role-playing. Advantages of these training methods include the potential for a high degree of transfer to the work situation, high participant involvement, providing specific feedback and helping learners deal with incomplete information.

Evaluating training and development programmes

It is necessary to evaluate training programmes (Kraiger *et al.*, 1993). Less effective programmes can be withdrawn to save time and effort. Weaknesses within established programmes can be identified and remedied. One way to approach the evaluation of training programmes is according to the model of Kirkpatrick (1959). According to Kirkpatrick, training programmes can be evaluated on four levels, namely reaction, learning, behaviour and results (see Focus 9.3).

Kirkpatrick levels of evaluation of training programmes

Reaction. Evaluating the reaction of a training programme answers the following question: 'How well did the trainees like the programme?' Reaction evaluation should consider topics such as programme content, programme structure and format, instructional techniques, instructor abilities and style, quality of the learning environment, extent to which training objectives were achieved and recommendations for improvement. Reaction evaluation is done directly after the training programme, or a few weeks thereafter. The shortcoming of reaction evaluation is that the enthusiasm of trainees cannot necessarily be taken as evidence of improved ability and performance (Warr, 2002).

Learning. Evaluating the learning after a training programme answers the following question: 'What facts, principles and concepts were learned in the training programme?'. Learning evaluation is concerned with how well the facts, principles and skills were understood by trainees. Paper and pencil or skill tests can be used to evaluate learning. In order to obtain an accurate picture of what was learned, trainees should be tested before and after the training programme (Wexley and Latham, 2002).

Behaviour. Evaluating the behaviour of trainees after a training programme answers the following question: 'Did the job behaviour of trainees change because of the programme?' (Warr, 2002). A systematic appraisal should be made of on-the-job performance on a before-and-after basis. The appraisal of performance should be made by the trainer, the trainees' superior, their subordinates or their peers. A statistical analysis should be made to compare performance before and after the training programme and to relate changes to the training programme. The post-training appraisal should be made several months after the training so that the trainees have an opportunity to put into practice what they have learned. An experimental group (who receive training) and a control group (who do not receive training) should be used.

Results. Evaluating the results of a training programme answers the following question: 'What were the results of the programme in terms of costs and productivity'?

ACTIVITY 9.1

The recent training and development perspective in a 100-year-old credo

The development and empowerment process has overtaken the training event in organizations. The focus is on learning through reframing the workplace problems, self-determined development, unfreezing barriers to learning and understanding what it means to be a learning organization (Mabey and Iles, 2001). However, if we investigate the life and philosophy of Dr Y.C. Yen, it is evident that this approach is not so new . . .

Dr Y.C. James Yen was born in China in 1893. He dedicated his life to mass education and rural reconstruction, first in China and then throughout the world. He committed himself to sensitizing the world's intellectual community to the tremendous losses the world suffers by ignoring the humanity of the poor, and by not acknowledging their productivity. During the First World War, he was stationed in France to supervise Chinese labourers. While there, he realized that the people's illiteracy was no fault of their own. Yen proclaimed, 'I began to realize that what these humble, common people of my country lacked was not brains, for God has given that to them, but opportunity. . . . They had potential powers waiting for development, waiting for release . . .'.

If one considers the principles of adult learning, the training cycle and training methods, the above observation of James Yen is still applicable today. James Yen developed a Credo of Rural Reconstruction, portraying the developmental approach that should be applied; the Credo speaks as follows:

Go to the people; Live among them
Learn from them; Plan with them; Work with them
Start with what they know; Build on what they have
Teach by showing; Learn by doing
Not a showcase but a pattern
Not odds and ends but a system
Not to conform but to transform
Not relief but release.

(James Yen)

Can you apply the approach portrayed in Yen's Credo to training and development approaches in the workplace? How?

Source: Mabey, C. and Iles, P. (2001). *Managing Learning*. London: Thompson Learning.

SUMMARY

- Induction has been defined as the introduction of new employees to the organization, work unit and job. The idea was expressed that it should be grouped with human resource management activities/subjects of study such as training and development because orientation involves learning. The objectives of induction are seen to be learning job procedures, establishing relationships with co-workers and fitting into the employer's way of doing things, to give the employee a sense of belonging and to create favourable attitudes towards the company. Both the personnel/human resource department and line managers/ supervisors are responsible for induction. The content of an induction programme can be divided into general organizational aspects and specific departmental/job aspects. Induction (programmes) should regularly be followed up and evaluated.

- Training is a form of job-specific education directed at improving the knowledge, skills and attitudes of employees. Effective organizations design their training programmes after assessing the individual's and organization's training needs and setting training objectives. Effective training programmes select trainees on the basis of their needs as well as the objectives of the organization. Various training methods can be used. Sound learning principles should, however, be applied to maximize trainees' learning.

- It is, however, important that training courses be evaluated to determine the reaction of participants, to evaluate the learning achieved, behavioural changes effected and the impact on work results after the completion of the training course.

KEY CONCEPTS AND TERMS

- Apprentice training
- Behaviour
- Coaching
- Computer-based training
- Conference
- Declarative knowledge
- Development
- Education
- Induction

- Job rotation
- Knowledge
- Learning-by-doing
- Learning principles
- Lecture
- On-the-job training
- Performance analysis
- Procedural knowledge
- Programmed instruction

- Reaction
- Results
- Skill
- Teleconferencing
- Training
- Training cycle
- Training need
- Training objective
- Vestibule training

SAMPLE ESSAY TITLES

- What are the main objectives of an induction programme for new employees?
- Why are training programmes one of the first areas to be eliminated when an organization's budget is cut?
- If you were asked to develop a training programme for taxi drivers, how would you do it? How would you evaluate the training programme?

FURTHER READING

Books

Swanson, R.A. and Holton, E.F. (2014). *Foundations of Human Resource Development*. New York: Berrett-Koehler.

Werner, J.M. and Simone, R.L. (2012). *Human Resource Development*. Mason, OH: South-Western.

Journal articles

Grant, A. M., Passmore, J., Cavanagh, M. J. and Parker, H. (2010). The state of play in coaching today: A comprehensive review of the field. *International Review of Industrial and Organizational Psychology*, 25, 125–167.

Salas, E., Tannenbaum, S.I., Kraiger, K. and Smith-Jentsch, K.A. (2012). The science of training and development in organizations: What matters in practice. *Psychological Science in the Public Interest*, 13(2), 74–101.

Sung, S.Y. and Choi, J.N. (2014). Do organizations spend wisely on employees? Effects of training and development investments on learning and innovation in organizations. *Journal of Organizational Behavior*, 35, 393–412.

10 Compensation management

This chapter introduces the reader to compensation in organizations. The first section focuses on the role of compensation in human resource management. The chapter then proceeds to the requirements for an effective compensation system. We look at the influences on compensation (including external and organizational influences). The next section focuses on job evaluation. More specifically, job evaluation will be defined, and the objectives and advantages/disadvantages thereof will be discussed. Furthermore, job evaluation methods will be explained and the steps in implementing a job evaluation system will be described. Lastly, incentive pay systems will be discussed.

LEARNING OUTCOMES

When you have completed this chapter you should be able to:

1 Discuss the role of compensation in human resource management.
2 Discuss the requirements for an effective compensation system.
3 Describe external and internal influences on compensation.
4 Explain the factors that affect the pay level decision.
5 Discuss job evaluation as a human resource management activity, and describe the steps in the implementation of a job evaluation project.
6 Evaluate different pay incentive schemes.

THE ROLE OF COMPENSATION IN HUMAN RESOURCE MANAGEMENT

Compensation is divided into financial compensation and non-financial compensation. Financial compensation includes pay and benefits. Non-financial compensation includes a variety of things people value and want to receive through their work.

Organizations use both financial and non-financial compensation to attract the quality and quantity of employees needed, retain these employees and motivate them towards organizational goal achievement. A fair and market-related financial compensation plays a key role in the organization's ability to attract, retain and motivate employee performance. A well-structured, flexible compensation package may enhance performance, especially if it is accompanied by recognition, good interpersonal relationships and other non-financial compensation (Rynes *et al.*, 2005).

REQUIREMENTS FOR AN EFFECTIVE COMPENSATION SYSTEM

An effective compensation system should be adequate (as set forth in minimum wage and other legislation and in line with market salaries), equitable (based on the value of a job relative to other jobs in the organization), incentive-providing (by making use of merit and raises), secure (adequate to satisfy the employee's basic needs), balanced (including pay, benefits and promotions), cost-effective for the organization and acceptable to the employee.

INFLUENCES ON COMPENSATION

Compensation is influenced by external and internal factors.

External influences

The external influences on compensation include the government, trade unions, the economy and the labour market.

- *The government.* The government directly influences compensation through laws directed at the establishment of minimum wage rates, wage regulations and the prevention of discrimination directed at certain groups.
- *Trade unions.* Unions have tended to be pacesetters in demands for pay, benefits and improved working conditions. There is reasonable evidence to suggest that the presence of unions tends to increase pay levels, although this is more likely where an industry has been organized by strong unions. The presence of the union is more likely to increase the compensation of its members when: a) the organization is financially and competitively strong; b) the union is financially strong enough to support a strike; c) the union has the support of other unions; and d) general economic and labour market conditions are such that unemployment is low and the economy is strong.
- *The economy.* The economic conditions of the industry, especially the degree of competitiveness, affect the organization's ability to pay high wages. The more competitive the situation, the less able the organization is to pay high wages. Ability to pay is also a consequence of the relative productivity of the organization, industry or sector. If a firm is very productive, it can pay higher wages. Productivity can be increased by advanced technology, more efficient operating methods, a harder working and more talented workforce or a combination of these

factors. The degree of profitability and productivity is a significant factor in determining the ability of organizations in the private sector to pay wages.

- *The labour market.* Although many people feel that human labour should not be regulated by supply and demand, it does in fact happen. In times of full employment, wages and salaries may have to be higher to attract and retain sufficient qualified employees; in depressions, the reverse is true. Pay may be higher if few skilled employees are available in the job market. Research evidence from the labour economics fields provides adequate support for the impact of labour market conditions on compensation.

Organizational influences on compensation

Several organizational factors, including the size and age of the organization, the labour budget and the goals of its controlling interests may influence pay levels. Although not much is known about the relationship between organization size and pay, it seems that larger organizations tend to have higher pay levels. Some people believe that new organizations tend to pay more than old ones.

The labour budget of an organization normally identifies the amount of money available for annual employee compensation. Every unit of the organization is influenced by the size of the budget. A firm's budget normally does not state the exact amount of money to be allocated to each employee, but it does state how much is available to an organizational unit. The discretion in allocating pay is then left to department heads and supervisors.

Another organizational influence on compensation is related to the goals of controlling interests and the specific pay strategy that managers select. The final authority in pay decisions is senior management. These are the managers who decide the overall strategic plan of the organization. Unfortunately, compensation is often an under-utilized tool in supporting overall strategic objectives. Therefore, many compensation plans have minimal impact on recruitment, motivation and retention of employees. To be part of the strategic plan, the compensation system must be directly linked to the strategic goals of the organization, provide strong incentives, not support undesired behaviour, offer valued rewards and be communicated clearly.

The views of managers and supervisors about pay differ as much as the employees' views do. Some managers and supervisors believe their employees should be compensated at high levels because they deserve it; they also accept or reject the idea that high pay leads to greater performance or employee satisfaction. These attitudes are reflected in the pay-level strategy chosen by the managers of the organization. Three pay-level strategies, namely high, low or comparable, can be chosen.

In the high pay-level strategy, managers choose to pay higher than average levels. In the low pay-level strategy, managers may choose to pay at the minimum level needed to hire enough employees. In the comparable pay-level strategy the pay level is set at the going wage level.

The pay-level decision

The pay-level decision is made by managers who compare the pay of persons working inside the organization with those outside it. The decision is affected by multiple factors

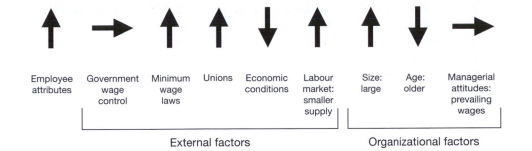

| Employee attributes | Government wage control | Minimum wage laws | Unions | Economic conditions | Labour market: smaller supply | Size: large | Age: older | Managerial attitudes: prevailing wages |

External factors   Organizational factors

FIGURE 10.1 Factors influencing the pay-level decision

(see Figure 10.1) in interaction with one another that affect pay levels upwards, downwards or laterally (Armstrong and Taylor, 2014; Truss *et al.*, 2012).

When factors such as managerial attitudes, the labour market and competition change, the pressures on pay levels shift. For example, if organizations experience little growth, it will put pressure on compensation in the downward direction. To help make the pay–level decision, managers use a tool called a pay or salary survey. Salary surveys are surveys of the compensation paid to employees by all employers in a geographic area, an industry or an occupational group. Surveys are the principal tool used in the pay-level decision. These surveys help managers to gauge the exact market rates for various positions. Obtaining valid, reliable salary surveys is critical to creating a compensation programme that supports the financial goals of the organization.

Salary surveys can be done by personal interviews. This method supplies the most accurate responses, but is also expensive. Mailed questionnaires are a frequently used method that is cheap. The jobs being surveyed by mail must be clearly defined, or the data may not be reliable. Telephone enquiries, as a follow-up to the mail questionnaires, can also be used. The organization must decide on the jobs to be covered, the employers to be contacted and the method to be used to gather data. Usually organizations compare themselves with similar competitors in their industry.

JOB EVALUATION

The organization must not only relate pay to pay levels paid for comparable jobs in other organizations, it must also determine the pay structures for its employees having different jobs within the organization. Managers can cope with the attempt to provide equal pay for positions of equal worth by making arbitrary management decisions, engaging in collective bargaining or using job evaluation. If managers try to make these decisions without help from tools such as collective bargaining and job evaluation, unsystematic decision-making is likely to lead to perceived inequities.

Definition of job evaluation

The implementation of a job evaluation system is the first step in developing a fair compensation structure. Job evaluation is a systematic process to determine the value of a given job relative to all other jobs in a specific organization. It involves the analysis of jobs for the purpose of writing job descriptions and specifications, rating of those jobs through use of a job evaluation plan, and conversion of relative job values to definite wage rates.

Job evaluation must not be confused with performance appraisal. The objective of performance appraisal is to determine the economic value of the job holder. The objective of job evaluation is to determine the economic value of the job, irrespective of the job holder. Job evaluation is a systematic, rather than a scientific, process. The subjective judgement of people is used to analyse, describe, assess and grade a job, which means that it is subjected to bias.

Objectives of job evaluation

The objectives of job evaluation are to:

* Establish a systematic and formal structure of jobs based on their worth to the organization.
* Justify an existing pay structure or develop one that provides for internal equity.
* Provide a basis for negotiating pay rates when an organization bargains collectively with a union.
* Provide a hierarchy of pay progression for employees.
* Develop a basis for a merit or a pay-for-performance programme.

Advantages and problems of job evaluation

The implementation of a job evaluation system has the following advantages for the organization:

* Personal bias in the determining of the value of the job is minimized.
* It forms the basis of a fair salary structure for all employees.
* An objective basis for collective bargaining is created.
* Job descriptions that can be used for selection, training and performance appraisal purposes are compiled.

The following problems are experienced with regard to job evaluation:

* Job evaluation can never be scientifically correct because it cannot be done according to scientific criteria.
* Pressure groups inside the organization can exercise pressure to grade certain jobs higher.

Job evaluation methods

The four most frequently used job evaluation methods include the job ranking method, the factor comparison method, the classification method and the point system.

- *The job ranking method.* The job ranking method is used in smaller, simpler organizations. Instead of analysing the full complexity of the job by evaluating parts of jobs, the job ranking method has the evaluator rank order in whole jobs, from the simplest to the most challenging. The problem with this method is that the difference between the highest job and the next highest job may not be exactly the same as that between the lowest and the next lowest. The method is not suitable for an organization with many jobs.

- *The job classification system.* This method groups a set of jobs together into a grade or classification. These sets of jobs are then ranked on levels of difficulty. The job evaluator decides how many categories the job has to be broken into. The next step is to write definitions of each class. Once the classes are defined, jobs to be evaluated are compared with the definitions and placed into appropriate classifications. The Paterson method (Paterson, 1972) is one of the most well-known job classification methods. This method divides jobs into levels based on decision–making.

- *The point system.* Most job evaluation systems use the point system. The point system requires evaluators to quantify the value of the elements of the job. On the basis of the job description and/or interviews with job occupants, points are assigned to the degree to which various factors are required to do the job. For example, points can be assigned based on skill required, physical and mental effort needed, degree of unpleasant working conditions involved and the amount of responsibility involved in the job. This method is reliable and assesses differentials between jobs. The disadvantage is that it is time consuming. The point system is, however, suitable in a unionized environment, because its validity can be demonstrated and union representatives can be trained in using it. The Hay system is an example of a point system.

- *The factor comparison method.* The factor comparison method permits the job evaluation process to be done on a factor-by-factor basis. It differs from the point method in that jobs are compared against a benchmark of key points. Five key factors are identified for the evaluation of jobs. Benchmark jobs are selected and the factors are then ranked in terms of their importance in each job. Monetary factors are assigned to the factors in each job. Others jobs in the organization are classified and paid in terms of their comparison to the benchmark jobs. This method can be suitable for small, homogeneous jobs, but is difficult to explain and does not allow any flexibility for prevailing market conditions.

The implementation of a job evaluation system

The steps in implementing a job evaluation system will now be discussed (Armstrong and Taylor, 2014).

Step 1: Establish the need for a job evaluation system

It is essential to determine if a job evaluation system is really necessary before such an expensive and timely project is initiated. The following factors may indicate a need for a job evaluation system:

1   An increase in the size of the organization. In a small organization it is possible to monitor salaries individually. If the organization, however, has more than 200 employees, salaries must be more structured.

2   Dissatisfaction among employees because of perceived inequality of compensation, which manifests in symptoms such as poor labour relations, and high labour turnover.

3   Perceived anomalies in compensation: for example, two employees on the same job level and with the same abilities earn different salaries.

Step 2: Get support from top management

Prior to implementing a job evaluation system, top management must be convinced that the project is necessary, and that the time and cost involved is justified. Their continuous interest and support is essential to ensure the successful implementation of the project. Employees, supervisors and managers (who will be affected by the implementation of the system) want to be sure that top management supports the project, and that it is not only a fad used by someone in the human resource department.

Step 3: Select a job evaluation system

An appropriate job evaluation system must be selected. The service of external job evaluation consultants can be used if expertise regarding job evaluation is not available in the organization. The organization can contact other organizations in the industry or area to enquire about their methods and successes regarding the implementation of a job evaluation system. A system that is good for one organization will not automatically be good for another one. The reason for this is that each organization has its own 'personality', and may require different systems. If a prefabricated system is used, it may be necessary to modify it to suit the needs of the specific organization.

Criteria for the selection of a job evaluation system include:

1   Credibility, e.g. how many organizations used the system, and are still using it successfully?

2   Relevancy, e.g. is the system applicable to all types of jobs and organizations?

3   Simplicity, e.g. is it easy to learn and understand the language of the system?

4   Objectivity, e.g. are the procedures of the system standardized?

5   Comparability, e.g. is it possible to compare the results of the evaluations with other organizations?

6   Flexibility, e.g. can the system be applied to all jobs that must be evaluated?

Step 4: Plan the implementation of the job evaluation system

The next step in the implementation of a job evaluation system is to finalize a time schedule. The following aspects regarding the time schedule must be considered:

1   The time schedule must include all phases of the job evaluation, including communication with employees.

2   The time schedule must be realistic and detailed. Interruptions affect the morale of employees and the credibility of the system.

3   The job evaluation must accompany the annual salary review.

Step 5: Communicate with employees

Employees tend to resist change, especially if change may affect their status and salaries. The timing of the communication is crucial. Rumours, which can be detrimental for the project, arise if you procrastinate with the employees' introduction to the project. It is essential to communicate important aspects regarding the project at an early stage to all employees. The information that is communicated must be simple and clear. Even unskilled employees must be able to understand it. Verbal and written communication with employees must include the reasons for and advantages of implementing the job evaluation system. No person is willing to invest energy in something that would have no advantages for him or her. The employee's first concern in implementing a new method, procedure or technique is: 'Which advantage or disadvantage will it have for me?' Advantages must be discussed with employees. The implementation of the job evaluation system must be approved by the trade union. A meeting must be held with representatives of trade unions to exchange information. Trade union representatives can also be included in job evaluation panels.

Step 6: Conduct job analyses and write job descriptions

The organization starts with the process of job analysis and job description.

Step 7: Rate and grade jobs

The rating of jobs is done by job evaluation panels. The job evaluation panel must include the following people: one or more representatives of the trade union(s), a senior representative from each department, a secretary and a neutral chairperson. The panel may include a consultant (as chairperson), a financial manager, a technical manager, the human resource manager, a work and organizational psychologist, and trade union representatives.

The panel must be trained in the specific job evaluation system and must be willing to spend time on job evaluation. The job evaluation panel must be representative of all the sectors of the organization. Each meeting of the job evaluation panel focuses on one section or department. The secretary provides copies of the job description to each member of the panel prior to the job evaluation meeting and records decisions of the job evaluation panel. The panel discusses and rates each job and the chairperson makes the final decision if they fail to reach consensus. A total score for each job is calculated by summing the panel ratings on each dimension of the job evaluation scale. The jobs are subsequently graded.

Step 8: Develop a salary structure

After each job has been graded, a salary structure, which accommodates present salaries within the range of reasonable, market-related salaries, must be developed. The first step is to plot current salaries of employees against the new job grades. A salary curve which gives the best representation of the data can be drawn. This can be done by calculating the linear regression, or by drawing a curve which best represents the data. The line of best fit will be the midpoint of the new scale. Salary ranges must be developed on each side of the salary scale. This range must accommodate most salaries within the grade, but must not be too wide. The salary range would normally be in the region of 10–20 per cent.

The following factors must also be considered before the scale can be finalized:

1   The scale must be in line with labour market data. National surveys could be consulted to find relevant market data and the scale should be adjusted.
2   The scale must conform to wage agreements, industrial legislation or be negotiated with the trade union. It is recommended that the salary scales are introduced at the time of a general increase or wage negotiations so that the organization can achieve the desired scales while adjusting salaries. Individual employees below the minimum should be given increases that will bring them to the minimum of the new scale. Employees above the maximum for a grade continue to receive standard increases while they are in those grades. They will be promoted or will leave the organization at some stage, and the salary curve of the organization would then be rectified.

Step 9: Communicate with employees

Employees should be notified verbally and in writing of their new grade and salary increase. They should also be informed how the grading system and salary structure operates and when increases will be given. Employees must receive a copy of their job description and be made aware that the job description may, in time, need to be altered and re-evaluated.

Step 10: Implement the system

The following should take place during implementation:

1   Salary increases should be awarded to employees.
2   New grades and salaries must be entered in the human resource records.
3   Procedures should be drawn up for job evaluation and updating of job descriptions.
4   A job evaluation manual should be distributed to personnel who need it.

Step 11: Maintain the job evaluation system

The job evaluation system should be maintained: that is, workable and documented procedures for its maintenance must exist.

INCENTIVE PAY SYSTEMS

Incentive pay plans attempt to relate pay to performance in an endeavour to reward above-average performance rapidly and directly. Although good performance can be rewarded through the salary structure – either by raising an individual's pay within the range of the job or by promoting the individual into a higher pay grade – these rewards are often subject to delays and other restrictions (Robbins and Judge, 2013). Such rewards are often not viewed by the employees as being directly related to performance. Incentive pay plans attempt to strengthen the performance–reward relationship and thus motivate the affected employees (Rynes et al, 2005).

The following basic requirements are necessary for an incentive plan to be effective:

- Employees must feel that their performance is accurately and fairly evaluated. Performance is easier to measure in some situations than others. The performance of a sales representative is easy to measure, while the performance of a middle manager is difficult to evaluate. It is difficult to quantify and measure some of the results that a manager must achieve.
- Incentives must be based on performance. Employees must believe that there is a relationship between what they do and what they get. Individual incentive plans require that the employees perceive a direct relationship between their performance and subsequent rewards. Group-based plans require employees to perceive a relationship between the group's performance and the subsequent rewards of group members.

An incentive plan can be effective in the long term. If it is only effective for a short time, there may be something wrong with the way in which it was implemented. Performance must be evaluated effectively and incentives must be based on the performance of employees. Therefore, delays and other restrictions in the implementation of the incentive plans must be prevented.

Individual incentives are based on the performance of the individual as opposed to the group or the organization. The advantage of the individual incentive systems is that the employees can readily see the relationship between what they do and what they get. With group and organization based plans, this relationship is often not so clear. The disadvantage of individual incentive systems is that they may cause competition between employees, which may have negative results (Rynes *et al.*, 2005). For example, sales personnel may not share their ideas with one another for fear that their peers might win a prize that is being offered to the top salesperson.

Because jobs are interdependent, it is sometimes difficult to isolate and evaluate individual performance. In these instances, it is wise to establish incentives based on group performance. For example, an assembly-line operator must work at the speed of the line. Thus, everyone working on the line is dependent on everyone else. With group incentives, all group members receive incentive pay based on the performance of the entire group. Many group incentive plans are based on factors such as profits or reductions in costs of operations.

Group incentive plans are designed to encourage employees to exert peer pressure on group members to perform. For instance, if a group member is not performing well and is lowering the production of the entire group, the group will usually pressurize the individual to improve, especially if a group incentive plan is in operation. A disadvantage of group incentives is that the members of the group may not perceive a direct relationship between their individual performance and that of the group (Rynes *et al.*, 2005). Organization-wide incentives reward members based on the performance of the entire organization. Group incentive systems include profit sharing and gain sharing, Scanlon-type plans, and employee stock ownership plans.

FOCUS 10.1

Scanlon-type plans

Scanlon-type plans provide employees with a bonus based on tangible savings in labour costs. These plans are designed to encourage employees to suggest changes that might increase productivity. Organizations establish departmental committees composed of management and employee representatives to discuss and evaluate proposed labour-saving techniques. Usually, the bonus paid is determined by comparing actual productivity with a predetermined productivity norm. Actual productivity is measured by comparing the actual payroll with the sales value of production for the time being measured. Any difference between actual productivity and the norm is placed in a bonus fund. Any cost savings are paid to all employees, not just the employees who made the suggestions.

SUMMARY

- Compensation is the human resource function that deals with every type of reward (financial and non-financial) that individuals receive in return for performing organizational tasks. The objective of compensation is to create a system of rewards that is equitable to the employee and the employer. Compensation should be adequate, equitable, cost effective, secure, incentive-providing and acceptable to the employee.
- Effective compensation administration is desirable in efforts to increase employee satisfaction and productivity. External influences on compensation systems include government, unions, economic conditions and the nature of the labour market. Internal influences on compensation systems include the labour budget and managerial pay strategies. Salary surveys are a valuable tool in determining the pay of employees. To ensure that salaries are internally fair, employers can compare jobs within the organization to determine their relative worth. Determining the value of a job is difficult because it involves measurement and subjective decisions. The use of systematic job evaluation procedures is recommended for determining a job's worth.
- The most important factors that influence the salary of an employee include the job content (as measured by job evaluation), the market value of the job and individual expertise. The market value of a job refers to the average wage or salary paid in a country, area or industry. The pay level of the individual is determined by expertise, that is, the qualifications and experience of the job incumbent.
- Incentive pay plans attempt to relate pay to performance in an endeavour to reward above-average performance rapidly and directly. Although good performance can be rewarded through the salary structure, either by raising an individual's pay within the range of the job or by promoting the individual into a higher pay grade, these rewards

are often subject to delays and other restrictions. Such rewards are often not viewed by the employees as being directly related to performance. Incentive pay plans attempt to strengthen the performance–reward relationship and thus motivate the affected employees (Rynes *et al.*, 2005).

KEY CONCEPTS AND TERMS

- Bonus
- Employee stock ownership plans
- Factor comparison method
- Financial compensation
- Group incentive
- Incentive pay system

- Job classification system
- Job evaluation
- Job grade
- Job ranking method
- Labour budget
- Stake
- Non-cash benefits
- Non-financial compensation

- Pay-level decision
- Pay-level strategy
- Plans based on saved time
- Point system
- Salary structure
- Scanlon-type plans
- Stock plans

SAMPLE ESSAY TITLES

- What are the differences between the job evaluation methods?
- What can an organization do to ensure fair payment?

FURTHER READING

Books

Armstrong, M., Cummins, A., Hastings, S. and Wood, W. (2003). *Job Evaluation: A Guide to Achieving Equal Pay*. London: Kogan Page.

Martocchio, J.J. (2014). *Strategic Compensation: A Human Resource Management Approach* (7th edn). Essex: Pearson Education.

Journal articles

Kahya, E. (2006). A revision of a job evaluation system. *Journal of Advanced Nursing*, 56, 314–324.

Treuren, G.J.M. and Frankish, E. (2014). The impact of pay understanding on pay satisfaction and retention: Salary sacrifice understanding in the not-for-profit sector. *Journal of Industrial Relations*, 56(1), 103–122.

11 Performance appraisal

This chapter introduces the reader to performance appraisal in organizations. The first section focuses on the definition of performance appraisal. The chapter then proceeds to the importance of performance appraisal for employees and organizations. We look at legislation affecting performance appraisal and the conditions for the successful implementation of performance appraisal (including a supportive philosophy and strategy of management, performance criteria and standards, establishing the system and performance appraisal methods). We also focus on the training of appraisers and describe the performance appraisal interview. Lastly, we will discuss guidelines for performance management.

LEARNING OUTCOMES

When you have completed this chapter you should be able to:

1 Define performance appraisal and discuss the importance thereof.
2 Discuss the uses of performance appraisal.
3 Describe the conditions for the successful implementation of a performance appraisal system.
4 Explain the content and methodology of a training programme for appraisers.
5 Discuss guidelines for performance management.

DEFINITION OF TERMS

Performance appraisal is a human resource management activity that is used to determine the extent to which an employee is performing the job effectively. It is a process of evaluation and documentation of personnel performance in order to make a judgement that leads to decisions regarding training and development, promotion, remuneration and selection (Gerber *et al.*, 1995).

In the past, organizations focused on performance appraisal. Currently, the focus is shifting to performance management (Cederblom and Pemerl, 2002). Performance management is a planned, systematic management system, which can be divided into a few integrated subsystems, directed at the improvement of individual, group and organizational effectiveness. The subsystems include the determination of performance objectives and standards, performance measurement, feedback and development of employees.

Performance management starts with the question, 'Which performance must be managed?' This has to do with where and what the organization wants to be and what it wants to achieve in the coming years. The long-term strategic plan is used to select the specific goals of the organization, and the behaviour that should be reinforced and rewarded to achieve the goals. Performance objectives, linked to the business plan, should be decided for each department and individual. Performance must be managed to bridge the gap between the current position (as shown by diagnosis) and desired position (as shown by the strategic plan) through the management of resistance to change.

Coaching and feedback form part of performance management (Latham and Mann, 2006). Feedback and coaching result in improved supervisor and employee relationships, increased commitment to the organization and reduced intentions to quit.

THE IMPORTANCE OF PERFORMANCE APPRAISAL

Performance management can be used to provide feedback about the strengths and weaknesses of employees, to distinguish between individuals to allocate rewards, to evaluate and maintain the human resource system of the organization (e.g. training and development, allocate rewards effectively) and to create a paper trail to document the reasons for certain actions, such as dismissing an employee.

Performance measurement and feedback are important for most individuals because they want to learn about themselves and find out whether they are making progress. Expectations can be made clear, employees can be managed more effectively and participative management practices can be established by using performance appraisal in the correct way. Satisfaction with performance appraisal might lead to high morale, motivation and productivity. Dissatisfaction with the system, however, may lead to decreased motivation, feelings of inequity and staff turnover (Mani, 2002).

Employees have conflicting goals concerning performance appraisal. They want to obtain the rewards and opportunities that come with favourable appraisals, so they present their performance in the best possible light, even denying problems or inflating accomplishments. When they want help with problems, they need to honestly share their difficulties. If they paint a very positive picture, they may not get the help they need. If they overemphasize their desire to improve, they risk giving the impression that they cannot do their jobs (Barnes-Farrell, 2001).

There is a conflict between the organization's and the individual's goals with performance appraisal. This can lead to feelings of ambivalence experienced by the manager and the employee. Accurate information is needed to allocate rewards and provide feedback, but employees may share only the most positive information for fear they will not be rewarded. Unpleasant interpersonal situations can arise because managers find it difficult to give negative feedback to poor performers.

Purposes of performance appraisal

The following purposes can be served with a well-designed, formal performance appraisal system:

- *Development*. Performance appraisal can determine which employees need more training and helps evaluate the results of training programmes.
- *Rewards*. Performance appraisal helps the organization decide who should receive pay rises and promotions.
- *Motivation*. Performance appraisal has a motivating effect because most employees want feedback about their performance.
- *Human resource planning*. Performance appraisal data are an important input to human resource planning.
- *Communication*. Performance appraisal is a basis for ongoing discussion between managers and employees about job-related matters.
- *Human resource management research*. Performance appraisal can be used to validate selection techniques (e.g. psychometric testing programmes).

LEGISLATION AFFECTING PERFORMANCE APPRAISALS

The performance appraisal process can serve as a tool to manage employee performance and to safeguard against litigation. In the USA, performance appraisal played an important role in cases involving personnel actions in organizations (Martin *et al.*, 2000). Performance appraisal practices are therefore subject to employment legislation (Werner and Bolino, 1997).

CONDITIONS FOR SUCCESSFUL IMPLEMENTATION OF PERFORMANCE APPRAISAL

Philosophy and strategy of management

The management of an organization has the following responsibilities regarding performance appraisal:

- They must be committed and actively manage the performance appraisal system.
- They should link the system to the strategy and policy of the organization and set specific objectives for the system.
- They should create a performance oriented climate.
- They have to maintain a participative, motivational approach. They must first focus the system on development of employees, and later on rewards.
- They should not regard performance management as a human resource function.

Performance criteria and standards

Performance appraisal should be based on the specific tasks that the employee accomplishes or fails to accomplish (Martin *et al.*, 2000). Performance standards should be narrow and job–focused (Arvey and Murphy, 1998). Performance standards can be determined by conducting a job analysis and a job description. An important part of the job description is to state the performance dimensions and standards expected from incumbents, as well as how it can be measured. Many things could be measured to determine performance. Although not often directly observed, individual characteristics combine with tasks and organization factors to produce behaviour that can be observed. Behaviour reflects an individual's attempts to perform; individual characteristics signal the causes of the behaviour.

The dimensions of performance against which an employee is evaluated are called the criteria of evaluation. Examples include quality of work, quantity of work and cost of work. One major problem of many performance appraisal methods is that they require supervisors to make person evaluations rather than performance appraisals. The criteria should be integrated with the strategy and business plans of the organization, and based on a job analysis. Multiple criteria, which include activities (e.g. the number of calls made) and results (e.g. value of sales), must be included. Focus 11.2 provides an overview of the different types of criteria which can be used in performance appraisal.

Criteria used in performance appraisal

- *Trait criteria*. Traits refer to observable dimensions of personality, such as initiative, friendliness and aggressiveness. Trait criteria are the most traditional performance criteria in use. Although they are convenient, they are poor criteria for performance appraisal. They confine the evaluator to making judgements strictly on ambiguous terms such as initiative, which result in unreliable appraisals among raters. Although traits may be potentially useful predictors of performance, situational and non-personality factors may also influence performance.

- *Behavioural criteria*. Behavioural criteria measure behaviour exhibited by the employee, such as asking subordinates for ideas and suggestions to solve job-related problems. These criteria permit the organization to specify the job behaviour relevant for getting the job done properly. These criteria are very useful for identifying employees' training and development needs, and communicating to them how they may improve their performance. Behavioural criteria are not useful for administrative purposes, because different behaviours may result in similar performance outcomes.

- *Output criteria*. Output criteria refer to the results of work such as sales or production volume and number of typing mistakes in a letter. Output criteria specify the employee's contribution to the achievement of organizational goals. These criteria are objective and there is little bias in evaluating someone's behaviour based on job results.

Output criteria are not useful for developmental purposes because they give little factual basis for suggesting how to improve performance. It is also difficult to obtain short-term output criteria for many jobs. The closer the relationship between the employee's performance and the outcome of that performance, the easier it is to invent output measures. Another problem with output measures is that situational factors, over which employees have little control, may affect their performance. Examples of situational factors are the quality of equipment available, the availability of materials, economic changes, budgetary support and co-operation of the people whose input is needed. The use of output measures as the only criteria may have the following negative effects on performance:

- It has a short rather than a long time-frame orientation.
- It may cause a results-at-any-cost mentality.
- It may lower the commitment of employees to the achievement of goals that are beyond their control.
- It may fail to let the employee know how to behave to maintain or increase performance.

It is essential to choose the objectives, standards and key performance areas in the performance measurement system and to give attention to the following aspects:

- It must be integrated with the strategy and business plans of the organization.
- Job analysis should be done to find performance dimensions and standards.
- Both behaviour and results (outputs) are important.
- Difficult objectives and standards must be established.
- It should be possible for individual behaviour to influence measurements.
- Limit key performance areas.
- Output/behaviour expectations and standards should be clear and quantifiable.

Establish the system

Top management must be involved and should participate in the establishment, evaluation and adjustment of the system. Performance management is a key performance area of every manager. Top, middle and first-level management are responsible for the management of the system. They assume ownership for the system, but ensure that it is carried over and shared. These people are important role models and should set the example. They will also be subjected to the system and process. Workers must be informed of the reasons for the system and how it works. It is important to involve them and give them a chance to participate so that they can identify with the system.

There are two decisions to be made regarding the timing of the appraisal. One is when to do it and the other is how often. In many organizations, performance evaluations are scheduled at arbitrary dates, such as the date the person was hired. Alternatively, each employee may be evaluated on or near a single calendar date. If the last alternative is selected, managers have to complete many performance evaluations on one day, which may lead them to quickly get it over with. It makes more sense to schedule the evaluation at the completion of a task or goal cycle. It seems better to conduct performance evaluations regularly.

Performance appraisal methods

A systematic process must be followed to ensure that accurate and reliable data are gathered. Users of appraisal systems often feel dissatisfied with these systems, not only because they are not valid, but also because they are not perceived as instruments that develop and motivate people (Latham and Mann, 2006). The requirements of a performance measurement system are given in Focus 11.3.

Evaluation against common performance standards

Three performance appraisal methods are based on evaluation against common standards. These methods are graphic rating scales, checklists and behavioural rating scales.

- *Graphic rating scales.* The rating scale requires the appraiser to rate the employee's performance among selected traits, behaviour or outputs on a descriptive scale that ranges from low performance to high performance. The outcome of the rating process produces a performance assessment on each performance category, and the ratings given for each standard can be summed to get an overall evaluation of performance. The use of graphic rating scales may result in evaluation errors. These scales are often low in job relatedness, reliability and validity.
- *Checklists.* Checklists are similar to graphic rating scales. Whereas the graphic rating scale uses traits as performance criteria, the checklist uses behaviour descriptions. In contrast to graphic rating scales, which are often not based on job analysis, checklists use the critical incident method of job analysis to arrive at the items for the scale. The rater is asked to specify agreement or disagreement with behavioural statements. Checklists vary in the degree of sophistication used in their development. A simple checklist may list ten to twenty items that are believed to reflect effective and ineffective job performance. In a weighted checklist the items are weighted in terms of their importance to job performance, as judged by those familiar with the job and its tasks. These checklists permit evaluations on each performance category to be summed for an overall performance assessment and allow employees to see their strengths and weaknesses along each performance category.

FOCUS 11.3

Requirements of a performance measurement system

- *Valid*: measures what it intends to measure.
- *Reliable*: measures accurately.
- *Objective*: applies clear procedures.
- *Standardized*: uses the same items for each worker.
- *Practical*: simple and easy to administer.

- *Behavioural rating scales.* Behavioural rating scales are called behaviourally anchored rating scales (BARS) or behavioural observation scales (BOS). Although these scales are similar to graphic rating scales, they are developed on the basis of a thorough analysis of the job and constructed in a sophisticated way. The critical incident method of job analysis is used to obtain information on effective and ineffective behaviour. The scales permit evaluation of overall performance by summing the scores obtained on each performance category. They also allow the identification of strengths and weaknesses in performance. BARS differ from BOS in the way the observed behaviour is scaled. In the BARS-scale, all behaviours are prefaced with the phrase 'could be expected to'. The intent of the phrase is to allow the appraiser to generalize what he or she has seen the employee do in the job situation to what the employee could be expected to do in a non-observed situation. BOS is a newer scale developed to overcome the complex judgements appraisers have to make in generalizing future behaviour by the BARS method. In the BOS, behaviour that measures similar concepts is grouped under a general behavioural performance category, called a performance dimension. Each behaviour is scaled from 1 to 5 and appraisers record how frequently they have observed the behaviour.

Evaluation against individualized performance standards

Appraisal systems that evaluate performance against individualized performance standards are called results-oriented, or output-oriented systems of performance management. Results-oriented systems take the organization's objectives for a given period and distribute them among the departments.

The following two methods evaluate performance against individualized performance standards: the direct index method and management by objectives.

- *The direct index method.* The direct index method is concerned with global outcomes of job performance. Global performance standards, which are derived from the job's required output, may be defined by the supervisor or negotiated between the supervisor and the employee. For example, a marketing job's required output may include performance goals regarding sales volume and profit from those sales. The level of performance for each goal is objectively defined, and numerical performance ratings reflecting each performance level for the goal are specified. Overall performance is determined by summing the numerical ratings.
- *Management by objectives (MBO).* MBO concerns itself with establishing goals for selected tasks whose performance is needed to attain departmental effectiveness in the short run. The MBO process consists of the following explicitly defined steps: a) set performance goals for a specified period; b) the supervisor and employee participate in goal setting; c) performance feedback. The MBO process starts with a meeting between the supervisor and each subordinate during which they agree on the major objectives of the employee's job for the next year and the performance outcomes required to achieve those objectives. The participative goal-setting process enables the supervisor to communicate the goals of the department to each employee and to discuss the ways he or she can contribute to departmental goal achievement. The supervisor and employee first assess the degree of success the employee had in achieving previous goals and the reasons for the

achievement or lack of achievement thereof. This helps to ensure that the work goals to be agreed upon are challenging but achievable, and are integrated with departmental goals and the career goals of the employee. The feedback step of MBO emphasizes the relationship between feedback and performance. Feedback influences performance when it is specific, timely, relevant and accepted by the employee.

Evaluation against others

The evaluation of employees against each other is important for making various decisions, such as who is ready for promotion. This leads to a rank order of employees according to their performance. Ranking is, however, of little use for employee feedback purposes, for compensation decisions and for identifying employee development needs. Ranking tells only who is the best and who is the worst, but it is difficult to determine the performance positions of the people in between.

Methods that evaluate employees against each other include simple ranking, paired comparison ranking and forced distribution.

- *Simple ranking.* Simple ranking is done by asking a judge to place a group of individuals in order of merit along some criterion. This process is easy at first, but gets harder. When the appraiser cannot distinguish between employees, a tie rank can be given to both.
- *Paired comparison ranking.* In the paired comparison method appraisers compare every possible pair of individuals on overall performance or against specific standards. The names of all people to be ranked are written on separate cards. The appraiser selects two names, compares them with the criterion in question and places the 'loser' in

FIGURE 11.1 The evaluation of employees against each other is important for making various decisions, such as who is ready for promotion

Source: © Michael D. Brown/Shutterstock.com

a new pile. The 'winner' and a new person are then compared. The process is repeated until all employees have been ranked from first place to last.

- *Forced distribution*. Forced distribution is a ranking method that requires the appraiser to distribute the employees to be ranked into specified performance categories. The appraiser can place the employees into one of five categories of performance. The proportion of employees to be placed in each category is also decided beforehand.

Selecting a performance appraisal method

All the performance appraisal methods are used regularly. The graphic rating scale is the most widely used technique. Management by objectives is used for managerial, professional and technical employees, not production and office personnel. It seems that the major problems are not with the techniques themselves, but how they are used and by whom. The appraiser is more crucial than the technique in developing effective measurement systems.

Traditionally, traits were used to measure the performance of employees. Frequently, these traits have no relationship with concrete behaviour. It is difficult to link rewards and development plans to this method. Sometimes a single rating of total job performance is used to measure performance and employees are compared with each other. It is difficult to use this method for feedback, development and goal-setting. Behaviourally anchored rating scales are used to measure observable behaviour, which leads to an improved task definition. Behavioural observation scales were found to be superior to all other appraisal methods in terms of eliciting favourable reactions (Latham and Mann, 2006). Objective-oriented methods (management by objectives) focus on predetermined goals and improve the objective measurement of results. The emphasis is on performance, not on the individual, and therefore this method is less emotional.

A results-oriented system can encourage behaviour that is functional for evaluation, but dysfunctional for organizational effectiveness. An activity-oriented system motivates activities rather than the accomplishment of results (objectives). A good performance measurement system measures activities (inputs).

Reward for performance

The integration of rewards with the performance management system should take place after two to three years of using the system. Compensation should be aimed at the acknowledgement and reward of 'correct behaviour and inputs'. Extrinsic and intrinsic rewards should be used. Non-financial compensation and recognition should form part of the system. The system should measure performance accurately and should lead to fair compensation. The total compensation administration of the organization should be healthy.

TRAINING OF APPRAISERS

Training in performance management and appraisal is essential for all managers and supervisors. Studies showed that trained raters were more accurate than untrained raters (Arvey and Murphy, 1998).

Content of appraiser training

Researchers distinguish between training in the mechanics and dynamics of performance appraisal. Training in the mechanics of the performance management system includes the use of performance appraisal forms. Training in the dynamics of performance appraisal includes the establishment and communication of performance standards, writing clear and measurable objectives, interpersonal skills, conflict management, rating errors, observation and measurement of performance, giving feedback, and the performance appraisal interview. Topics that could be included in the training are shown in Focus 11.4.

Performance feedback

Appraisers must learn that ongoing feedback is the most important factor in maintaining or improving employee performance. The supervisor has the opportunity to observe the employee's performance, discuss that performance and, if necessary, help the employee to improve that performance.

Rating errors

Appraiser bias is regarded as one of the problems associated with performance appraisal. Latham and Mann (1996) summarize some of the recent research findings regarding appraiser bias as follows:

- Ratings were a stronger reflection of raters' overall biases than true performance factors.
- Supervisors' positive regard for subordinates results in leniency and halo errors, and less inclination to punish poor performance.
- Gender and race bias play a role when ratings are made. Men are rated as more effective than women. Blacks and Asians are rated as less effective than whites.

FOCUS 11.4

Content of appraiser training

- The underlying management philosophy of the system.
- The underlying values of the system.
- Techniques used in the system.
- Negotiation of goals and communication of standards.
- Human relations aspects.
- Preparation of employees for performance appraisal.
- Handling of performance appraisal problems.
- Feedback interviews.
- Discussing low performance with workers.
- Observing and recording skills and rating errors.
- Performance dimensions and standards.
- Linking performance with rewards.
- Administrative aspects.

Ratings errors reduce the reliability, validity and utility of the performance appraisal system (Roberts, 1998). Therefore, raters should be aware of rating errors. The most common appraiser errors are reported in Focus 11.5.

The ability to identify and define rating errors should minimize their occurrence. Raters should know that they could prevent errors by justifying and recording their ratings (Feldman, 1992). According to Latham and Mann (2006), appraiser bias can be solved by finding ways to increase user acceptance of the appraisal process, basing appraisals on multiple sources, and training observers not only to be objective but also to coach employees throughout the year.

Evaluating performance

Although many organizations say that they teach supervisors and managers in performance appraisal, they usually merely train them on how to fill in the performance appraisal form. Supervisors are instructed to make sure that the appraisals they give to their employees are normally distributed. This type of training is inconsistent with the goals of performance appraisal. Effective training should teach appraisers to increase their rating accuracy and not to distribute the ratings along a normal curve.

FOCUS 11.5

The most common rating errors

- *Halo effect*. An extremely good or poor rating in one performance category induces the appraiser to give correspondingly good or poor ratings on all the other performance categories.
- *Central tendency*. The employee's ratings on all performance standards cluster around the middle point of the rating scale. Although most people are average performers overall, most can also be differentiated along specific performance standards. Giving average ratings can be unfair towards outstanding performers.
- *Leniency rating effects*. The appraiser rates everyone on the positive end of the rating scale regardless of actual levels of performance.
- *Strict rating effects*. The appraiser rates everyone lower than their actual level of performance.
- *Recency effects*. The appraiser is influenced by the employee's most recent positive or negative behaviour.
- *Similar/dissimilar to me effect*. People tend to like others who hold similar opinions, values and attitudes and behave similarly under similar conditions. The appraiser may positively appraise employees who are similar to him or her and negatively appraise those who are different.
- *Initial/first impressions*. An appraiser forms an initially positive or negative impression of the employee and ignores any subsequent information that may distort that first impression.

The performance appraisal interview

Supervisors and managers must be trained how to conduct the performance appraisal interview.

Methodology of performance appraisal training

Case studies and video material of different jobs must be discussed with managers and supervisors and they must prove that they can assess performance accurately. Adequate opportunities for practice must be given. Frequent discussions of ways to overcome rating errors take place. It is not enough to make trainees aware of rating errors. They must practise ways to overcome rating errors and should receive feedback on their performance. Inter-rater reliability in respect of different case studies should be determined to get the ratings to an acceptable level of accuracy. Special attention must be given to trainees who rate too high or too low.

Training alone will probably not solve performance appraisal problems. Unless raters are motivated to use the system effectively and unless they are given the opportunity for observing their subordinates' performance, performance appraisal errors will not be solved.

ACTIVITY 11.1

Performance appraisal training

Why would training in how to conduct performance appraisals be an important issue for organizations to consider?

SOURCES OF APPRAISAL

Supervisors, peers, subordinates and the employees themselves could be involved in the appraisal. Based on the work of Latham and Mann (2006), the research findings regarding the different appraisers can be summarized as follows:

- *Supervisory appraisals*. A subordinate's performance tends to increase in years when performance appraisals take place. However, supervisors spend little time on the appraisals of their subordinates. Poor appraisals result when the supervisor had limited opportunity to observe the behaviour of a subordinate, and when the subordinate is hostile towards the supervisor. The supervisor's role should be to gather data and to make a final decision about the appraisal of a subordinate after gathering data from multiple sources.
- *Peer appraisals*. Peer appraisal is regarded as a reliable source of performance information. Peers tend to place more emphasis on interpersonal relationships and motivation than on task performance. However, inadequate instruments are often

used to do appraisals. They are seen as useful when they are done with behaviour observation scales.

- *Self-appraisals.* There is a poor relationship between self-appraisals and appraisals of others. Employees tend to rate their performance more favourably than their supervisors. Cross-cultural differences seem to exist between Eastern cultures and Western cultures. In Eastern cultures, self-criticism is regarded as an important way to improve performance. It seems that individuals with a high self-esteem tend to seek self-verifying feedback, even if it is negative, while individuals with a low self-esteem seek positive feedback.
- *Subordinate appraisals.* Anonymous feedback from subordinates tends to promote positive changes in a supervisor's behaviour and performance. Subordinates who were not allowed to provide anonymous feedback viewed appraisals more negatively than those who were allowed to provide anonymous feedback.

THE PERFORMANCE APPRAISAL INTERVIEW

It is a demotivating experience for an employee to receive an unexpected negative appraisal rating (Roberts, 1998). Research has shown that many performance appraisal interviews have the following effects:

- Employees feel more uncertain where they stand after the interview than was the case before the interview.
- Many employees evaluate their supervisors less favourably after the interview (than before it).
- The interview is sometimes conducted in an authoritarian way, which is inconsistent with democratic values.
- The interview does not lead to constructive behaviour change.

Research shows that interview effectiveness will increase when the interview is approached in a problem-solving manner. This includes setting a climate in which the supervisor and subordinate discuss the performance goals and standards, and the employee's performance relative to these goals or standards. A problem-solving approach encourages employees to think about their job problems in a non-threatening atmosphere and to provide their own solutions to encountered performance problems. Participation by the employee is one of the most important factors influencing the success of the review.

Evaluation should not be viewed as a once-a-year completion of rating forms. To help with this communication, the manager should hold an appraisal interview with each subordinate to discuss the appraisal and to set objectives for the upcoming appraisal period. Experts advise that employee development and salary action discussions should not occur in the same interview.

The effectiveness of the interview will be increased when the supervisor or manager prepares for the interview. Preparation for the interview includes reviewing:

- *The performance appraisal format.* He or she must be able to explain the rating scales, how the ratings are derived, and how the numbers on the rating scales are related to performance standards used on the measure.

- *The employee's performance*. He or she must be able to answer any employee questions and to justify the rating given to the employee.
- *Knowledge of the self*. The supervisor or manager must review his or her own strengths and weaknesses in interacting with people, in particular the ability to give negative feedback in a constructive manner.

The following behaviour may lead to effective performance appraisal interviews:

- *Structure and control the interview*. The purpose of the interview must be stated, control over the interview must be maintained, and an organized and prepared approach must be shown. No interruptions should occur during the interview. The employee should be oriented towards future performance by emphasizing the development of strengths. Ways to accomplish performance improvements should be discussed. At the end of the interview, a summary should be provided of all the major points.
- *Establish and maintain rapport*. An appropriate climate for the interview must be set, the interview must be opened in a warm and non-threatening manner, and the supervisor or manager must be sensitive to the needs and feelings of the employee.
- *Reacting to stress*. The interviewer must remain cool and calm during an employee's outbursts, apologize when appropriate (without retreating unnecessarily) and maintain composure and perspective.
- *Obtain information*. The interviewer must ask appropriate questions, probe to ensure that meaningful issues are discussed and seek meaningful information. The interviewer should focus on a limited number of topics so that each topic can be discussed comprehensively. Work goals should be reviewed and attainable objectives should be set.
- *Provide feedback*. The focus should be on facts rather than opinions and evidence should be available to document the claims. The manager should open with specific positive remarks, be specific regarding performance shortcomings and orient the discussion to performance comments, not personal criticisms. The manager should guard against overwhelming the employee with information. Too much information can be confusing, while too little information can be frustrating. Probably no more than one or two negative points should be brought up at one evaluation. The handling of negative comments is critical. They should be phrased specifically and be related to performance. Conclude with positive comments and total evaluation results.
- *Resolve conflict*. The interviewer should manage the conflict in the interview, make appropriate commitments and set realistic goals to ensure conflict resolution.
- *Develop the employee*. The interviewer should offer to help the employee develop his or her career plans, specify development needs and recommend sound developmental actions.
- *Motivate the employee*. The interviewer should provide incentives for the employee to stay with the organization and perform effectively, provide commitments to the employee to encourage high performance levels and support the employee's excellent performance.

THE PERSONAL MANAGEMENT INTERVIEW

The personal management interview is an application of which consists of an initial, one-time only role negotiation meeting, and a regular, one-on-one, on-going interview meeting between a manager and his or her direct reports (Cameron, 2014). There should be an on-going programme of regular, one-to-one interviews between a manager and each of his or her direct reports. This interview should take place regularly and privately. Its major goals are continuous improvement, team building and personal development, and feedback. The first agenda item should be to follow up on action items from the previous session. Agenda for the meeting (which lasts from 45 to 60 minutes) are organizational and job issues, information sharing, training and development, resource needs, interpersonal issues, obstacles to improvement, targets and goals, appraisal and feedback, and personal issues (Cameron, 2014).

SUMMARY

- Performance appraisal is a human resource management activity that is used to determine the extent to which an employee is performing the job effectively.
- A well-designed performance appraisal system can serve various purposes, namely developmental, reward, motivational, human resource planning, communication and human resource management research purposes.
- The successful implementation of performance appraisal is affected by the philosophy and strategy of management, performance criteria and standards, the way in which the system is established, the methods used to appraise performance, the link between rewards and performance, and the training of appraisers.
- Training in performance management and appraisal is essential for all managers and supervisors. Trained raters are more accurate than untrained raters.
- Supervisors, peers, subordinates and the employees themselves could be involved in the appraisal.
- It is a demotivating experience for an employee to receive an unexpected negative appraisal rating. It seems that interview effectiveness will increase when the interview is approached in a problem-solving manner. Participation by the employee is one of the most important factors influencing the success thereof.
- Performance appraisal should not be viewed as a once-a-year completion of rating forms. The manager should hold an appraisal interview with each subordinate to discuss his or her appraisal and to set objectives for the upcoming appraisal period. Employee development and salary action discussions should not occur in the same interview.
- Performance management is a planned, systematic management system that can be divided into a few integrated subsystems, directed at the improvement of individual, group and organizational effectiveness. The subsystems include the determination of performance objectives and standards, performance measurement, feedback and development of employees. Coaching and feedback form part of performance management.

ACTIVITY 11.2

Forced ranking: friend or foe?

Jack Welch, retired Chief Executive Officer of General Electric (GE), is associated with forced ranking. GE annually used this performance management tool to eliminate the bottom 10 per cent of employees who were rated as poor/low performers by means of the forced ranking system.

Forced ranking systems are performance evaluation programmes under which managers rank employees against each other, and then use the rankings to determine who receives rises, rewards, bonuses, promotion and, in some instances, who is terminated (www.aarp.org/work/employee-benefits/info-2006/forced_ranking_systems.hmtl). Predetermined percentages of employees are forced into categories, sometimes designated by letter grades such as A, B and C; in other cases the categories are numerical, and in others there are labels such as 'superior' and 'needs improvement'. The distribution typically follows a bell-shaped curve with 10 or 20 per cent in the top category, 70 or 80 per cent in the middle and 10 per cent in the bottom. The top-ranked employees are considered 'high-potential' employees and are often targeted for a more rapid career path and leadership development programmes. In stark contrast, those ranked at the bottom are denied bonuses and increases. They may be given a probationary period to improve their performance but are often terminated if they fail to show improvement.

Fans of forced ranking argue that ranking employees enables companies to reward top performers, eliminate unproductive workers and raise the overall level of productivity. On the other hand, its critics assert that forced ranking creates an overly competitive workplace where employee co-operation and teamwork are replaced with ruthless competition to outrank and outlast co-workers.

The AARP argues that one of the most common criticisms of forced ranking systems is that the criteria used to rank employees are not objective and, consequently, are subject to bias. The forced ranking systems adopted by Ford, Goodyear, General Electric, Conoco, Microsoft, Capital One and Sprint all have been challenged as being designed to get rid of workers of a specific race, age or gender rather than poor performers.

Debate the pros and cons of forced ranking as a performance evaluation system. Which ethical challenges might be inflicted by this method?

For more opinions and information visit:
www.aarp.org/work/employee-benefits/info-2006/forced_ranking_systems.html
www.businessweek.com/careers/content/feb2007/ca20070212_272450.htm
Why 'Forced' Job Rankings Don't Work by Liz Ryan
edweb.sdsu.edu/people/arosset/pie/Interventions/forcedranking_1.htm
Performance Management: Forced Ranking by Charlotte A. Donaldson

KEY CONCEPTS AND TERMS

- Appraiser training
- Behavioural criteria
- Behavioural rating scale
- Central tendency
- Checklist
- Coaching
- Direct index method
- First impression
- Forced distribution
- Graphic rating scale
- Halo effect
- Management by objectives
- Output criteria
- Paired comparison ranking
- Peer appraisal
- Performance appraisal
- Performance appraisal interview
- Performance criteria
- Performance management
- Rating errors
- Recency effects
- Self-appraisal
- Simple ranking
- Strict rating
- Subordinate appraisal
- Supervisory appraisal
- Trait criteria

SAMPLE ESSAY TITLES

- What are the content and methodology of a training programme in performance appraisal for managers?
- What are the advantages and disadvantages of the different performance appraisal methods?
- Which method could be used for the appraisal of performance of sales staff?

FURTHER READING

Books

Aguinis, H. (2014). *Performance Management* (3rd edn). Essex: Pearson Education.

Journal articles

DeNisi, A. and Smith, C.E. (2014). Performance appraisal, performance management, and firm-level performance: A review, a proposed model, and new directions for future research, *The Academy of Management Annals*, 8(1), 27–179.

Haines III, V.Y. and St-Onge, S.(2012). Performance management effectiveness: Practices or context? *The International Journal of Human Resource Management*, 23(6), 1158–1175.

12 Career development

This chapter introduces the reader to the topic of career development. The first section focuses on the definition of terms such as career development, career planning and career management. The chapter then proceeds to the importance of career development. We also look at career theories, and the role of life and career stages in career development. The third section looks at career success. This is followed by a discussion of career planning and career management as components of career development. Lastly, we focus on the evaluation of career management.

LEARNING OUTCOMES

When you have completed this chapter you should be able to:

1 Define career, career development, career planning and career management, and discuss the importance of career development.
2 Evaluate theories of career development.
3 Define life stages, career stages and career success, and the role they play in career development.
4 Discuss career planning as a component of career development.
5 Discuss career management as a component of career development.
6 Point out the importance of evaluating career development.

DEFINITION OF TERMS

A career is a sequence of positions/jobs/occupations held by one person over his or her entire working life. The word 'career' comes from the Latin for 'carriageway' or roadway on which the Roman charioteers drove their chariots. Hall (1976) defines a career as 'the individually perceived sequence of attitudes and behaviours associated with work-related experiences over the span of the person's work life'. The term career is also associated with paid employment, or at the least self-employment. If we take this view, then you might very well think of other types of careers. What about the career of a house-person who does not work outside the home, but who is in charge of the smooth running of a household? Is this a case of paid employment or not? What about the career of the professional criminal or thief? Does such a person really have a career?

Career development encompasses career planning and the implementation of career plans by means of education, training, job search and acquisition, and work experiences. From the perspective of the organization, career development is the process of guiding the placement, movement and growth of employees through assessment, planned training activities and planned job assignments. Therefore, career development includes both personal career planning and organizational career management (Armstrong and Taylor, 2014).

Career planning is a personal process through which workers plan their work life by identifying and implementing steps to attain career goals. Career planning includes evaluating one's own abilities and interests, examining career opportunities, setting career goals and planning appropriate developmental activities. Career planning is mainly an individual process, but the employing organization can assist through career counselling offered by the work and organizational psychologists and supervisors. More specifically, organizations can present workshops to assist workers in evaluating themselves and in deciding on developmental programmes by making career planning workbooks available to interested workers, and by disseminating information about jobs within and outside the organization.

ACTIVITY 12.1

Relationship between human resource planning and career development

What is the relationship between human resource planning, career development, personal career planning and organizational career planning?

Career management, the other subset of career development, focuses on plans and activities of the organization (Armstrong and Taylor, 2014). In career management the management of the organization matches individual employee career plans with organizational needs and implements programmes to accomplish these joint objectives.

THE IMPORTANCE OF CAREER DEVELOPMENT

Recent changes in career patterns are mainly because of external factors, such as globalization, rapid technological changes, labour market deregulation and changes in organizational structures (Kidd, 2002: 179). Often skilled workers have been displaced because of automation. Deregulation in the UK and USA reduced job security and increased the need to adapt to more flexible forms of working. In addition, employability (regularly updating knowledge and skills) became important, because life-long employment is no longer guaranteed.

In general, workers want interesting and meaningful work, and they want to utilize and develop their skills and abilities. Career development actions enable both an individual and the organization that employs him or her to meet these expectations. Depending on the state of the economy, many workers change organizations quite a few times during their working lives. This emphasizes the important role that career planning plays in an individual's life.

The importance of career development can also be deduced from other reasons for career development in organizations. If an organization pays the necessary attention to the career development of employees, it will be able to attract the required qualified workers because the word quickly travels around. Many qualified people would like to be employed by such organizations. It also leads to lower turnover among employees, because they now see that their expectations are being met. Employees tend to be more productive and to perform better when their abilities are being utilized more fully.

CAREER THEORY

Person–environment fit

Person–environment fit refers to the degree of congruence between workers and their environments. Applying this perspective to career planning implies that reliable and valid data should be gathered regarding individual differences (such as abilities, interests, personality and values) and jobs. Person–environment fit is positively related to employee well-being and negatively related to employee discontent (Tinsley, 2000). Person–environment fit is measured in terms of rewards sought by the individual and satisfaction offered, as well as between individual abilities and the demands of the work. The following theories focus on person–environment fit:

- *The Minnesota theory of work adjustment* (Dawis and Lofquist, 1984). Work adjustment refers to the process by which an individual seeks to achieve and maintain correspondence with the work environment. This model focuses on rewards sought and abilities used.
- *The attraction–selection–attrition (ASA) model* (Schneider *et al.*, 1995). The ASA model suggests that organizational homogeneity increases over time through three stages. In the first stage, called 'attraction', people who hold values similar to those espoused by the organization are attracted towards the organization as potential employees. In the second stage, called 'selection', the organization actively chooses the applicants who are perceived to be most similar to the employees already in the organization. Finally, the third stage, called 'attrition', occurs when employees realize that they are not as similar to the organization as was once believed. The result of these three stages is that the personal values and preferences of the people within an organization should grow more similar over time. Fit, according to this theory, is a result of recruitment and selection of limited people.

- *The theory of vocational choice* (Holland, 1997). Holland's theory proposed that individuals seek occupational environments that are congruent with their vocational interests. Individuals can be classified in terms of six personality types, namely realistic, investigative, artistic, social, enterprising and conventional. Work settings can also be categorized according to this model. Because individuals search for environments that allow them to express their interests, skills, attitudes and values, and take on interesting problems and agreeable roles, work environments become populated by individuals with related occupational personality types.

The role of life stages in career development

The term 'career development' implies a developmental process. It is a fact that developmental psychology and individual differences form two of the three bases of career development. The third basis is the fact that positions/jobs/occupations also differ from one another because they place different demands on people and they 'compensate' people in different ways.

A few years back, developmental psychology did not play a major role in career development. There were two reasons for this. First, much emphasis in developmental psychology was placed on the development of children and adolescents. It was only later that researchers also started looking into the development of adults. Second, researchers concentrated to a large degree on the matching of individual differences with the differences between jobs. However, it is obvious that both individuals and jobs change over time.

Developmental psychologists have established that most people move through a sequence of 'orderly' life stages. There are different ways of describing these life stages. One way to classify life stages is in terms of stages such as early childhood, middle childhood, late childhood, early adolescence, middle adolescence, late adolescence, the youth stage, early adulthood, middle adulthood and late adulthood. Daniel Levinson (1978) also identified transition stages or life structures which can be found when, for instance, a person moves from early adulthood to middle adulthood (or midlife). It is important to take note of these life stages because each stage brings its own issues that an individual has to face and tasks that have to be carried out.

Even though many of the tasks and issues that an individual has to face have to do with a person's own development (for instance, partaking in sporting activities or hobbies) and with family issues, these tasks and issues are often intertwined with career tasks and issues. This is because everyone is a 'whole' person. The main implication of viewing an employee as a 'whole' person is that organizations should take note of the fact that much of what happens at work influences the family and personal life of an employee. This, for instance, means that if an organization deems it necessary to transfer an employee to another town or city, the management should consider what the influence of such a relocation will be on the employee's family and on the employee's personal adjustment.

The role of career stages in career development

Running parallel to life stages, but not quite identical to them, are different career stages. As in the case of life stages, there are models or approaches to identifying and describing these career stages. Even more than in the case of life stages, not every person's career stages perfectly fit the different career stages one supposedly moves through. An individual has to a certain degree more 'influence' over his or her career than over his or her life stages. One's career is also more open to influences such as the state of the economy and the profitability of the organization for which one works.

Career choice

Career choice is a developmental process. This means that there may even be substages in occupational choice. This is not hard to understand. Take, for instance, a young boy who wishes to be a firefighter because he sees it as an exciting job, or the young girl who wishes to be a nurse at all costs. Once they start growing older, they realize that these jobs may not be as glamorous as they first thought them to be. They also start to notice that they are better at certain tasks than at others. A little later they realize that they need to look earnestly at an occupation that matches their skills, abilities and personality characteristics. In the occupational choice stage a person moves through the substages of fantasy, realism and specification.

The individual should understand him- or herself as well as the world of work very well to make a meaningful occupational choice. This means that he or she should have self-insight regarding his or her needs, abilities, interests and personality characteristics. Such an individual should also have knowledge of different occupations and the requirements that should be met to successfully practise those occupations.

Once an occupational choice is made, preparation to enter that occupation is needed. This may take on many different forms. One of these forms can be the choice of specific school/college/university subjects. It can be in the form of doing some kind of apprenticeship. Some people view occupational choice and preparing for the world of work as one big career stage.

The next (sub-)career stage may be that of finding a position/job and entering the world of work by joining an organization or by becoming self-employed. This has become one of the major tasks young people have to accomplish, considering the loose labour market that exists. The individual should have qualified him- or herself to enter the chosen occupation. Such an individual should also know where to look for possible job openings and how to write a letter of application, complete an application form, compile a curriculum vitae and act during a selection interview.

The early career

The next big career stage is that of the early career. Some people view this stage as consisting of two main substages, namely the stage of becoming established in the world of work and the achievement stage. This early career runs somewhat parallel to that of the life stage of early adulthood. It is important to note that the time that an individual has to establish him- or herself in the world of work roughly corresponds with the time the person in early adulthood is likely to get married and start a family. This places quite a burden on a person. Most people at that stage of life also have the energy, vigour and enthusiasm that it takes to accomplish these tasks.

An individual who finds him- or herself in the establishment stage should show willingness to learn and to work hard. Such a person should try to fit into the organization and into the way things are done. At the same time he or she should also show initiative and a willingness to make a contribution to the organization. He or she should also keep in mind that in the beginning he or she is, in a certain sense, 'on probation' and that other organizational members are busy trying to decide whether he or she will be a worthy member of the organization.

One of the most important things an organization can do is to present the new-comer with challenging work as soon as it is possible. In this way the new employee can test him- or herself. At the same time the organization can get an indication of whether the new employee will be able to make a contribution to the organization in the long run. It is also important that the organization gives the individual some feedback on performance.

Note that we talk about the substage of achievement, rather than the substage of advancement. Achievement might lead to advancement, but sometimes this is not the case. A person might perform in such a way that he or she is eligible for promotion, but it is not forthcoming because the promotional channels might be blocked or clogged by more senior personnel. This condition is aggravated by the processes of downsizing and rightsizing, and by the fact that organizational structures nowadays tend to be much 'flatter' than in previous times. If a person at this stage does not want to leave the organization, other ways will have to be found to keep him or her interested and productive.

Midcareer

The next career stage is that of midcareer, which roughly corresponds with the life stage of middle adulthood. Some people especially find moving from the last part of early adulthood to the first part of middle adulthood a very trying time. Some people call this the midlife transition, or even the midlife crisis. A person facing a midlife crisis is likely to ask him- or herself many questions. Some of these questions might be: 'Why am I working so hard?'; 'Is there more to life than work?'; 'Have I been neglecting my family?'. The person in midcareer starts to question things again. Not every person experiences a midlife crisis. This means that there is nothing wrong with someone who does not experience a midlife crisis. On the other hand, there is nothing 'abnormal' about experiencing a midlife crisis either.

Many people at this stage ask themselves questions that are associated with work/careers. This is the time for a person to do some stocktaking concerning the career goals that he or she set him- or herself at the start of his or her career. A person in this stage realizes that there is only so much time left to accomplish certain tasks or to reach certain goals. For the first time, many people really become aware of the fact that they are mortal beings, whose life might end sooner than they might think. No wonder, then, that some people talk about people experiencing a midcareer crisis. An organization can make counselling facilities available to employees who wish to use such a service.

One of the main tasks of the midcareer stage is to stay productive in a job and to strive to update skills. If the latter does not happen, a person's skills become obsolete. An individual should always try to keep up with developments and changes in his or her field of specialization or employment. An organization could assist workers to upgrade their knowledge and skills on a continuous basis. Another task is to handle the reaching of a possible plateau in a career. When a worker reaches a plateau, it means that he or she cannot advance further in the organization. It may be due to changes in the person, such as the lack of (updated) skills or the loss of speed, and the like.

Sometimes the plateau is caused by organizational factors, such as a lack of promotional opportunities.

The late career

The final career stage is that of the late career. Because more people opt for early retirement or receive severance packages before reaching retirement age, many people do not really reach this stage in organizations. For those who do, there are two main tasks to be accomplished in this stage. The one task is basically the same as that of the middle career stage, namely to still be productive in a person's work. This again implies that a person needs to ensure that his or her skills remain up to date. The other main task is that of adequately preparing for retirement.

Adequate preparation for retirement takes on many forms. Financial planning for retirement should actually start in the early career. If one leaves it until late career, it is usually too late to really do anything about it. When preparing to retire, the worker should look into aspects such as housing, medical care, relations with friends and relatives, and one's state of health. Psychological preparation for retirement is perhaps one of the most important, but often also one of the most neglected, aspects.

When thinking about psychologically preparing for retirement, a person must remember that work plays an important role in the lives of most people. By working, a person ensures a livelihood for him- or herself and for their dependants. But work also fulfils other needs. Here one can think of such needs as the need for social interaction, the need to make a meaningful contribution to society, the need to keep busy and to make use of one's abilities and skills, and perhaps even to fill the time that is available. When someone retires, work ceases to fulfil these needs. Something else will then have to fulfil these needs, and the person will have to reorientate him- or herself to the new situation.

Career success

In the past it was assumed that a person was successful in his or her career when he or she had a job that was paying a good salary and having a high status (Armstrong and Taylor, 2014). Other signs of career success were the fact that a person was moving upwards to positions of greater responsibility. At the same time the person was a loyal employee and the organization rewarded the person in different ways for his or her hard work and dedication. In some instances, this scene has drastically changed. The changing nature of the workforce can also be seen in a difference in orientation with regard to career success. Nowadays, people place much more emphasis on personal freedom, self-determination and a personal view of career success.

This new orientation regarding career success manifests itself in the following ways (Ivancevich and Konapaske, 2013):

- The individual wants to control his or her own career development, by deciding when or whether to undergo additional training/acquire additional skills, to apply for particular positions/jobs and when to leave the organization.
- Personal values, such as freedom, growth and self-determination, play an important role in any career decision that an individual makes.

- The individual wants to maintain a healthy balance between involvement in work/career, with family and friends and his or her own developmental activities (such as the practising of sport or hobbies).
- Each individual has his or her own view of what it takes and what it means to be successful. This means that career success is a very personal thing. It might still be the attainment of a senior position in an organization or receiving a fat pay cheque. On the other hand, it might be something like experiencing personal freedom, experiencing self-respect or being heavily involved in non-work activities.

All that has been said so far implies that the person who wishes to experience career success will have to play an important and active role in his or her own career planning and personal career management. Such a person does not wait for the organization to do something about his or her career development, but assumes full responsibility for his or her destiny, as far as it is under his or her own control.

Career planning as a component of career development

Career planning is defined as the personal process of planning one's own work life. It was also pointed out, however, that an organization can, in different ways, assist an individual with personal career planning. Bearing in mind that it is important to match an individual's personal career planning with the career management efforts of the organization, the way in which this assistance is presented plays an important role in career development.

The primary responsibility for career planning lies with the individual concerned. Only the individual can know what he or she wants out of his or her career. This means that career planning is to a large degree an individualized and personalized process, and that each employee should develop his or her own career plan. An individual should take the necessary time and put in the necessary effort to develop a sound career plan. An organization can and actually should assist an individual in career planning. There are different ways of going about this. Another party that plays an important role in an individual's career planning is the immediate supervisor or manager of the particular individual. It is suggested that an organization should prepare a supervisor/manager to efficiently play this role.

The individual should develop a personal career plan. This involves four steps, namely (Byars and Rue, 2011):

- an assessment by the individual of his or her other abilities, interests and career goals;
- an assessment by the organization of the individual's abilities and potential;
- communication of career options and opportunities within the organization, and
- career counselling to set realistic goals and plans for their accomplishment.

When an individual engages in career self-management, he or she usually has some decision to make regarding his or her career. In order to make this decision, he or she should first do some career exploration. This means that he or she should find out more about him- or herself, and about the opportunities and demands presented by the world of work. On the basis of this, the individual should set career goals and identify different strategies that can be followed to reach these goals.

Once a decision has been made on strategies, these strategies should be implemented. One such strategy might be to perform as best as someone can in his or her present job. Once a strategy is implemented, the individual must use the feedback received from work and non-work sources to make the necessary adjustments in the strategy being followed. For instance, the individual's supervisor might be pleased that the individual puts in a lot of overtime and rewards him or her for doing this. On the other hand, the individual's family, at the same time, may rebuke him or her for not spending enough time with them.

An organization could play the following roles in assisting an employee with career planning (Armstrong and Taylor, 2014):

- *Assisting the individual in appraising him- or herself.* Individuals can be assisted in appraising themselves by providing them with different career planning workbooks. The purpose of these workbooks is to let the individual engage in self-exploration and self-assessment. The individual should be assisted in identifying his or her own strengths and weaknesses, abilities, skills and interests. Besides completing the workbooks, the individual might also be assisted in taking aptitude, interest and personality tests in order to learn more about him- or herself. Sometimes individuals can take part in assessment centres and receive feedback on their performance in these centres. Sometimes organizations may organize career planning workshops.

- *Assisting the individual in identifying different career opportunities.* Once an individual has identified his or her abilities, interests and other career-related characteristics, the individual should be assisted in identifying jobs/occupations where these characteristics can be put to use. An individual should be encouraged to make use of these opportunities. Sometimes it might mean that a particular individual might be encouraged to look outside the organization for possible job openings. If an organization encourages an individual to look for career opportunities outside the organization, then the possibility exists that the individual might leave the organization.

- *Assisting the individual in setting personal career goals.* The individual should set operational and conceptual goals. An operational goal is usually seen as one that is tied to the attainment of a specific position. A conceptual goal is one in which the values that a person wishes to attain in his or her career are found. Such a value might, for instance, be to render service to people in need of assistance. Because goal setting in general enhances the likelihood of an individual reaching a certain point, it is very important to pay close attention to the way in which career goals are set. For instance, they should not be too easy or too difficult to reach, but should at the same time be challenging enough to the individual, so that he or she needs to utilize his or her abilities in order to reach the goals. The goals should also be specific enough, so that a person is able to tell if he or she has reached his or her goals.

- *Assisting the individual in planning career strategies.* Sometimes these strategies are called career plans.

- *Assisting the individual in implementing career strategies.* Once an individual has decided on strategies, he or she should be encouraged to implement it/them. Here an organization should see to it that the necessary developmental or training opportunities are made available to the individual.

CAREER MANAGEMENT AS A COMPONENT OF CAREER DEVELOPMENT

Integrating career management with human resource planning

Human resource planning is the basis of human resource management. In this case it is important to remember that through human resource planning, the future demand and supply of human resources is determined. The present employees form part of the supply of human resources. Through the process of human resource planning one can determine in what developmental and training activities present employees should partake in order to prepare them for future job openings. That is why it is important to integrate human resource planning with career management.

Identifying career paths/ladders

The process of human resource planning should help to identify the different ways in which individuals can progress through the ranks of an organization. This is depicted by means of career paths or career ladders that individuals can follow. It also shows what training and developmental activities an individual needs to undergo, as well as the skills needed to fill these jobs. Sometimes this is called the traditional approach to career pathing. A typical traditional career path is depicted in Figure 12.1.

Because of changing circumstances, organizations need to look at the traditional career paths that have been identified. Organizations need to ensure that a realistic approach to career pathing is followed. This approach is not an easy one to follow

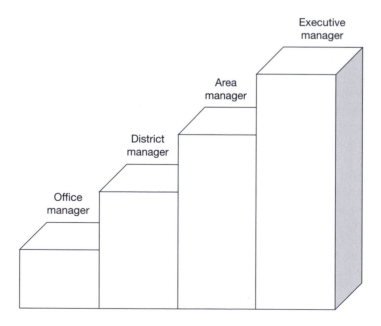

FIGURE 12.1 An example of a traditional career path

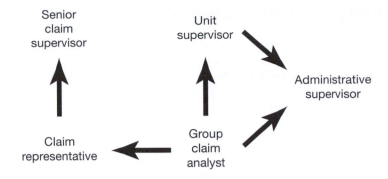

FIGURE 12.2 An example of a realistic career path

because of the characteristics of these realistic career paths. These characteristics are (Ivancevich and Konapaske, 2013):

- They would include lateral and downward possibilities, as well as upward possibilities, and they would not be tied to 'normal' rates of progress.
- They would be tentative and responsive to changes in organizational needs.
- They would be flexible enough to take into account the qualities of individuals.
- Each job along the paths would be specified in terms of acquirable skills, knowledge and other specific attributes, not merely in terms of educational credentials, age or work experience.

An example of a realistic career path is given in Figure 12.2.

Informing employees of career paths/ladders

Once career paths have been identified, employees should be informed of these paths. This will enable them to engage in realistic personal career planning that is integrated with the career management efforts of the organization. Employees should also be informed of the results of the human resource planning forecasts that have been done.

Doing job posting

Once vacancies become available, employees should be informed of them. They must then be allowed to 'bid' or apply for these vacancies. It can thus be seen that career management should also be integrated with the recruitment effort.

Assessing employees

The assessment of employees should be done in an ongoing way in organizations and should not be left until vacancies occur. Through the process of performance appraisal, information on the potential of each employee should be available on a continuous basis. Usually, an employee's immediate supervisor/manager is responsible for keeping the performance appraisal up to date. Because of the fact that performance appraisals are to a large degree based on the judgement and views of one person (the supervisor/manager), organizations sometimes use assessment centres to assess employees. Although an assessment centre is a rather costly method, it does have the advantage of resulting in judgements of different observers about the performance and potential of a particular employee being pooled. Especially if an assessment centre is geared towards development, these pooled judgements can be of tremendous value when used to give feedback to participants in an assessment centre. In this way, their own career planning can be enhanced. At the same time, the organization can utilize the information gained at the assessment centre for organizational career management. The information on each employee contained in the human resource information system can also be used in the assessment process, especially if this information is continually being updated.

Offering career counselling

Although counselling is, strictly speaking, the domain of counselling psychologists, it often happens that counselling aspects come into play when undertaking career management. When feedback is given to an employee after attending an assessment centre, it can well be argued that an element of counselling was present in that situation. The same can be said when a supervisor/manager discusses an employee's performance appraisal with him or her. If an employee talks to his or her supervisor/manager or to someone in the human resource department about the availability of career opportunities inside or outside the organization, elements of counselling are again present. Earlier, we mentioned the possibility of offering career planning workshops to employees for doing their personal career planning. During such workshops, usually some career counselling takes place.

When an employee talks to his or her supervisor/manager about a career problem he or she experiences, elements of counselling are again present. That is why it is important to train supervisors/managers in basic counselling skills. This does not mean that they can fulfil the role of a counselling or a clinical psychologist. It does mean, however, that they will be in a position to decide when to refer a person experiencing career or personal problems to an expert, such as organizational and work, counselling or clinical psychologist.

Career counselling is in order when employees experience career problems such as plateauing and obsolescence. It is also appropriate when there is a mismatch between an individual's personal career planning and the career management actions that the organization wishes to carry out. Sometimes individuals also face career-related problems when they move from one life or career stage to the next. In this regard one can think about the problems faced by a person experiencing a midlife or midcareer crisis.

Using work experiences

Sometimes people tend to forget that one of the best methods of career management that can be utilized by an organization is the type of work experiences the employee is subjected to. It does imply, however, that these experiences are structured in a meaningful, planned and co-ordinated way. These work experiences can take on

Hierarchy of authority

The organizational chart specifies who reports to whom in the organization. In this regard it is necessary to consider the appropriate levels of responsibility and authority to be delegated. Centralization versus decentralization refers to the degree to which authority is retained by higher level managers in the organization. In a *decentralized* organization a significant amount of authority and decision–making is delegated to lower levels, while in a *centralized* organization a limited amount of authority and decision-making is delegated to lower levels.

Decentralization is advocated by those who believe in the empowerment of people. If most decisions are made by managers, employees tend to act as unthinking executors of their commands. The amount of centralization will depend on the size and complexity of the organization, geographical dispersion of activities and competence of staff. Managers in large organizations are forced to delegate more authority. Decentralization of authority is also necessary when the activities of the organization are geographically dispersed. However, the degree of competence (abilities, skills and motivation) of employees might make it difficult to decentralize authority.

Division of labour

The organizational chart indicates who is responsible for what activities. *Department-alization* is used to group related work activities into manageable units. Functional similarity can be used as a basis to divide labour. Jobs with similar objectives and requirements are grouped to form a section. The achievement of functional similarity depends on various factors, including the volume of work, traditions, preferences and work rules, the nature of departments and the possibility of conflict of interest. If the organization is large, more *specialization* occurs. Although tasks may be similar, traditions, preferences and work rules might prevent their assignment to one individual. Similar functions may also occur in different departments. Separation of functions may occur to prevent conflict of interest. Departmentalization can be done based on function, customer, geographical territory or project.

Spans of control

The span of control refers to the number of people reporting to a specific manager. The span of control can vary from narrow to wide. The narrower the span of control, the closer the supervision and the higher the administrative costs as a result of a higher manager–to–worker ratio. Leanness and administrative efficiency dictate *wide* spans of control. There is no hard and fast rule regarding the optimum span of control. A *narrow* span of control is applicable when the work is complex, if jobs are interdependent and if the organization is operating in an unstable environment.

A narrow span of control does, however, have some disadvantages. It is expensive because it adds levels of management. It makes vertical communication more complex and slows down decision-making. It discourages employees from acting autonomously. To a great degree the span of control depends on the nature of the tasks which are being performed. If the task is of a routine and repetitive nature, employees need less supervision than in the case of highly complex tasks being carried out. Also, when employees have the necessary training for and experience of carrying out tasks (perhaps even complex tasks) they need less supervision. In such cases the span of control can be widened.

Line and staff positions

Line managers occupy formal decision-making positions within the chain of command. *Staff* managers do background research and provide technical advice and recommendations to line managers, who have the authority to make decisions. Line people, who are directly involved in the production of goods and services, often feel that they are the experts in their own fields and that they do not need or want advice from staff departments. People in staff departments might feel that the people in line departments have too narrow a focus, and that they actually need the advice and input from staff departments. Often, top management accepts the advice from staff departments over that of the line departments. It is obvious that the line–staff relationship can be a difficult one, and one which should certainly be taken into consideration when thinking about organizational structures and organizational design.

Types of organizational structures

Mechanistic versus organic structures

Mechanistic organizations are characterized by less flexible and more stable organizational structures (Armstrong and Taylor, 2014). Activities are specialized into clearly defined jobs and tasks (e.g. in an assembly line). Workers of high rank typically have greater knowledge of the problems facing the organization than those at lower levels. Policies, procedures and rules guide much of the decision-making in the organization. Rewards are mainly obtained through obedience to the directions of supervisors and managers.

Organic organizations have flexible organizational designs and can adjust rapidly to change (Armstrong and Taylor, 2014). These organizations put less emphasis on job description and specialization. Workers become involved in decision-making when they have the knowledge or skills that will help to solve the problem. Workers holding higher positions are not necessarily assumed to be better informed than workers on lower levels. Horizontal relationships are considered as important as vertical relationships. Status and rank differences are de-emphasized, and the structure of the organization is less permanent.

The choice between mechanistic and organic structures depends on various factors, including the culture in a country and organization, and the personality and values of workers.

Matrix organizations

The matrix organizational design is characterized by dual hierarchies (a functional hierarchy and a product hierarchy) and a balance of power between these two hierarchies. The responsibilities of the functional manager include recruiting and hiring functional specialists, maintaining their expertise by training and ensuring that products meet technical specifications. Product managers recruit specialists for each product, ensure that each product is completed on time and within budget, and ensure that functional specialists comply with the product goals.

Matrix organizations allow for the good use of limited resources since resources can be shifted between products or projects. Workers gain experience from both a functional and general management perspective. However, the dual lines of authority lead to conflicts, which may result in frustration, anxiety and stress. This type of structure requires that workers spend more time in meetings. Matrix managers also need to have particular skills.

New design options

New structural options with fewer layers and emphasis on the opening of the boundaries of the organization have been developed. Two designs are the virtual organization and the boundaryless organization (Robbins and Judge, 2013: 524–527).

- *The virtual organization.* This is a small, core organization that outsources its major business functions. This type of organization is highly centralized with little departmentalization. This structure allows each project to be staffed with the talent best suited to its demands. It minimizes bureaucratic overhead because there is not a lasting organization to maintain. Teams are disbanded when projects are completed.
- *The boundaryless organization.* This type of structure eliminates vertical and horizontal boundaries in an organization, and breaks down barriers between the organization and its customers and suppliers. This type of organization eliminates the chain of command and replaces departments with empowered teams. The breakdown of vertical boundaries flattens the hierarchy and minimizes status and rank. Functional departments create horizontal boundaries that stifle interaction among functions and units. Cross-functional teams replace functional departments and activities are organized around processes.

The consequences of a poor structure

The business environment and the organization's product should in part determine the structure of an organization. Therefore, there are no good or bad structures. A poor structure is one which is inappropriate for the specific goal that the organization wants to achieve.

A poorly designed organizational structure might have the following outcomes:

- It may suit the aims and personality of powerful individuals who created them rather than the needs of the organization. The structure should not follow the skills profile available but rather a comprehensive analysis of the task and organization.
- It can lead to stress for workers, especially if duties are not clearly described.

Structural deficiencies may result in low motivation and morale (because of insufficient delegation, unclear roles, overload and inadequate support systems), late and inappropriate decisions (because of poor co-ordination and delegation), conflict and poor response to change.

ORGANIZATION DEVELOPMENT

Definition of organization development

Brown (2011) defines organization development (OD) as a long-range effort to improve an organization's ability to cope with change and its problem-solving and renewal processes through effective management of the organizational culture. It is a planned, systematic approach to change and involves changes to the whole organization or important segments of it. Anderson (2012: 3) defines OD as 'the process of increasing organizational effectiveness and facilitating personal and organizational change through the use of interventions driven by social and behavioural science knowledge'.

The purpose of OD is to increase the effectiveness of the system, and also to develop the potential of all individual members. It makes use of planned behavioural science interventions which are carried out in collaboration with organization members to help find improved ways of working together towards individual and organizational goals. OD is a discipline applying behavioural science to help organizations adapt to changes. It is aimed not only at improving the organization's effectiveness, but also at enhancing the effectiveness of organization members (Brown, 2011).

The importance of organization development

Organization development is aimed at improving the effectiveness of the organization and its members by means of a systematic change programme (Palmer *et al.*, 2006). An effective organization is one in which both the individual and organization can develop. Healthy organizations' strengths lie in change – the ability to transform their products and organization in response to changes in the economy. Organizations find themselves in a changing environment, and the only thing which is constant is change. Most people are unprepared to cope with it. Organizations are never completely static. They are in continuous interaction with external forces. Focus 14.1 summarizes the external forces that lead to a need for OD.

FOCUS 14.1

External forces that lead to a need for organization development

- Socioeconomic factors, such as international competition, unemployment, low productivity, low economic growth and crime.
- Customer expectations regarding quality products, and safety and health.
- Government factors, such as laws and regulations.
- Technological advancements, such as new information technology.
- Stakeholders' expectations for high dividends and return on their investment.
- The changing nature of expectations of employees and unions.
- Globalization and increased competition.

These changes imply that organizations should focus on adding value. This manifests in a tendency to move from autocracy to democracy in organizations, flatter organization structures, a focus on core business, a tendency to split up into business units and the use of self-regulating work groups.

Characteristics of organization development

Organization development has the following characteristics (Brown, 2011; French and Bell, 1999):

- *Planned change.* OD is a planned strategy to bring about organizational change. The change effort aims at specific objectives and is based on a diagnosis of problem areas.
- *Collaboration.* OD involves a collaborative approach to change, which includes the involvement and participation of those organization members most affected by the changes.
- *Performance.* OD programmes include an emphasis on ways to improve and enhance performance and quality.
- *Humanistic values.* OD relies on a set of humanistic values about people and organizations which aims at gaining more effective organizations by opening up new opportunities for increased use of human potential.
- *Systems.* OD represents a systems approach concerned with the interrelationship of various divisions, departments, groups and individuals as interdependent subsystems of the total organization.
- *Scientific approaches.* OD is based on scientific approaches to increase organizational effectiveness.

The organization as a socio-technical system

Organization development may be referred to as a systems approach to change (Weick, 2000). An organization is viewed as an open socio-technical system of co-ordinated human and technical activities. The organizational processes and functions are not considered as isolated elements, but as parts reacting to and influencing other system elements. According to Brown (2011), an organization is an open system consisting of five components (see Focus 14.2)

Stages in organization development

Organization development programmes are based on a systematic analysis of problems and a top management actively committed to the change effort. Many organization development programmes use the action research model (Cummings and Worley, 2005). Action research involves collecting information about the organization, feeding this information back to the client system, and developing and implementing change programmes to improve system performance.

Action research provides at least two benefits for organizations. First, it is problem focused. The change agent objectively looks for problems and the type of problem determines the type of change action. Many change activities are solution–centred

Characteristics of an open system

1 *The structural subsystem.* The structural subsystem includes the formal design, policies and procedures of the organization. It is set forth by the organization chart, and includes the division of work and patterns of authority.

2 *The technical subsystem.* The technical subsystem includes the primary functions, activities and operations, including the techniques and equipment used to produce the outputs of the system.

3 *The psychosocial subsystem.* The psychosocial subsystem includes the network of social relationships and behavioural patterns of members, such as norms, roles and communications. It is referred to as the culture of the organization.

4 *The goals and values subsystem.* The goals and values subsystem includes the vision and mission of the organization (e.g. profits, growth and survival).

5 *The managerial subsystem.* The managerial subsystem spans the entire organization by directing, organizing and co-ordinating all activities towards the basic mission. The managerial subsystem is important in integrating the activities of the other subsystems.

rather than problem-centred. The change agent has a favourite solution – for example, implementing teams or management by objectives – and then seeks out problems his or her solution fits. Second, because action research so heavily involves employees in the process, resistance to change is reduced. Once employees have actively participated in the feedback stage, the change process takes on a momentum of its own. The employees and groups who have been involved become an internal source of sustained pressure to bring about change.

Stage 1: Anticipating change

Before an OD programme can be implemented, the organization must anticipate the need for change. The first step is the manager's perception that the organization is somehow in a state of disequilibrium or needs improvement. The state of disequilibrium may result from growth or decline, or from competitive, technological, legal or social changes in the external environment. There must be a felt need, since only felt needs convince individuals to adopt new ways. Managers must be sensitive to changes in the external environment.

Stage 2: Developing the consultant–client relationship

After an organization recognizes a need for change and a consultant contacts the system, a relationship begins to develop between the consultant and the client system. The development of this relationship is an important determinant of the probable success or failure of the OD programme. As with many interpersonal relationships, the exchange of expectations and obligations (the formation of a psychological contract) depends to a high degree on a good first impression or match between consultant and the client system. The consultant may be a manager or other member of the organization, referred to as an internal consultant, or an outside source referred to as an external consultant. The consultant attempts to establish a pattern of open communication, a relationship of trust and an atmosphere of shared responsibility. Issues dealing with responsibility, rewards and objectives must be clarified, defined or worked through at this point.

The consultant must decide at what point to enter the system, and what his or her role should be. The consultant may intervene with the sanction and support of top management, and either with or without the sanction and support of the members in the lower levels of the organization. On first entering the client system, the OD consultant begins evaluating its readiness for organization development. It is a mistake to assume that because most organizations can benefit greatly from an OD programme, they must have one. Answers to the following questions will help to assess the client's readiness for OD (Brown, 2011):

- Are the learning goals of OD appropriate?
- Is the cultural system of the client ready for OD?
- Are the key people involved?
- Are members of the client system adequately prepared and oriented to OD?

Stage 3: Organizational diagnosis

After the consultant has intervened and developed a working relationship with the client, the consultant and the client begin to gather data about the client system. The collection of data is an important activity providing the organization and the client with a better understanding of client system problems.

Diagnosis is a systematic approach to understanding and describing the present state of the organization. The purpose of the diagnostic phase is to specify the nature of the exact problem requiring solution, to identify the underlying causal forces and to provide a basis for selecting effective change strategies and techniques. Focus 14.3 shows the issues which are critical in organizational diagnosis (Brown, 2011).

One rule for the consultant is to question the client's diagnosis of the problem because the client may be biased. After acquiring data relevant to the situation which is perceived to be in disequilibrium, the consultant and client analyse the data together to identify problem areas and causal relationships. A weak, inaccurate or faulty diagnosis can lead to a costly and ineffective change programme. The objective of the diagnostic phase is to determine the exact problem that needs solution, to identify the causal forces in the situation, and to provide a basis for selecting effective change strategies and techniques.

Two other concerns are important in organizational diagnosis. First, it is important to use a diagnostic model when diagnosing organizations. A diagnostic model is a representation of how organizations function and is crucial in understanding organizations. Diagnostic models include the analytical model of Lawrence and Lorsch

Critical issues in organizational diagnosis

- *Simplicity*: keep data as simple as possible and use simplicity in presentation.
- *Visibility*: use visible measures of what is happening.
- *Involvement*: emphasize participation and involvement of organization members in diagnosis.
- *Primary factors*: use undistorted collection of primary operating variables in diagnosis.
- *Measure what is important*: pursue the straightforward assessment of variables which are critical to success.
- *Sense of urgency*: during diagnosis, gain an overall sense of urgency for change.

(1986), the socio-technical systems model and the force field analysis model. Although these models are not discussed here, they are important and should be kept in mind when approaching an organization for a diagnosis. Second, the data collection process should be considered. The most obvious step in data collection is defining the goals and objectives of the change programme. This step is necessary to determine which information is relevant. The next step is to identify the central variables involved in the situation (e.g. production, turnover, culture and values). The last step is to select a data-gathering method. Although organizations generate a large amount of 'hard' data, it may present an incomplete picture of organizational performance. The consultant and client may decide to increase the range and depth of the available data by using interviews, direct observation and/or questionnaires as a basis for further action programmes.

Stage 4: Interventions

The diagnostic phase leads to a series of interventions, activities or programmes aimed at resolving problems and increasing organization effectiveness. An intervention is defined as an instrument or tool that will enact and accomplish a state or goal (Burke, 2005). Intervention is regarded as part of the implementation phase of an organization change, which is the core of an organization change effort. Interventions aim to change some aspects of an organization (e.g. its climate, employees, structure or procedures) to improve the health or functioning of the client system.

The definition of an intervention includes various important elements (French and Bell, 1999). First, an intervention refers to something that happens in an organization's life. Interventions include educational activities, methods, techniques observations, interviews and questionnaires which are used to bring about organizational improvements. Second, an intervention refers to different levels of activities, e.g. a single task, a sequence of related tasks, activities that are related but also different, and an overall plan for the improvement of the organization. Third, an intervention implies joint collaboration between an organization and a client. For organization development interventions to be successful, the interdependencies between various subelements of the organization must be considered.

Argyris (1970) distinguished between three tasks of an intervener, namely to generate valid and useful information, to help the client to make free and informed choices, and to assure the client's internal commitment to choices made:

- Generating valid and useful information. Valid and useful information refers to the factors and their interrelationships that create problems for the client system.
- Helping the client to make free and informed choices. The second task of the intervener is to help the client system to make free, informed choices and to provide the client with alternatives for action.
- Assuring the client's internal commitment to choices. The third task of the intervener is to assure that the client is committed to choices made.

Interventions can be categorized based on the target group, namely: a) personal and interpersonal interventions, b) team interventions, c) intergroup interventions and d) organizational interventions (Brown, 2011).

Personal and interpersonal interventions

The central theme of personal and interpersonal interventions is learning through the examination of underlying processes. These interventions also focus on individuals and their development and growth within the organization.

- *Sensitivity training laboratories*. Sensitivity training groups are also known as training groups (T-groups). T-groups is an approach to human relations training which provides individuals with the opportunity to learn more about themselves and their impact on others, in particular to learn how to function more effectively in face-to-face situations.
- *Transactional analysis*. Transactional analysis involves a system of interaction analysis, which assists people to understand their feelings and behaviour, and which helps them to form satisfactory interpersonal relationships.
- *Behaviour modelling*. Behaviour modelling is a structured, effective and reliable method that can be used to train people in interpersonal skills. The rationale of behaviour modelling is that behaviour is shaped by external stimuli, that behaviour is learned through the observation of other persons (models), that behaviour is shaped and maintained by the consequences thereof, and that behaviour is repeated because of the reinforcement of similar behaviour in the past.
- *Life and career planning interventions*. Life and career planning interventions are used to assist individuals to focus on their life and career goals so that they can be empowered to exert better control over their own destinies.
- *Wellness promotion and stress management interventions*. Stress management interventions have embedded a range of practices that offer opportunities for individual development and employee well-being.
- *Counselling and coaching*. Counselling is used to help employees cope with personal problems which are interfering with their work. Coaching is used to help employees perform new tasks and/or improve their performance of old tasks or skills.

Team/group interventions

Team/group interventions are focused on group development and the interaction between individuals within groups or teams. Team interventions can be applied to family groups (i.e. intact work teams) and special groups (i.e. special project teams). The following team-building designs are applicable to work teams (Dyer *et al.*, 2013):

- *The family group diagnostic meeting.* This type of team intervention is used to analyse and evaluate the current functioning of the team and to identify problems that the team should work on.
- *The family group team-building meeting.* The family group team-building meeting is used to improve the effectiveness of the group by focusing on task accomplishment, relationships in the team and group processes.
- *Process consultation interventions.* Process consultation is a philosophy of helping which involves joined diagnosis by client and consultant. Schein (1969: 11) defines process consultation as a 'set of activities on the part of the consultant that help the client to perceive, understand, and act upon the process events that occur in the client's environment in order to improve the situation as defined by the client'. A process consultant helps the client to become aware of and improve group and interpersonal processes.
- *Role analysis team building.* Role analysis team building is used to clarify roles in a team when a unit is newly organized and team members do not know what others do and what others expect of them, changes and reassignments have been made in the team and members are no longer sure how functions fit together, job descriptions are outdated, conflict and interpersonal disruptions in the team are increasing, and the manager engages primarily in one-to-one management.
- *Role negotiation team building.* Role negotiation team building is used when the causes of a team's effectiveness are based on people's behaviour that they are unwilling to change. Using this technique, team members ask each other to change behaviours that will make it possible for the other person to do his or her job more effectively.

Intergroup interventions

Intergroup interventions are necessitated because of interdependency between teams and groups in organizations, conflicting objectives of teams, perceived power imbalance between groups, role conflict, and role ambiguity and personality conflict.

- *Intergroup team-building interventions.* In intergroup team-building interventions, key members work on issues of interface. The meeting typically involves five steps, namely:
  - Working separately, the two work groups make lists of how they see themselves, how they think the other group sees them, and how they see the other group.
  - The two groups meet and a person from each group presents their lists.
  - The two groups meet separately to discuss.
  - Subgroups are formed by mixing members of the two groups and these groups develop action plans.
  - A follow-up evaluation meeting is held.

- *Organizational mirror interventions.* These give feedback to teams on how other elements of organization view them. Units meet together to process data with the objectives of identifying problems and formulating solutions.
- *Third-party peacemaking interventions.* A third-party peacemaking intervention is a technique that can be used to resolve the conflict between two or more people. Confrontation is an essential feature of third-party peacemaking (French and Bell, 1999). The parties involved in the conflict must be willing to confront the fact that conflict exists and should realize that it has implications for their effectiveness.

Organizational interventions

- *Confrontation meeting.* The confrontation meeting as an organizational development intervention was developed by Richard Beckhard as a one-day meeting of the entire management of an organization in which they take a reading of their own organizational health.
- *Strategic planning intervention.* Strategic interventions link the internal functioning of the organization to the larger environment and transform the organization to keep pace with changing conditions (Cummings and Worley, 2005). Organization development practitioners should become experts in strategic management processes and need to have thorough knowledge of strategic management content (French and Bell, 1999).
- *Survey feedback.* Survey feedback intervention is the most effective if the organization wants to include a large group of people. This type of intervention is mostly used in diagnosing situations that need attention within the organization, and to plan and implement organizational improvements. This approach of organization development surveys the unit of analysis through questionnaires and feedback to all the relevant role-players.
- *Grid OD.* The Grid was designed by Robert R. Blake and Jane S. Mouton as a six-phase programme which will last about three to five years. The programme utilizes a considerable number of instruments, enabling individuals and groups to assess their own strengths and weaknesses; it focuses on skills, knowledge and processes necessary for effectiveness at the individual, group, intergroup and total-organization levels. The Grid OD programme is effective because it showed greater profits, lower costs and less waste.
- *Job design.* Job design is the process of incorporating tasks and responsibilities into jobs to make them more meaningful, productive and satisfying. Various models can be followed in redesigning jobs, including the job characteristics model (Hackman and Oldham, 1976), the job demand-control model (Karasek, 1979) and the interdisciplinary approach of Campion and Berger (1990).
- *Quality circles.* Quality circles are focused on customer satisfaction through continuous improvement and teamwork.
- *Management by objectives.* Management by objectives is based on the philosophy that the manager and employee ought to negotiate or collaborate on defining the objectives that the worker is to pursue over the next time period (Drucker, 1954; Odiorne, 1965).
- *Socio-technical systems.* According to Trist *et al.* (1963), a socio-technical system design is based on the premise that an organization or a work unit is a combination of social and technical parts that is open to its environment. A socio-technical

system focuses on the interdependencies between and among people, technology and environment in order to optimize both social and technical elements in organizations. The social system aims to design a work structure that is responsive to the psychological needs of employees.

The OD consultant should consider the following three aspects in selecting the appropriate intervention (Brown, 2011; French and Bell, 1996). First, the potential results of the technique of the intervention should be considered. The interventions should solve the intended 'problems' and result in positive outcomes. Second, the possibility to implement the interventions should be considered. The expected costs of interventions should be weighed against the potential benefits thereof. Last, it is important to assess clients' willingness to participate in the interventions beforehand.

Stage 5: Self-renewal, monitoring and stabilizing action programmes

Once an OD programme is implemented, the next step is to monitor the results and stabilize the desired changes. This stage concerns the assessment of the effectiveness of change strategies in attaining stated objectives. Each stage of an OD programme needs to be monitored to gain feedback on member reactions to change efforts. The system members need to know the results of change efforts in order to determine whether they ought to modify, continue or discontinue the activities.

Once a problem has been corrected and a change programme implemented and monitored, means must be devised to make sure that the new behaviour is stabilized and internalized. If this is not done, the system tends to regress to previous ineffective modes or states. The client system needs to develop the capability to maintain innovation without outside support.

Management of change

According to Kurt Lewin (1952), any change process consists of three phases, namely unfreezing the status quo, movement to a new state (change), and refreezing the new change to make it permanent (see Figure 14.1).

The status quo can be considered to be an equilibrium state. To move from this equilibrium – to overcome the pressures of both individual resistance and group conformity – unfreezing is necessary. It can be achieved in three ways (see Figure 14.2). The driving forces, which direct behaviour away from the status quo, can be increased. The restraining forces, which hinder movement from the existing equilibrium, can be decreased. A third alternative is to combine the two approaches.

Organization members should be unfrozen to overcome resistance to change. Individuals must be prepared for change, and must release physical and psychic energy

FIGURE 14.1 Lewin's three-step change model

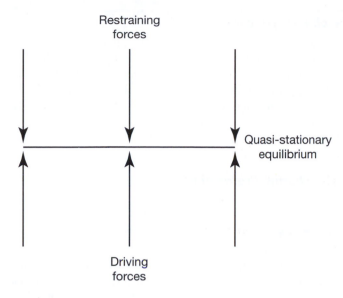

FIGURE 14.2 Force field analysis (Kurt Lewin)

for it (Anderson, 2012). Dissatisfaction with the status quo can be created to encourage employees to experiment with new behavioural forms. Focus 14.4 shows that dissatisfaction can be generated by engaging in specific behaviours (Anderson, 2012).

As soon as employees understand the necessity of change, they must be convinced that the proposed changes are workable. This can be facilitated by pilot projects which involve employees, which may indicate that the assumptions underlying changes are valid. Pilot projects will promote feelings of security, which will help employees to change.

FOCUS 14.4

Creating dissatisfaction with the status quo

- Make employees aware of the need for change by presenting the reality of the situation to them (e.g. a decrease in sales figures, an increase in costs, high labour turnover and rate of absenteeism). It is easier to generate motivation for change if a competitive crisis is present.
- Disclose the differences between the present and the desired situation.
- Describe a more desirable future situation, i.e. develop a vision of a future state that could energize people. Leaders should be more concerned about the determination of a desired state than how to get there.
- Communicate positive expectations regarding the change. Expectations of employees may serve as a self-fulfilling prophecy and encourage them to invest energy in change programmes which they expect to succeed.
- Inform employees about the expected advantages of changes for them.

Manage the change process

Change implies the learning of new attitudes and/or behaviour by making the person aware of new sources of information, or by helping him or her to look at old information in a new way. Change can take place in two ways, namely: a) by identifying with a role model, mentor, friend or other person and by learning to see things from his or her frame of reference, and b) by scanning the environment to find a specific problem. It is difficult to manage the change process because people seldom react as was planned. Organizational politics are also involved, and people's perceptions, emotions and behaviour are affected by changes.

Stabilizing the change ('refreezing')

Refreezing involves the stabilizing of changes by helping the person to integrate the new activities in his or her routine activities. Various mechanisms can be used to stabilize changes (Anderson, 2012), namely:

*   The individual should be given the opportunity to determine if the new attitudes and/or behaviour really fit his or her self-concept, are congruent with other parts of his or her personality and if they can be integrated comfortably.
*   The individual should be given the opportunity to test if others will accept and confirm the new attitudes and behaviour. It is important to tell people which things would not change. The latter serves as an anchor to provide stability to manage changes. The reward system can be used to reinforce behaviour. Formal and public acknowledgement of employees who help to move the organization in the desired direction may help to specify what acceptable behaviour is. Guardians may be employed to serve as role models and norm carriers of the new culture and changes.

ORGANIZATIONAL CULTURE

Definition of organizational culture

Organizational culture is defined as 'how things are done around here' (Drennan, 1992: 1). As employees work together, specific procedures or ways in which work is done, problems are handled and decisions are made become established, and in time these procedures and ways become the accepted way in which such actions are performed (Cartwright et al., 2001). Schein (1990: 111) defined organizational culture as follows:

> a pattern of basic assumptions, invented, discovered, or developed by a given group, as it learns to cope with its problems of external adaptation and internal integration, that has worked well enough to be considered valid and therefore is to be taught to new members as the correct way to perceive, think and feel in relation to those problems.

Organizational culture is not necessarily the overt behaviour which can be observed when visiting an organization. It is not only the written policy or values, but also the basic assumptions which influence the behaviour, architecture and layout of offices (Armstrong and Taylor, 2014; Schein, 1985). Organizational culture includes traditions, events and established practices which created patterns of relating and problem solving in the organization. It is the rules and guidelines prescribing to participants how they should participate, how they should act and what they should not do.

Organizational culture should not be confused with organizational climate. Organizational climate can be observed and measured more directly, and has a longer research history than organizational culture (Schein, 1990). Organizational climate can be described as a psychological state which is strongly influenced by organizational factors such as systems, structures and management behaviour.

Components of organizational culture

Organizational culture consists of the following four components (Armstrong and Taylor, 2014; Cummings and Huse, 1989):

- *Assumptions*. Assumptions describe what is important and how problems in the organization are solved. These assumptions could be studied through intensive observation, focused questions and intensive self-analysis. People are normally unaware of these assumptions.
- *Values and beliefs*. People cannot easily become aware of their values and beliefs. Values describe the things which are important for organization members. Values can be studied by using interviews, observation and questionnaires. A questionnaire is normally less useful in measuring values, because it makes assumptions about the dimensions which should be studied.
- *Behavioural norms*. Behavioural norms are unwritten behavioural rules of which people can be aware. These norms prescribe how people should behave in specific situations.
- *Artefacts*. Artefacts are the highest level of cultural awareness and refer to creations which are visual manifestations of other cultural levels. They include the observable behaviour of employees, dress, structures, systems, policies, procedures, rules, records, annual reports and physical layout of the organization. It is, however, difficult to judge artefacts accurately – they are not necessarily a reliable indicator of how people behave.

The development of organizational culture

Organizational culture develops as a result of previous crises, achievements, successes and failures in an organization. These aspects lead to the formation of assumptions regarding the following aspects: reality, truth, time, human nature and human relations (Schein, 1990). The founders of an organization traditionally have a major impact on the organization's culture (Schein, 1985). They are unconstrained by previous customs or ideologies. The culture develops as employees identify with the leader as role model. Once an organization's culture is started and begins to develop, there are a number of practices which can help solidify the acceptance of core values and ensure that the culture maintains itself. These practices include:

- *Selection of entry-level personnel*. The first step is to select candidates whose characteristics and values fit those of the organization. Evidence indicates that those candidates who have a realistic job preview of the culture will turn out better.

- *Placement in the job.* New personnel are subjected to a series of different experiences, the purpose of which is to enable them to question the organization's norms and values, and to decide whether or not they can accept them.
- *Job mastery.* Once the initial cultural shock is over, the next step is that the employee should master his or her job.
- *Measuring and rewarding performance.* The next step of the socialization process consists of meticulous attention to measuring operational results and to rewarding individual performance.
- *Adherence to important values.* The next step involves careful adherence to the organization's most important values. Identification with these values helps employees reconcile personal sacrifices brought about by their membership of the organization.
- *Reinforcing the stories and folklore.* The next step involves reinforcing organizational folklore. This entails keeping alive stories which validate the organization's culture and way of doing things. The folklore helps to explain why the organization does things in a particular way.
- *Recognition and promotion.* The final step is the recognition and promotion of individuals who have done their jobs well and who can serve as role models to new people in the organization.

Changing organizational culture

Before an organization can change its culture, it should become aware of the current culture. Organizations which do not have knowledge of their culture are vulnerable, especially because of the covert nature of organizational culture. Awareness could be regarded as the first step which is necessary to facilitate change. Outsiders can play an important role in helping organizations to become aware of their culture.

Brown (2011) points out that culture change requires a change in the hearts and beliefs of employees. Motivation to change can be enhanced by creating dissatisfaction with the status quo, and by encouraging employees to believe that the change is possible and wanted. Cultural change should not be forced on people. A participative approach is required to influence the deepest level of culture. A top-down approach to change may be used when a single culture exists or when the focus is on changing norms rather than assumptions. Strategies which could be implemented to change organizational culture include developing a shared vision and mission, defining objectives and target behaviour, and the implementation and evaluation of interventions. The proactive involvement of the manager and management staff is crucial for cultural change. Employees should be encouraged to change, and a fair performance appraisal and reward system should be used to recognize performance.

SUMMARY

- Organizational structure is characterized by four dimensions, namely hierarchy of authority, division of labour, spans of control, and line and staff positions.
- Types of organizational structures include mechanistic versus organic structures and matrix organizations.

- There are no good or bad structures. A poor structure is one which is inappropriate for the specific goal that the organization wants to achieve.
- Organization development is a long-range effort to improve an organization's ability to cope with change and its problem solving, and renewal processes through effective management of the organizational culture.
- Organization development is aimed at improving the effectiveness of the organization and its members by means of a systematic change programme.
- Forces that lead to a need for organization development include socioeconomic factors, customer expectations, government factors such as laws and regulations, technological advancements, stakeholders' expectations, the changing nature of expectations of employees and unions, and globalization and increased competition. Organization development has six characteristics, namely planned change, collaboration, performance, humanistic values, a systems approach and a scientific approach.
- The stages in organization development are anticipating change, developing the consultant–client relationship, organizational diagnosis, interventions, self-renewal, monitoring and stabilizing action programmes, and the management of change.
- Organizational culture includes traditions, events and established practices which created patterns of relating and problem solving in the organization. It is the rules and guidelines prescribing to participants how they should participate, how they should act and what they should not do. It consists of four components, namely assumptions, values and beliefs, norms and artefacts.
- Organizational culture develops as a result of previous crises, achievements, successes and failures in an organization.
- Before an organization can change its culture, it should become aware of the current culture. Motivation to change can be enhanced by creating dissatisfaction with the status quo, and by encouraging employees to believe that the change is possible and wanted. A participative approach is required to influence the deepest level of culture.

KEY CONCEPTS AND TERMS

- Anticipating change
- Behaviour modelling
- Centralization
- Change
- Coaching
- Collaboration
- Complexity
- Confrontation meeting

- Consultant–client relationship
- Co-ordination
- Counselling
- Division of labour
- Hierarchy of authority
- Humanistic value
- Inter-group interventions
- Intervention

- Life and career planning
- Management by objectives
- Matrix organization
- Organic structure
- Organization
- Organizational design
- Organization development

- Organizational diagnosis
- Performance
- Planned change
- Quality circle
- Refreezing
- Scientific approach
- Sensitivity training laboratories
- Socio-technical system
- Span of control
- Staff positions
- Strategic planning
- Survey feedback
- System
- Transactional analysis
- Unfreezing
- Wellness promotion

SAMPLE ESSAY TITLES

- Which changes necessitate organization development?
- How can organizational change be effectively managed?
- What are the differences between organizational climate and culture?
- What are the dimensions of organizational culture?
- How can organizational culture be studied?

FURTHER READING

Books

Anderson, L. (2012). *Organization Development: The Process of Leading Organizational Change* (2nd edn). Thousand Oaks, CA: Sage.

Dyer, W.G., Dyer, J.H. and Dyer, W.G. (2013). *Team Building: Proven Strategies for Improving Team Performance* (5th edn). San Francisco, CA: Wiley.

Lewis, S. and Passmore, J. (2011). *Appreciative Inquiry for Change Management: Using AI to Facilitate Organizational Development*. London: Kogan Page.

Journal articles

Bryson, A., Barth, E. and Dale-Olsen, H. (2013). The effects of organizational change on worker well-being and the moderating role of trade unions. *Industrial Labor Relations Review*, 66(4), 989–1011.

Drzensky, F., Egold, N. and Van Dick, R. (2012). Ready for a change? A longitudinal study of antecedents, consequences and contingencies of readiness for change. *Journal of Change Management*, 12(1), 95–111.

Mohrman, S.A. and Lawler, E.E. (2012). Generating knowledge that drives change. *Academy of Management Perspectives*, 26(1), 41–51.

References

Adams, J.S. (1963). Toward an understanding of equity. *Journal of Abnormal and Social Psychology*, 67, 422–436.

Agars, M. and Kotke, J. (2005). 'Innovations in diversity management'. In: R. Burke and C. Cooper (eds), *Reinventing Human Resource Management*. London: Routledge.

Ajzen, I. (2001). Nature and operation of attitudes. *Annual Review of Psychology*, 52, 27–58.

Ajzen I. and Fishbein, M. (1977). Attitude-behavior relations: A theoretical analysis and review of empirical literature. *Psychological Bulletin*, 84, 888–918.

Ajzen, I. and Fishbein, M. (1980). *Understanding Attitudes and Predicting Social Behaviour*. Upper Saddle River, NJ: Prentice Hall.

Allport, G.W. (1961). *Pattern and Growth in Personality*. London: Holt, Rinehart & Winston.

Amunkete, S. and Rothmann, S. (in press). Authentic leadership and psychological capital in state-owned enterprises: Effects on job satisfaction and intention to leave. *International Journal of Human Resource Management*.

Anderson, L. (2012). *Organization Development: The Process of Leading Organizational Change* (2nd edn). Thousand Oaks, CA: Sage.

Argyris, C. (1970). *Intervention Theory and Method: A Behavioral Science View*. Reading, MA: Addison-Wesley.

Argyris, C. (1990) *Overcoming Organizational Defenses: Facilitating Organizational Learning*. Boston, MA: Allyn & Bacon.

Argyris, C. and Schön, D.A. (1978). *Organizational Learning: A Theory of Action Perspective*. Reading, MA: Addison-Wesley.

Argyris, C., Putnam, R. and Smith, D.M. (1985). *Action Science*. San Francisco, CA: Jossey-Bass.

Armstrong, M. and Taylor, T. (2014). *Armstrong's Handbook of Human Resource Management Practice* (13th edn). London: Kogan Page.

Armstrong, M., Cummins, A., Hastings, S. and Wood, W. (2003). *Job Evaluation: A Guide to Achieving Equal Pay*. London: Kogan Page.

Arnold, J., Cooper, C.L. and Robinson, I.T. (1995). *Work Psychology: Understanding Human Behaviour in the* Workplace (2nd edn). London: Pitman Publishing.

Aronsson, G. and Gustafsson, K. (2005). Sickness presenteeism: Prevalence, attendance-pressure factors, and an outline of a model for research. *Journal of Occupational and Environmental Medicine*, 47, 958–966.

Aronsson, G., Gustafson, K. and Dallner, M. (2000). Sick but yet at work: An empirical study of sickness presenteeism. *Journal of Epidemiological Health*, 54, 502–509.

Aronsson, G., Svensson, L. and Gusstafson, K. (2003). Unwinding, recuperation, and health among compulsory school and high school teachers in Sweden. *International Journal of Stress Management*, 10, 217–234.

Arthur, D. (1995). The importance of body language. *HR Focus*, 72, 22–23.

Arvey, R.D. and Faley, R.A. (1988). *Fairness in Selecting Employees* (2nd edn). Reading, MA: Addison-Wesley.

Arvey, R.D. and Murphy, K.R. (1998). Performance evaluation in work settings. *Annual Review of Psychology*, 49, 141–168.

Ashforth, B.E. and Mael, F. (1989). Social identity theory and the organization. *Academy of Management Review*, 14, 20–39.

Axtell, R.E. (1991). *The Dos and Taboos of Body Language Around the World*. New York: Wiley.

Azar, B. (1996). People are becoming smarter: Why? *APA Monitor*, 27, 20.

Bales, R.F. (1953). 'The equilibrium problem in small groups'. In: T. Parsons, R.F. Bales and E.A. Shils (eds), *Working Papers in the Theory of Action*. Glencoe, IL: Free Press, 111–161.

Bandura, A. (1977). Self-efficacy: Toward a unifying theory of behaviour change. *Psychological Review*, 84, 191–215.

Barker, R.T., Johnson, I.W. and Pearce, G. (1995). Enhancing the student listening skills and environment. *Business Communication Quarterly*, 58, 28–33.

Barkhuizen, N., Rothmann, S. and Van de Vijver, A.J.R. (2014). Burnout and engagement of academics in higher education institutions: Effects of dispositional optimism. *Stress and Health*.

Barling, J., Kelloway, K. and Zacharatos, A. (2002). 'Occupational safety'. In: P. Warr (ed.), *Psychology at Work* (5th edn). London: Penguin Books, 253–275.

Barnard, C.I. (1938). *The Functions of the Executive*. Cambridge, MA: Harvard University Press.

Barnes-Farrell, J. (2001). 'Performance appraisal'. In: M. London (ed.), *How People Evaluate Others in Organizations*. London: LEA, 135–150.

Bar-On, R. (1997). *BarOn Emotional Quotient Inventory*. Toronto: Multi-Health Systems.

Barrick, M.R. (2001). Personality testing: Controversial no more. Paper presented at the 4th Annual Conference of the Society for Industrial Psychology, Pretoria, South Africa, June.

Barrick, M.R. and Mount, M.K. (1991). The big five personality dimensions and job performance: A meta-analysis. *Personnel Psychology*, 44, 1–26.

Barrick, M.B. and Mount, M.K. (2005). Yes, personality matters: Moving on to more important matters. *Human Performance*, 18, 359–372.

Barrick, M.R., Mount, M.K. and Judge, T.A. (2001). Personality and performance at the beginning of the new millennium: What do we know and where do we go next? *International Journal of Selection and Assessment*, 9, 9–30.

Barry, B. and Stewart, G.L. (1997). Composition, process and performance in self-managed groups: The role of personality. *Journal of Applied Psychology*, 82, 62–78.

Bass, B.M. (1981). *Stogdill's Handbook of Leadership: A Survey of Theory and Research*. New York: The Free Press.

Bass, B.M. (1985). *Leadership and Performance Beyond Expectation*. New York: Free Press.

Bass, B.M. (1990). From transactional to transformational leadership: Learning to share the vision. *Organizational Dynamics*, 18, 19–31.

Bass, B.M. (1997). 'Concepts of leadership'. In: R.P. Vecchio (ed.), *Leadership: Understanding the Dynamics of Power and Influence in Organizations*. Notre Dame, IN: University of Notre Dame Press, 3–23.

Bass, B.M. (1998). *Transformational Leadership: Industrial, Military, and Educational Impact.* Mahwah, NJ: Erlbaum.

Baumeister, R.F. (1982). A self-presentational view of social phenomena. *Psychological Bulletin,* 91, 3–26.

Bell, G. (2013). Cary Cooper on engagement, wellbeing, and the persistence of the glass ceiling. *Human Resource Management International Digest,* 21(4), 41–44.

Berry, J.W. (1989). Imposed etics–emics–derived etics: The operationalizations of a compelling idea. *International Journal of Psychology,* 24, 721–735.

Berry, J.W., Poortinga, Y.P., Segall, M.H. and Dasen, P.R. (2002) *Cross-cultural Psychology: Research and Applications.* Cambridge: Cambridge University Press.

Bion, W.R. (1961). *Experiences in Groups.* London: Tavistock Publications.

Blake, R.R. and Mouton, J.S. (1964). *The Managerial Grid.* Houston, TX: Gulf.

Block, J. (1995). A contrarian view of the five factor approach to personality description. *Psychological Bulletin,* 117, 187–213.

Boehm, J.K. and Lyubomirsky, S. (2008). Does happiness promote career success? *Journal of Career Assessment,* 16(1), 101–116.

Borman, W.C. and Motowidlo, S.J. (1997). Task performance and contextual performance: The meaning for personnel selection research. *Human Performance,* 10, 99–109.

Bormann, E.G. (1996). *Effective Small Group Communication* (5th edn). Minneapolis, MN: Burgess.

Bormann, E.G. and Bormann, N.C. (1988). *Effective Small Group Communication.* Minneapolis, MN: Burgess.

Bowling, N.A., Eschleman, K.J. and Wang, Q. (2010). A meta-analytic examination of the relationship between job satisfaction and subjective well-being. *Journal of Occupational and Organizational Psychology,* 83, 915–934.

Brayfield, A.H. and Crockett, W.H. (1955). Employee attitudes and employee performance. *Psychological Bulletin,* 52, 396–424.

Breckler, S.J. (1984). Empirical validation of affect, behavior, and cognition as distinct components of attitude. *Journal of Personality and Social Psychology,* 47, 1191–1205.

Brewerton, P. and Millward, L. (2004). *Organisational Research Methods.* London: Sage.

Brodsky, C. (1976). *The Harassed Worker.* Lexington, MA: D.C. Heath and Company.

Brown, D.R. (2011). *An Experiential Approach to Organization Development* (8th edn). Upper Saddle River, NJ: Prentice Hall.

Brown, M.E., Treviño, L.K. and Harrison, D.A. (2005). Ethical leadership: A social learning perspective for construct development and testing. *Organizational Behavior and Human Decision Processes,* 97, 117–134.

Bryson, J. and Hosken, C. (2005). What does it mean to be a culturally competent I/O psychologist in New Zealand? *New Zealand Journal of Psychology,* 34, 69–76.

Bundel, T. (2004). *Effective Organizational Communications.* London: Prentice-Hall.

Burke, R. and Cooper, C. (2004). *Leading in Turbulent Times.* Oxford: Oxford University Press.

Burke, R. and Cooper, C. (2006). *Inspiring Leaders.* London: Routledge.

Burke, W.W. (2005). 'Implementation and continuing the change effort'. In: W.J. Rothwell and R.L. Sullivan (eds), *Practicing Organization Development* (2nd edn). San Francisco, CA: Pfeiffer, 313–326.

Burns, T. and Stalker, G.M. (1961). *The Management of Innovation*. London: Tavistock.

Byars, L.L. and Rue, L.W. (2011). *Human Resource Management* (10th edn). New York: McGraw-Hill.

Cameron, K. (2008). *Positive Leadership*. San Francisco, CA: Berrett-Koehler Publishers.

Cameron, K. (2014). The personal management interview program: A technique for enhancing engagement, empowerment, and positive deviance. Paper presented at the Positive Organizations Conference. Johannesburg: Knowledge Resources.

Cameron, K. and Spreitzer, G.M. (2012). 'What is positive about positive organizational scholarship?' In: K. Cameron and G.M. Spreitzer (eds), *The Oxford Handbook of Positive Organizational Scholarship*. New York: Oxford University Press, 1–16.

Campion, M.A. and Berger, C.J. (1990). Conceptual integration and empirical test of job design and compensation relationships. *Personnel Psychology*, 43, 525–553.

Caprara, G.V., Barbaranelli, C., Hahn, R. and Comrey, A.L. (2001). Factor analysis of the NEO PI-R inventory and the Comrey Personality Scales in Italy and the United States. *Personality and Individual Differences*, 30, 217–228.

Cartwright, S., Cooper, C. and Earley, C. (2001). *International Handbook of Organizational Culture and Climate*. New York: Wiley.

Carver, C.S. and Scheier, M.F. (2002). 'Optimism'. In: C.R. Snyder and S.J. Lopez (eds), *Handbook of Positive Psychology*. Oxford: Oxford University Press, 231–243.

Cascio, W.F. (2001). Knowledge creation for practical solutions appropriate to a changing world of work. *South African Journal of Industrial Psychology*, 27, 14–16.

Castellana, M.J. (2013). 'Teamwork in financial institutions: Does it really matter?' In: E. Salas, S.I. Tannenbaum, D.J. Cohen and G. Latham (eds). *Developing and Enhancing Teamwork in Organizations: Evidence-based Best Practices and Guidelines*. San Francisco, CA: Jossey-Bass.

Cattell, R.B. (1965). *The Scientific Analysis of Personality*. London: Penguin Books.

Cederblom, D. and Pemerl, D.E. (2002). From performance appraisal to performance management: One agency's experience. *Public Personnel Management*, 31, 131–140.

Chamorro-Premuzic, T. (2007). *Personality and Individual Differences*. London: Blackwell.

Chen, C., Gostafson, D. and Lee, Y. (2002). The effect of a qualitative decision aid on group polarization. *Group Decision and Negotiation*, 11, 329–344.

Cheung, F.M., Leung, K., Zhang, J.X., Sun, H.F., Gun, Y.G., Song, W.Z. and Xie, D. (2001). Indigenous Chinese personality constructs: Is the five-factor model complete? *Journal of Cross-Cultural Psychology*, 32, 407–433.

Cheung, F.M., Van de Vijver, F.J.R. and Leong, F.T.L. (2011). Toward a new approach to the study of personality in culture. *American Psychologist*, 66(7), 593–603.

Church, A.T. and Lonner, W.J. (1998). The cross-cultural perspective in the study of personality: Rationale and current research. *Journal of Cross-Cultural Psychology*, 29, 32–62.

Clarke, S. and Robertson, I. (2005). A meta analytic review of the big five personality factors and accident involvement in occupational settings. *Journal of Occupational and Organizational Psychology*, 78, 355–376.